TAKING A LEARNER-CENTRED APPROACH TO MUSIC EDUCATION

Adopting a fresh approach to the assumptions and concepts which underlie musical learning, *Taking a Learner-Centred Approach to Music Education* provides comprehensive guidance on professional and pedagogical aspects of learner-centred practice.

This essential companion offers a pedagogy which is at once informed by theoretical understandings, and underpinned by experience, practical examples, case studies and self-reflection. Initial chapters explore the theoretical dimensions of learner-centred music education, touching on aspects including collaborative learning, the learning environment and pedagogical sensitivity. Latter chapters delve deeper into the practical application of these teaching strategies and methods. The book invites its reader to reflect on topics including:

- music, emotions and interaction
- the voice and body as instruments
- making music visible and tangible
- improvising and learning music with instruments
- working with groups in creative activities
- the music pedagogue as a sensitive and creative instrument.

Taking a Learner-Centred Approach to Music Education will deepen understanding, facilitate reflection and inspire new approaches to teaching in the field of music. It is essential reading for current and future practitioners involved in music education, early childhood music practice, community music, music therapy and special needs education.

Dr Laura Huhtinen-Hildén is Senior Lecturer, Researcher and Head of Early Childhood Music Education and Community Music at Metropolia University of Applied Sciences, Finland.

Dr Jessica Pitt is a researcher and early childhood music education consultant. She leads the MA in early years music at CREC (Centre for Research in Early Childhood), UK.

TAKING A LEARNER-CENTRED APPROACH TO MUSIC EDUCATION

Pedagogical Pathways

Laura Huhtinen-Hildén and Jessica Pitt

Routledge
Taylor & Francis Group

LONDON AND NEW YORK

First published 2018
by Routledge
2 Park Square, Milton Park, Abingdon, Oxon OX14 4RN

and by Routledge
711 Third Avenue, New York, NY 10017

Routledge is an imprint of the Taylor & Francis Group, an informa business

British Library Cataloguing-in-Publication Data
A catalogue record for this book is available from the British Library

Library of Congress Cataloging-in-Publication Data
Names: Huhtinen-Hildâen, Laura, author. | Pitt, Jessica, author.
Title: Taking a learner-centred approach to music education : pedagogical
    pathways / Laura Huhtinen-Hildén and Jessica Pitt.
Description: Abingdon, Oxon ; New York, NY : Routledge, 2018.
Identifiers: LCCN 2017059161 (print) | LCCN 2017060097 (ebook) |
    ISBN 9781315526539 (eb) | ISBN 9781138695597 (hb) | ISBN
    9781138695627 (pb)
Subjects: LCSH: Music—Instruction and study. | Student-centered learning.
Classification: LCC MT1 (ebook) | LCC MT1 .H92 2018 (print) |
    DDC 780.71—dc23
LC record available at https://lccn.loc.gov/2017059161

ISBN: 978-1-138-69559-7 (hbk)
ISBN: 978-1-138-69562-7 (pbk)
ISBN: 978-1-315-52653-9 (ebk)

Typeset in Bembo
by Apex CoVantage, LLC

CONTENTS

PREFACE

Welcome to adventures into possibility spaces. We hope this book becomes as much a part of a creative process for you as writing it has been for us.

The practice that has influenced our thinking has grown through our music teaching in the community, schools and higher education, as well as research in the music education field. In our experience, there is a need to highlight the practical pedagogical wisdom that our colleagues live and breathe.

The thoughts, reflections and ideas about music education are always shaped and formed by those we encounter, work with and learn from. We are grateful to all the children and families, colleagues and students of teaching with whom we have worked. Most of these thoughts and ideas have been developed and enriched by collaborating, sharing and teaching.

Without the support of others, this book would never have been written. We want to thank Soili Perkiö for her generosity in reading the manuscript and her wise comments. Eve Alho, Charlotte Arculus, Olly Armstrong, Margareta Burrell, Jane Parker, Soili Perkiö, Susan Young – thank you for sharing your pedagogical thinking for Theme 7. We are most grateful to those colleagues who have generously given their permission to use their beautiful compositions and lyrics: Eve Alho, Margaret Corke, Hilkka Hautsalo, Hannele Huovi, Markku Kaikkonen, Soili Perkiö and Debbie Pullinger. We also want to thank the Moomin Characters company for giving permission to use Tove Jansson's text excerpts and The Association of Finnish Non-fiction Writers for financial support.

We are also grateful to those special colleagues who have encouraged and supported us over many years: Hanna-Maija Aarnio, Linda Bance, Cecilia Björk, Maureen Brookson, June Boyce-Tillman, Pam Burnard, Lori Custodero, David Hargreaves, Inkeri Simola-Isaksson, Minna Lamppu, Inger-Lisa Møen, Amanda

Niland, Alison Street, Marjanka Van Maurik, Sara Sintonen, Sanna Vuolteenaho and Susan Young.

We are indebted to our families. Hildén family: Kaarlo, thank you for the decades of dialogue in music education that has been an invaluable professional support in this work. Thank you Linnea, Aarni and Elias for your contribution and for being such a source for inspiration. Pitt family: Julian, thank you for your precision with reading the text, the great discussions and your wisdom. Thank you, Hannah and William, for your support and encouragement.

Inspired by Debbie's poem, we wish for you to sing the songs that spring from your heart, as you play with music into the spaces you go to on your pedagogical journey.

Laura Huhtinen-Hildén & Jessica Pitt
Kirkkonummi and Norwich 14.11.2017

EX-TEMPORE

Some re-arranged notes from a music conference

In music we discover what we know.
The spring and rhythm sounded from the start.
We play into the spaces as we go.

Our songs cut to the quick; our words are slow.
Childlike, we strive to speak of any art;
In music we discover what we know.

We improvise – i – e – i – e – i – o –
Mastery and mystery both part
Of playing into spaces as we go.

Bright sound in light: a synaesthetic flow!
Boundaries dissolve and colours slant.
In music we uncover what we know.

Our searching roots go down so shoots can show.
Weaving, they entangle and enchant
And play into the spaces as we go.

From sounding womb to noisy world we're thrown,
To where the space is thin, the going hard;
But music will recover what we know.

So in the minor key, sing long, sing low.
And sing the song that springs within the heart.
In music we discover what we know.
We play into the spaces as we go.

Debbie Pullinger 2017

Published with permission from the poet

ABOUT THE AUTHORS

Dr Laura Huhtinen-Hildén (PhD, MMus, Music Therapist) is Senior Lecturer, Researcher and Head of Early Childhood Music Education and Community Music at Metropolia University of Applied Sciences, Finland. She is a former board member of EuNet MERYC (Music Educators and Researchers of Young Children) and collaborates internationally in research and development. Her research has focused on the formation process of professional knowledge and identity in becoming a music educator. As a researcher and developer of the field, she is also interested in the use of arts and arts-based methods in new contexts in society.

Dr Jessica Pitt (PhD) is a music researcher and education consultant. She leads the MA in early years music at CREC (Centre for Research in Early Childhood), Birmingham City University, and is an Honorary Research Fellow at the University of Roehampton, Applied Music Research Centre. She is a trustee of MERYC-England and a former board member of EuNet MERYC (Music Educators and Researchers of Young Children). She has wide experience of research and evaluation in the field of music psychology, arts-based education and wellbeing, and is a reviewer for academic journals in the field of music education and arts in early childhood.

IMAGE CREDITS

INTRODUCTION

This book is in two parts: the first is a journey through theoretical aspects that frame and support learner-centred music education; the second opens practical explorations for deeper understanding and working with this approach.

This book can accompany professionals teaching music in different contexts as facilitators of another's creative and artistic learning, and those educating music teaching professionals. It also works as course material for students of teaching, providing ideas for reflective workshops that are easily adaptable for use in many contexts. It is an invitation to discuss and reflect on the underlying assumptions and concepts that affect music education practice. It can facilitate reflection in early childhood music education, school and instrumental music teaching, working with the elderly, special education and animateurs working with orchestras or in community settings (museums, libraries, family music making). No matter where this book meets you, we hope that it will provide a useful companion for your pedagogical journey.

Chapter 1 introduces the landscape with perspectives that underpin learner-centred thinking in music education. In Chapter 2, we examine the dimensions and understanding of learning. Chapter 3 looks to collaborative learning and understanding the group as a learning environment. Chapter 4 explores the essential elements of professional practice and pedagogical sensitivity. Chapter 5 considers planning musical activities through a learner-centred approach. These chapters illustrate the theoretical territory through which we can understand our experiences in music education practice.

Part II is a workbook to deepen understanding of, and reflection on, working with a learner-centred approach. Important perspectives of practice have been themed, and serve as ways to enter the complex systems of group teaching and learning music.

The themes are:

- The group as an orchestra, team and learning environment
- Music, emotions and interaction
- Voice and body as first instruments
- Making music visible and tangible
- Improvising and learning music with instruments
- Creating learning environments through imagination
- The music pedagogue as a creative instrument

The two parts of the book work together to bridge the theoretical world and the practical world, so that these two domains merge through the sensitive pedagogue's interaction with the text, materials and a group of participants, to become an embodied theory-practice synergised pedagogy.

Throughout the book, practical exercises encourage reflection both in and on pedagogical thinking.

PART I

Underpinning a learner-centred approach to music education

1

OPENING POSSIBILITIES FOR LEARNING

This chapter begins the journey of reflection on practice by focusing on concepts that underpin learner-centred teaching. This holistic approach to music education sees learning music as an essential element of living a fulfilled life.

IMAGE 1.1 Starting the journey

Exploring learner-centred thinking in music education

Learner-centredness in education is a prominent discourse that needs ongoing dialogue to foster understanding, especially with regard to the implications of its approach to practice. This evolution of understanding develops through re-framing the ideas about how learning occurs and the role that the teacher might play. Gert Biesta (2013) sees education at the heart of a dialogical process and raises the point that education always involves a risk and therefore has an element of "weakness" in it (pp. 1–9). This unpredictable, indeterminate and in-the-moment nature of a learning situation calls for pedagogical sensitivity (see Van Manen, 1991, 2008) in order to realise the potential of this creative process both from the learner's and the teacher's points of view. Sawyer (2011, pp. 1–3) conceives of teaching as an improvisational activity, that attempts to achieve a delicate balance between structure and improvisation. He sees this as the essence of the art of teaching.

Focusing on learners and the pedagogical actions that support learning leads to the concept of pedagogy from the holistic perspective that is embodied in the whole being of the person. Max Van Manen (1991) suggests that teaching viewed through this lens "has the quality of opening up possibilities of being and becoming" (p. 14). Through this lens, teaching could be seen as opening possibilities for learning (see Huhtinen-Hildén, 2017) with a pedagogy that is "willing to engage the beautiful risk" (Biesta, 2013, p. 9).

Learning – seen from this broader perspective – has been re-framed by many in the field of music education. David Elliott and Marissa Silverman (2015, p. 108) highlight humanity's concern for education being fundamentally aimed at "achieving and living a meaningful and fulfilling personal and social life" or, a good life for all. Learning in music activities can be seen as meaningful in changing how a person perceives themselves and life. Following this trajectory of understanding learning, musical interactions and group musical processes are a way of entering an attuned state in the participatory process, which can lead to constructing meaningful life experiences. With a focus on possibilities for learning, different layers and abilities can be present and nurtured at the same time. The group is engaged in a creative process of learning (see Biesta, 2013, pp. 5–9), and the focus is not on the act of teaching but on learning and scaffolding the growth of individuals and interaction. Learning and knowledge may be seen as co-constructed in a dialogic process between 'learners' and 'teachers'. Learning and teaching form a complex system. Together they lead to growth in knowledge and understanding through practice that has meaning for both the teacher and the learner (Loughran, 2006).

In this book, the term 'music pedagogue' is used to refer to someone who educates or teaches music (there are various terms used in different countries for those who work in music education in its broadest sense). Originating from the Greek *ped*, meaning 'child', and *agein*, 'to lead', this allows not only those with teaching qualifications, but also those not formally qualified as teachers, to be included in the title. Thus, music pedagogues work in various contexts and settings, for example with pre-school children and their families, the elderly, those with mental health difficulties, children with special needs and countless other community contexts.

The music pedagogue can be seen as a professional facilitator of another's creative and artistic processes, learning and expression.

By reflecting on the assumptions and values about professional teaching practice, some of the established ways of thinking about music education have been challenged (see Björk, 2016). Deeper articulation, analysis and framing of learner-centred music education are needed to give voice to the practical, pedagogical tacit knowledge (see Polanyi, 1966) that music pedagogues experience. Pedagogical actions that support learning can develop a sense of awe and wonder in what may lie 'beyond' (Boyce-Tillman, 2016) and of what remains hidden and intangible when learning or experiencing music.

There are – in both practice and professional discourse and policy – many examples where teaching is referred to in terms that imply giving instructions or focusing on things that are visible and/or audible and where learning is seen as predictable and caused by the controlled delivery of instruction. Although these conceptualisations have been challenged by researchers and practitioners in the field (see e.g. Barnett, 2004; Biesta, 2013; Custodero, 2010; Korthagen, 2004; Loughran, 2006), the need remains for shared enterprise to develop the vocabulary that bridges the research-based theoretical framework and the learner-centred practice in music education.

John Loughran (2006) describes those pursuing what might be considered teacher training as 'students of teaching'. This expression could also refer to professional practitioners to emphasise the ongoing reflection on practice as a lifelong pursuit. Thus, a professional could be seen as someone who is in the constant process of becoming. With reflection on the experience in practice, combined with theoretical frameworks and notions, a deepening of understanding occurs in collaboration with the professional's communities of practice (see Wenger, 1998), which includes both colleagues and learners that they work with. In this process, both students of teaching, as well as professionals in the field, are in the process of reflection and "learning for an unknown future" (Barnett, 2004, p. 247). Looked at from this point of view, professional practice is always in a state of 'becoming' and not in a state of having arrived. In Korthagen's 'onion model' (Korthagen, 2004, p. 80), which describes levels of change towards new directions in teacher education, he refers to the innermost part of a teacher's professional identity as the 'mission level', where professional reflection is bound up with a deep sense of calling, beliefs and values.

Music education as part of life

For a plant to flourish, certain conditions are needed: suitable soil, a perfect growing position and the right amount of sun and rain at the right time. It needs tending, pruning and feeding in order to perform well year after year. A similar set of conditions may be needed for human flourishing. What do we need to live a good life in and through music?

Elliott and Silverman (2015) suggest 'Praxis' as a concept that can be applied to music education. At the heart of the framework is the idea that music education seen through the praxial lens should have the empowerment of people as a central tenet, "to develop the abilities and dispositions required to pursue important life goals and values for themselves and others", leading to what they call 'human flourishing' through creative, participatory music making (or education). This idea of music as a source of human flourishing is a driving thought behind learner-centred music education (pp. 17–18).

Integral to the praxial approach is the concept that musical activities should be "embedded in and creatively responsive to both traditional and ever-changing musical/cultural/social values" (Elliott & Silverman, 2015, p. 17). Achieving a good life for all should surely be a key driver for education and the arts, and music in particular is an effective and suitable vehicle for this.

The lifelong musical learning journey begins before birth with muffled sounds; later, in the first few years of life, music can become an intrinsic part of important relationships. The child's own artistic world can, with the help of scaffolding from others more expert, be nurtured and flourish. 'Pruning' and 'feeding' along the way enable continued flourishing and the emergence of unexpected shoots of creative outburst and learning. Year upon year, the love and interest in music can grow and become rooted in the lives of young people as they mature.

Sounds combine in some way with our hearing, thoughts and feelings to produce an internal response. We must therefore acknowledge that "musical experiences are corporeal – located in body" (Custodero, 2010, p. 62). Music connects the learner to their primal humanity, felt in their bodies. This embodiment enables learners to integrate their feelings with their actions, which together provide a foundation for higher-order conceptualisation (Custodero, 2010, p. 84). This is one notion for how we 'know' in and through music. Mihály Csikszentmihalyi suggests that a 'flow' experience can lead to positive affect and happiness through personal development in order to achieve more than the individual felt was possible. Through observing individuals totally absorbed in a task, it is suggested that they are utterly committed to the present moment – that is referred to as being in a state of flow. This state generates positive emotional feelings or a state of wellbeing (Csikszentmihalyi, 1990). Musical activities in a group can lead to a 'group-flow' experience, described by Victor Turner as 'communitas' (1974).

Elliott and Silverman (2015) base their praxial philosophy of music education upon Aristotle's conception of Praxis – comprising four distinct parts: theoria, poiesis, techne and phronesis. Each of these has a different role to play in music teaching. Theoria – the theories and research-based knowledge about music, child development and education – is an underpinning to actions in teaching but not all that is required. Poiesis refers to those aspects of music making that rely on what is known about music prior to creating something new – such as familiar compositional structures such as 12-bar blues or rondo form. Techne includes the technical skills required of music making – drills and practise exercises, for example. Phronesis is the dimension that drives the music pedagogue's thoughts, decisions and actions made in unique practical situations (pp. 44–45). Phronesis is also known as practical reasoning, and this is the aspect that can influence what is taught, how it is taught and when it is taught. The capacity to make 'right' choices in a given moment for a particular group of learners carries with it an ethical dimension that can lead to good results and outcomes. Praxis is an embodied integration of the four dimensions, a dynamic and sensitive philosophical view of music education that depends on our sensitivity as pedagogues to effect good decisions based on our knowledge of theory, musical forms and structures, technical skill, and practical wisdom that are all deployed appropriately, in the moment, for the group of learners and their learning needs. Praxis requires an element of caring about the decisions that one takes in terms of others' wellbeing (Chubbuck, Burant, & Whipp, 2007). This can also be referred to as pedagogical sensitivity (Van Manen, 2008). Pedagogical sensitivity in teaching music is a layer of the professional knowing that allows us to feel, to analyse in action and to combine this with the knowledge that we have, merging them all in our pedagogical actions to support learning in the specific moment and context (see also Huhtinen-Hildén, 2012).

Music teaching can be seen as nurturing the learner's relationship with music, endorsing their creativity and being sensitive to their needs. This adds to the learning of musical skills by deepening the personal significance to the individual learner through the embodiment of the experience in the whole being of the person.

 Reflection and discussion

IMAGE 1.2 How has your relationship with music been nurtured through your life?

Take a moment to think about

- What made music special for you?
- What threats have there been, or might there be, to your love of, or participation in music?
- How has your relationship with music been nurtured through your life?

References

Barnett, R. (2004). Learning for an unknown future. *Higher Education Research & Development*, *23*(3), 247–260.

Biesta, G. J. (2013). *The beautiful risk of education*. London: Routledge.

Björk, C. (2016). *In search of good relationships to music: Understanding aspiration and challenge in developing music school teacher practices*. Åbo: Åbo Akademi University Press.

Boyce-Tillman, J. (2016). *Experiencing music: Restoring the spiritual: Music as well-being*. Oxford: Peter Lang.

Chubbuck, S. M., Burant, T. J., & Whipp, J. L. (2007). The presence and possibility of moral sensibility in beginning pre-service teachers. *Ethics and Education*, *2*(2), 109–130.

Csikszentmihalyi, M. (1990). *Flow: The psychology of optimal experience*. New York: Harper Row.

Custodero, L. A. (2010). Meaning and experience: The musical learner. In H. F. Abeles & L. A. Custodero (Eds.), *Critical issues in music education: Contemporary theory and practice* (pp. 61–86). New York: Oxford University Press.

Elliott, D. J., & Silverman, M. (2015). *Music matters: A philosophy of music education* (2nd ed.). New York: Oxford University Press.

Huhtinen-Hildén, L. (2012). *Kohti sensitiivistä musiikin opettamista: Ammattitaidon ja opettajuuden rakentumisen polkuja [Towards sensitive music teaching: Pathways to becoming a professional music educato]*. Jyväskylä Studies in Humanities 180. Jyväskylä: University of Jyväskylä.

Huhtinen-Hildén, L. (2017). Elävänä hetkessä: Suunnitelmallisuus ja pedagoginen improvisointi [Present in a moment: Systematic planning and pedagogical improvisation]. In A. Lindeberg-Piiroinen & I. Ruokonen (Eds.), *Musiikki varhaiskasvatuksessa – käsikirja [Music in early childhood education – a handbook.]* (pp. 389–411). Helsinki: Classicus.

Korthagen, F. A. (2004). In search of the essence of a good teacher: Towards a more holistic approach in teacher education. *Teaching and Teacher Education*, *20*(1), 77–97.

Loughran, J. (2006). *Developing a pedagogy of teacher education: Understanding teaching and learning about teaching*. London: Routledge.

Polanyi, M. (1966). *The tacit dimension*. London: Routledge and Kegan Paul.

Sawyer, R. K. (2011). What makes good teachers great? The artful balance of structure and improvisation. In R. K. Sawyer (Ed.), *Structure and improvisation in creative teaching* (pp. 1–24). Cambridge: Cambridge University Press.

Turner, V. (1974). *Dramas, fields, and metaphors: Symbolic action in human society*. Ithaca and London: Cornell University Press.

Van Manen, M. (1991). *The tact of teaching: The meaning of pedagogical thoughtfulness*. New York: State University of New York Press.

Van Manen, M. (2008). Pedagogical sensitivity and teachers practical knowing-in-action. *Peking University Education Review*, *1*(1), 1–23.

Wenger, E. (1998). *Communities of practice*. New York: Cambridge University Press.

2

LEARNING IN AND THROUGH MUSIC

In this chapter we look at the dimensions and understanding of learning. It includes theoretical notions and perspectives on play and anticipation, before exploring musical interaction and learning through music.

IMAGE 2.1 Learning

Approaching different understandings of learning

As we attempt to understand learning, different ideas and thoughts come together in various discourses. At one end, there is a discourse of learning that centres on the teacher and the act of teaching that leads to a predetermined outcome. This discourse implies that there are facts and truths about knowledge waiting to be discovered through hypotheses and experimental research designs involving testing and control groups. Assessment and measurement of learning according to predetermined outcomes at various stages of development may be found in this paradigm (referred to as a 'Positivist' or 'Behaviourist' discourse). At the other end is a discourse of learning where the learner is conceptualised as the active agent in the learning process, which can in turn vary according to the learner's experiences, cultural context, time and place, and social situation. Teaching includes consideration of the learning environment to allow focus and inquiry that are appropriate and meaningful for the learner or group of learners. This set of ideas sees knowledge as co-constructed in a collaborative learning process. The focus is on building a shared learning context and process (the 'Social-Constructivist' discourse).

Sami Paavola, Lasse Lipponen and Kai Hakkarainen (2004) describe different views of learning via three metaphors: learning as knowledge acquisition, learning as participation in a social community, and learning as knowledge creation (p. 557). Learning as knowledge acquisition conceives of the mind as a container of knowledge that can acquire information and transfer it to others. The second, in contrast, views learning as participation in a social community; knowledge is not seen as existing alone, or in an individual mind, but as a shared understanding within a community group. The third, learning as knowledge creation, includes elements of the previous two, combined with the view that knowledge comprises a collective creation of knowledge for the development of a shared activity focus, "knowledge and social practices are constructed by learners." These researchers view the third metaphor as a form of constructivism, with the emphasis on the creation of "something new in the process of learning" (p. 569).

Conceptualising learning as a collective creation of knowledge is a helpful way to understand taking a learner-centred approach to music education, where every process of learning can be the creation of something new.

Theories of learning

Psychological and educational theorists have proposed different notions about how we learn. Jean Piaget suggested that young children take a scientific approach when seeking to understand the world in which they live. They explore and learn by experimenting and self-discovery. He conceived of child development as broadly occurring in stages; a child moves from one stage to the next in a linear fashion. His research of young children was based on experiments, some of which tested a child's developing 'Theory of Mind' and understanding of the perceptions of others, and the age/stage at which these empathetic skills emerge (see Piaget and Inhelder, 1969; Robson, 2012, pp. 84–108).

Lev Vygotsky's ideas have become influential in recent thinking about the way we learn. He suggests that society has an important contribution to make to individual development, and that interaction between parents, carers, peers and the wider cultural context contribute to an individual's higher-order functions. Such higher-order functions include a range from voluntary attention and memory through to the formation of concepts (Vygotsky, 1978).

He proposes that human mental functions originate socially, between people first – the 'interpsychological' aspect – and then within the child or individual – the 'intrapsychological' domain. He saw this as a dynamic interchange in which society is viewed as influencing people, and in which people exert a reciprocal influence on society (Vygotsky, 1978).

A significant concept that Vygotsky (1978) posits is a 'zone of proximal development':

> that an essential feature of learning is that it creates the zone of proximal development; that is learning awakens a variety of internal developmental processes that are able to operate only when the child is interacting with people in his environment and in cooperation with his peers. Once these processes are internalised, they become part of the child's independent developmental achievement.
>
> *(p. 90)*

This concept describes how instruction and learning take place – children's development proceeds through participation in activities slightly beyond their competence (in the 'zone of proximal development') with the help of adults or skillful peers. The process of learning and instruction occurs within a social context. Jerome Bruner and colleagues built on Vygotsky's theory to suggest that the more skillful 'other' scaffolds the child's learning in ways that allow the child to move through the zone to the next level of challenge (see Bruner, 1957; Wood, Bruner, & Ross, 1976). These ideas about learning and teaching are radically different to Piagetian notions of children's exploration through stages of development. Here, learning is social and set within the context of a cultural environment. The prevalent culture of the social group would situate the learning within accepted norms of behaviour (Lave & Wenger, 1991; Wenger, 1998).

Barbara Rogoff (1991, 2003) draws on Vygotskian notions to suggest that learning may be seen in cultural aspects of collaboration: children learn how to participate in cultural activities through observation of adults, who act as guides to the process.

Thinking about the work of music pedagogues, Vygotsky and theorists espousing his notions have helped enrich thinking about group musical and creative processes. Group musical activity could be thought of as a zone of proximal development with more expert 'others' scaffolding the learning of individuals within the group in a dynamic, reciprocal process. Indeed, Lois Holzman (2009) reports on work with a social therapy group where the practitioner worked with the group as a whole, rather than as individuals, with the purpose of creating an 'emotional' zone of proximal development. She found it was a dynamic and ever-changing situation as the different group members were encouraged to create the group's level of emotional development (p. 35).

Ethological thinkers consider that language emerged as a means to communicate propositions with an immediacy, whereas music fostered and sustained social interaction over a longer time scale. Together, they allow for humans to acquire a social and individual cognitive flexibility (Cross, 2001; Cross & Morley, 2009). Music appears to have a social function and integrates thinking across domains to communicate beyond words, or at least in a different way and with a different purpose.

The idea of groups working together, sharing and creating an emotional zone of proximal development, is intriguing and offers relevant concepts to music pedagogues. Through the group process, music and the environment it creates, become a zone of proximal development where rich social–cultural–emotional learning takes place (Pitt, 2014; Pitt & Hargreaves, 2016; Pitt & Hargreaves, 2017).

Perspectives on play, participation and learning

Over the course of the last century, developmental psychology emerged, ethological studies developed, the works of Piaget and Vygotsky became widely known, and the understanding that children learn through play became a dominant discourse.

IMAGE 2.2 Play

Piaget and Inhelder (1969) regarded play from the developmental psychology perspective as starting in the sensori-motor level with repetition, for pleasure, of activities acquired for adaptation during this phase, calling this 'exercise play'. Play then becomes an important aspect of the semiotic function,[1] with the instruments of signs and symbols becoming differentiated signifiers. Signs resemble the signified item, although they may not emulate the size, shape and dimensions of the three-dimensional object that they represent for example, a visual image of an object bears little resemblance to it. Language is considered to be the essential instrumental sign of social adaptation, not invented by the child but transmitted in "ready-made, compulsory and collective forms" (p. 58).

'Symbolic play', according to Piaget and Inhelder (1969), generally occurs during the pre-school period and is superseded by 'games with rules' as children progress to compulsory schooling. Symbolic play was seen by Piaget as the way a child adapts to the adult world, attempting to assimilate reality to the needs of the self. His belief was that play at this 'pre-operational stage of development' helped in reliving events for conflict resolution, compensation for unsatisfied needs or role-inversion (p. 60).

This theory of play is based on an approach focused on cognitive achievements of the individual child and their abilities to reason. It is a developmental theory that presupposes that children follow similar pathways to adulthood and that play follows a sequential order. If we think about musical playfulness from this view-point, children's musical play would follow certain stages through different levels of development. Children might be expected to play in a particular way at a particular age/stage, and there would be generalised, sequential pathways of musical play that would be anticipated as the child matures.

Other theories assume that development progresses in multiple ways, with children following different pathways. Donald Winnicott (1941, 1953, 1971) outlines the role of transitional objects in an infant's development – such as moving away from the mother's breast. One aspect in developing attachment to an object that is 'not me' is an infant's ability to create and imagine. He suggests that infant babbling and an older child singing familiar songs as they fall asleep may also be seen as 'transitional phenomena' (Winnicott, 1971, p. 2), so that thinking and fantasising become caught up with functional experiences of self-comfort. Transitional phenomena such as a soft blanket or a particular cuddly toy get imbued with symbolic value, and this external object helps the child initiate a relationship with the world (p. 2). These first steps in creativity lead to play, and then shared playing. However, gender differences have been found in the ways young children socialise and interact when playing (Evangelou, Sylva, Kyriacou, Wild, & Glenny, 2009).

Vygotsky (1978, p. 94) suggested a theory of cooperation as the basis of the development of moral judgment through rules in game play, proposing that "there is no such thing as play without rules", and maintaining that the role of play in a child's development is fundamental. A stage is reached at which a child can "see one thing but acts differently in relation to what he sees. Thus a condition is reached in which the child begins to act independently of what he sees" (pp. 96–97). In his example, a child playing with a stick can call it a horse and apply meaning to the stick that could be applied to a horse.

Rogoff (2003) applies Vygotsky's notion that play creates its own zone of proximal development, suggesting that children emulate, experiment and practise adult roles in which they may later participate (pp. 298–299). Children also rehearse playing with routines and rules through what Rogoff calls 'guided participation' – "children's active learning in the context of socio-cultural activity, with the guidance of more skilled partners"(Rogoff, 1991, p. 91).

This play involves interpersonal communication, cognitive development and it occurs in the course of everyday social life. It depends on a shared understanding between the novice and the expert (Rogoff, 1991, p. 8) and is concerned with the transmission of culturally appropriate rules, behaviours and practices. Vygotsky (1978) suggests that "an interpersonal process is transformed into an intrapersonal one" (p. 57), that is to say that a child's cultural development occurs first at the social level and then at the individual level. Through this internalisation of cultural forms of behaviour, there is a reconstruction at the inner, psychological level. He asserts that "higher functions originate as actual relations between human individuals" (p. 57). Bert Van Oers (2010) argues that play is also a cultural invention to explore cultural experiences and try out different actions without risk and that enculturation happens for children through 'playful' participation in cultural practices (p. 200). Teaching and learning in music can be thought of as both social and cultural (DeNora, 2000; Wiggins & Espeland, 2012). From this socio-cultural perspective, Rogoff (2003) states, "Humans develop through their changing participation in the socio-cultural activities of their communities, which also change" (p. 11). These cultural processes are around us and often involve taken-for-granted ways of doing things; they constitute a series of interconnected variables such as economic resources, family size and urbanisation – thus one community's way of doing something may vary from another's. There are many right ways.

It is clear that social, emotional and cultural learning are closely linked, perhaps inseparable, and that music represents the traditions and values of a culture, yet also provides affective (emotional) interaction (social) between members of a group. The synthesis of these three dimensions that occurs through music make it a powerful medium for learning. Music embodies values and beliefs of a culture in time and place, through its sound characteristics, its structure and organisation (Clarke, Dibben, & Pitts, 2012). Pamela Burnard (2012, p. 22) suggests that both students and teachers need more awareness of musical creativity as a "situated cultural and social activity".

The music group setting provides a rich environment for playful participation in the cultural practices that predominate (or are accepted or preferred) in that location. The way that musical materials and practices are valued and used, influences how an individual or group construct their identity (Hargreaves & Marshall, 2003), their sense of gender and musical style preferences (Marshall & Shibazaki, 2012). Activities that are playful build on learners' ideas – scaffolded by a more expert guide – and allow for creative cultural experiences that have meaning for the learner and deepens their sense of self in a particular cultural context. If we think about musical playfulness through this socio-cultural lens, we might see that the context of the music making becomes significant: who am I making music with? Who can help me? Who understands me, and who is my companion in my learning?

 Reflection and discussion

1   Recall an example of a child's independent musical play (e.g. a child exploring an instrument alone in a nursery setting).
    • What are the ways you might meet that child in their play?
    • Reflect on the scaffolds you have thought about. How do these support children in what might be meaningful for them in that moment?
    • Can you imagine situations where the scaffold is not to interfere in the physical activity?

Musical interaction from the beginning of life

From our earliest moments, being a good communicator is fundamental to our survival. We need to make ourselves attractive and interesting in order to gain the attention that will keep us alive. We are sophisticated communicators with a keen ear and desire to interact with those closest to us. Research suggests that hearing is the first sense to be fully developed in the foetus. From 30–35 weeks in utero (Lecanuet, 1996; Lecanuet & Schaal, 2002), we can perceive sound and start to become attuned to the voices of our probable primary caregivers. Music can be heard in the womb; indeed pitch and timbre perception starts before birth (Parncutt, 2009; Särkämö, Tervaniemi, & Huotilainen, 2013), and although the sounds are muffled (Woodward & Guidozzi, 1992), they gain attention, soothing and calming premature and newborn babies (Polverini-Rey, 1992; Standley, 1998). We are already becoming attuned to the rhythmic and melodic shapes and frameworks that are likely to surround our early life. This prior knowledge is rapidly built upon in the post-natal period as adult–infant interactions become a key feature of our early existence and seems to play a part in sustaining these initial, primal connections. Not only are we prepared and able to listen to and discern sounds, but we also use this discrimination to interact with a familiar 'sound maker', our primary caregiver. From the start of life, we are listening and responding to sounds for the purposes of bonding and connection with the most important person to our survival. Deaf infants have been found to display vocalisation-related behaviours including touch and visual signals to convey the desire for proximity with their caregiver (Thomson, Kennedy, & Kuebli, 2011, p. 36). The need to develop close attachment and bonding early in life is caught up with maintaining contact and communicating with primary caregivers.

Developmental psychologists, ethnomusicologists and neuroscientists have become increasingly interested in infant-parent interactions. Their studies have revealed startling information: the earliest intimate interactions are exquisite, rhythmically sustained narratives that have an 'intersubjective' quality that is essentially musical in nature. These findings have been defined as 'communicative musicality' (Trevarthen & Malloch, 2000) and refer to the empathetic meaning shared by both parties in early infant-significant other interactions. What seems to help sustain these interactions is what has been referred to as 'motherese'/infant-directed speech (Fernald, 1989; Papoušek & Papoušek, 1981), namely the way that vocalisations with infants seem to take on a melodic rise in pitch, repetition and the widening of eyes and smiling. The interchange also demonstrates cooperation and synchrony (Papoušek, 1996). These adaptations to our speech seem to help and sustain the interaction and are emotionally satisfying.

'Interactional synchrony' (Condon & Ogston, as cited in Sawyer, 2005, p. 52) was referred to by R. Keith Sawyer in relation to group musical performance that requires attunement and flexibility to modify one performer's actions in response to another. He compares musical interaction in jazz to the interactional synchrony between mother and infant. Young children use their instinctive ability to synchronise with another's interaction to adapt to adult social life (Trevarthen, 1979; see also Tronick, Als, & Brazelton, 1980).

IMAGE 2.3 Learning together

From birth, humans utilise sound patterns, organised in time, to express to one another a connectedness that may be essential for survival and could be seen as paving the way for the acquisition of the rules of social interaction in their cultural circumstance. Music is at the core of these pioneering attempts at socialisation by young children. This evidence suggests competency of young children in directing their learning from the start of life. This learning relies on social connections, inter-action with others that also have an emotional and musical component that helps understanding, and the growth of knowledge about the world the infant inhabits.

 Reflection and discussion

1   Find a video clip of a parent and baby vocalising together (there are plenty on the internet). Observe the interactions closely and reflect on this in relation to what you have read and understood from this chapter so far.

- What insights have you gained about infant musicality and parent-infant bonding?
- Write some adjectives that describe your thoughts about young children.

Brain development and musical learning

It is essential to be aware of the contribution that music makes to brain function and to therefore value the importance of music and musical activities through life. By the age of three, the synaptic density of the cerebral cortex is at its highest (at least 50% denser than the adult brain). It is not until puberty that elimination of synapses takes place (DiPietro, 2000). The synapse is the junction between nerve cells where signals may be transmitted from one to another – neural networks are established through regular synaptic exchanges. Learning and development in early childhood are concerned with the maintenance of those neural networks that are used and the elimination of those that are not. Janet DiPietro points out that development across cognitive, socio-emotional, language and motor domains are inter-related, thus enrichment or deprivation in one modality can affect devel-opment in others (DiPietro, 2000). Thinking is clearly a complex cocktail of modalities working together.

Musical training in early childhood was found to improve musically relevant motor and auditory skills, demonstrating structural brain changes (Fujioka, Ross, Kakigi, Pantev, & Trainor, 2006; Hyde et al., 2009; Shahin, Roberts, & Trainor, 2004; Trainor, Shahin, & Roberts, 2003). Informal musical activities carried out at home between parents and young children (2–3 years old) were found to have a beneficial effect on children's auditory discrimination and attention (Putkinen, Tervaniemi, & Huotilainen, 2013). Furthermore, professional musicians' brain images show struc-tural changes when compared with non-musicians (Schlaug, 2001; Schlaug, Jäncke,

Huang, Staiger, & Steinmetz, 1995). These changes probably occurred as a result of a lifetime of musical practise (Gaser & Schlaug, 2003; Johansson, 2006), especially when music training started in early childhood (Bailey & Penhune, 2012; Steele, Bailey, Zatorre, & Penhune, 2013). Children as young as three years old who had received some musical training showed an enhanced ability to distinguish subtle differences in speech sounds (neural differentiation of 'ba' and 'ga' stop consonants) in the auditory brainstem. This enhanced perception is helpful in language acquisition and was found to persist in adult musicians (Strait, Parbery-Clark, O'Connell, & Kraus, 2013). It seems that the malleable brain of the infant can become changed in those individuals who persist with music practise.

Different instruments effect different changes on the practising musician's brain structure , depending on the instrument's left or right hand fine motor skill requirements (Schlaug, Forgeard, Zhu, Norton, Norton, & Winner, 2009, p. 200). The corpus callosum – the neural pathway that transfers information between left and right hemispheres in the brain – has been found to be larger in male musicians compared to male non-musicians, especially those who began music training before the age of seven (Schlaug et al., 1995). Musicians also have an increased efficiency in their sensory level perception and cognitive level auditory processing (see Brattico, Tervaniemi, Näätänen, & Peretz, 2006, pp. 304–314). These studies are mainly of adult professional musicians and confirm that years of music practise can influence the structure of the human brain.

What is clear from neuroscience and developmental psychology research is that the human ability to process sounds and to prefer melodic information is present from birth and perhaps before, and regular engagement in musical activities affect the structure of the brain in the areas of auditory and motor skills (Fujioka, Mourad, & Trainor, 2011; Hannon & Trainor, 2007). This structural change may be beneficial to other areas of learning where auditory processing is helpful, such as language acquisition.

John Flohr (2010) suggests that the brain may be more malleable in the first decade of life, with the brain's plasticity even able to accommodate changes in environmental circumstances. Studies of Romanian orphans who were later adopted found that persistent effects of their previous deprivation were subtle and remained only in the socio-emotional domains (DiPietro, 2000, p. 461). It would appear that the brain can recover from challenging circumstances – change is not permanent unless behaviours are repeated over time.

Young children have malleable and active brains, and learning and development occur across many domains. Humans need to integrate stimuli from all the senses in order to be in an optimal state of being. This involves our entire body, all our senses and our brain (Ayres, 1972). A learning environment that facilitates this integration provides an optimal state for learning and wellbeing (McIntosh, Miller, Shyu, & Hagerman, 1999). Diane Persellin (1992, p. 314) suggests that we learn music through a variety of modalities and that the most effective learning about music happens with a multimodal approach. Learning modalities in this context include visual, kinaesthetic, rhythmic and auditory modes, which all have a place in the learning required to play an instrument. None is more important than the other, and this suggests that using movement, listening to music, using visual elements and playing with all of these should be included in learning music.

Sensory integration theory was proposed by A. Jean Ayres (an occupational therapist), who defined it as "the neurological process that organizes sensation from one's own body and from the environment and makes it possible to use the body effectively within the environment" (Ayres, 1972, p. 11). This explains the relationship between our brains and our behaviour, giving a rationale for how we respond to sensory experiences in our behaviour. In addition to the five senses: touch, taste, sight, smell and sound, there are two others to be aware of. The vestibular sense (movement and balance) tells us where the head and body are in space and in relation to the ground, and the proprioception sense (joint/muscle) gives feedback on how our body parts are moving together (Ayres, 1972). Winnie Dunn (1997) suggests that there is a neurological thresholds continuum; some individuals have low thresholds, the neurons trigger easily, and they can become sensitised rapidly; others with high thresholds do not react as quickly and may need greater sensory stimulation. All of us are somewhere on the continuum.

When we experience music in different ways, using our bodies as instruments, interpreting auditory experiences into visual expression either with our body or with paint or drawing, we get a pleasant feeling of sensory integration. The holistic learning environment opens up possibilities for learning that would not otherwise be available. There is the opportunity for transmodal redesign (Tomlinson, 2012, 2015); interpretation of information from one sense is processed with supporting information from another sense to make learning deeper, richer and more fulfilling (e.g. dancing to the phrases of music).

Learning through music

There is plenty of research to support the benefits of arts-based methods in health and social care and the promotion of wellbeing (e.g. Boyce-Tillman, 2016; Clift & Hancox, 2010; Clift, Hancox, Morrison, Hess, Kreutz, & Stewart, 2010; Kilroy, Garner, Parkinson, Kagan, & Senior, 2007; Staricoff, 2004). Choral singing has been found to contribute to quality of life scores and measurements of wellbeing in adults (see Clift & Hancox, 2010; Clift et al., 2010) and to help with emotional, social and cognitive engagement (see Bailey & Davidson, 2003). Attempts are being made to explore the value of arts-based interventions in public health in terms of wellbeing (see APPGAHW, 2017; Crossick & Kaszynska, 2016; Kilroy et al., 2007).

In education, the transfer benefits of music can be used to justify the inclusion of music activities in the curriculum. With curriculum targets and outcomes to meet, it can be a challenge to justify music for its own sake. Music has been found to be helpful across a number of domains of learning (Hallam, 2010, 2015). In the area of young children's spatial-temporal reasoning, an experimental group and a control group of 4- to 5-year-old children were tested for steady beat, rhythmic pattern and vocal pitch, as well as given a series of Stanford Binet tests (a popular cognitive assessment testing procedure used to measure intelligence or IQ) including a bead memory test – where children reproduced strings of beads that varied in colour and shape having viewed an image of the beads. After the experimental group had received active music training classes for 30 weeks, significant differences were found between the two groups, the music group performing better in all the music-related tasks and the bead memory test (Bilhartz, Bruhn, & Olson, 1999). Six months of music training showed an improvement in spatial-temporal reasoning in 3-year-olds (Gromko & Poorman, 1998). Processing sound has been associated with cognitive sequencing ability; disturbances in sequencing skills of serial-order information have been found in deaf children. It is suggested that sound provides auditory scaffolding for time and serial-order information (Conway, Pisoni, & Kronenberger, 2009).

Groups of pre-school children who studied either piano or voice demonstrated significant improvements in IQ scores compared with children in control groups. However, the children allocated to a drama group scored higher in social skills (Schellenberg & Weiss, 2013; Schellenberg, 2005). These studies also showed strong correlations between parental involvement and post-treatment scores, evidencing the importance of the intersubjective nature of music making as well as the cognitive improvements.

In the realm of speech perception and language acquisition, longitudinal studies with young children aged 8 years showed that those attending music training were significantly better able to identify speech segments than those who attended a painting group (Chobert, François, Velay, & Besson, 2014; François & Schön, 2011; François, Chobert, Besson, & Schön, 2013). Music instruction over four months improved phonemic segmentation fluency ability in a group of kindergarten children compared to a control group (Gromko, 2005). Musical perception skills were found to be associated with phonological processing and early reading ability in pre-school children. Music has also been found to be beneficial for early word use and social and emotional development (Anvari, Trainor, Woodside, & Levy, 2002; Bolduc, 2008). Rhythmic ability was found to be related to phonological awareness and word recognition skills in kindergarten children (Moritz, Yampolsky, Papadelis, Thomson, & Wolf, 2013).

Michael Forrester (2010) studied one child's naturalistic, music-related behaviour for three years. Around 30 examples of musical behaviour were analysed, and the 36 months were divided into three time periods: under 2 years, between 2 and 2.5 years, and from 2.5 to 3 years 10 months (p. 136). Over these time periods, three distinct phases of development were discovered: firstly, social-affective – demonstrated by sound imitation and rhythmic rocking, secondly, 'song-word' play – exemplified by musical independence and word-association song play, and finally narrative-related musicality – the examples given are of frequent spontaneous song play with narrative song-dialogue interdependence (p. 137). Findings suggest that as children are learning language, they hear words as sounds, and that musical play and word play are interlinked. Indeed in the second time period, musical repetition seemed to serve as word-production scaffolding and in the final period became part of the characterisation and realisation of narrative structures. Musical behaviours were used for purposes other than music making for its own sake (p. 150).

Correlations have been found between number concept development and the performed accuracy of rhythm patterns in groups of children aged two to four years, suggesting links between motor development, numeric skill, working memory and conservation capacity (Habegger, 2010). In the domain of emotional learning, practical music activity was found to enhance non-verbal skills and communication of emotion (Boone & Cunningham, 2001). Music can entrain and synchronise social partners' movements in a joint activity, encouraging social behaviour (Kirschner & Tomasello, 2009, 2010). Susan Hallam (2010, pp. 791–817) outlines ways that individuals benefit from affective experiences in music: expressing emotion and developing personal and social skills such as awareness of others, wellbeing and confidence, as well as benefits transferred to other learning areas. Music group interaction over the course of a school year with a group of 8- to 11-year-old children (Rabinowitch, Cross, & Burnard, 2013) showed increased emotional empathy scores after the study compared to the beginning and higher scores than the control group. These results suggest that music group interaction develops social-emotional capacities in children. The group shares a sense of empathy through several characteristics including entrainment, shared intentionality and intersubjectivity (p. 485).

IMAGE 2.4   Music and a playful attitude can help us make sense of the world

The effectiveness of a school-readiness music programme was assessed in terms of children's social-emotional readiness to move from pre-school to kindergarten (Ritblatt, Longstreth, Hokoda, Cannon, & Weston, 2013). A hundred and two children in this study were assigned to two school-readiness music programmes and two non-music control groups. Those in the music groups improved in social skills as measured by cooperation, interaction and social independence scales. Results indicated that using a music-based curriculum facilitated learning social skills that were helpful for making transitions to pre-school (ibid., 2013).

There is much evidence to indicate the ways in which music and music education can be at the heart of fostering lifelong learning in music, arts and self-expression, which contributes to a good quality of life. Musical play and a playful attitude can help us make sense of the world, and this is not limited to childhood. Learning can be multi-sensory, and the creation of holistic environments can open possibilities for learning.

 Reflection and discussion

Reflective working with pictures of different learning situations

These workshop and discussions help us to focus on our own thoughts about teaching and learning. You need pictures of different teaching situations. You can find these with an Internet search using words such as "music lesson" (explore a variety: one-to-one lessons, group lessons, pictures from different decades, learners of different age groups etc.)

- Look at the pictures for a while.
- Write your thoughts on the learners and teachers in these learning situations on post-it notes. Every interpretation is correct.
- Sticking the post-it notes beside the pictures on a wall might be helpful if you are working with a group of students.
- Discuss in small groups.

Note

1 Semiotic function – the ability to mentally represent events and objects – this occurs in the pre-operational stage of development (Piaget & Inhelder, 1969, pp. 52–56)

References

Anvari, S. H., Trainor, L. J., Woodside, J., & Levy, B. A. (2002). Relations among musical skills, phonological processing and early reading ability in preschool children. *Journal of Experimental Child Psychology, 83*(2), 111–130. doi: 10.1016/s0022-0965(02)00124-8

APPGAHW. (2017). All-Party Parliamentary Group on Arts, Health and Wellbeing. *Creative health: The arts for health and wellbeing report*. artshealthandwellbeing.org.uk/appg/inquiry

Ayres, A. J. (1972). *Sensory integration and learning disorders*. Los Angeles: Western Psychological Services.

Bailey, B. A., & Davidson, J. W. (2003). Amateur group singing as a therapeutic instrument. *Nordic Journal of Music Therapy, 12*(1), 18–32.

Bailey, J., & Penhune, V. B. (2012). A sensitive period for musical training: Contributions of age of onset and cognitive abilities. *Annals of the New York Academy of Sciences, 1252*(1), 163–170.

Bilhartz, T. D., Bruhn, R. A., & Olson, J. E. (1999). The effect of early music training on child cognitive development. *Journal of Applied Developmental Psychology, 20*(4), 615–636. doi: 10.1016/s0193-3973(99)00033-7

Bolduc, J. (2008). The effects of music instruction on emergent literacy capacities among preschool children: A literature review. *Early Childhood Research & Practice, 10*(1).

Boone, R. T., & Cunningham, J. G. (2001). Children's expression of emotional meaning in music through expressive body movement. *Journal of Nonverbal Behavior, 25*(1), 21–41. doi: 10.1023/a:1006733123708

Boyce-Tillman, J. (2016). *Experiencing music: Restoring the spiritual: Music as well-being*. Oxford: Peter Lang.

Brattico, E., Tervaniemi, M., Näätänen, R., & Peretz, I. (2006). Musical scale properties are automatically processed in the human auditory cortex. *Brain Research, 1117*(1), 162–174.

Bruner, J. S. (1957). *Going beyond the information given*. New York: Norton.

Burnard, P. (2012). Rethinking "musical creativity" and the notion of multiple creativities in music. In O. Odena (Ed.), *Musical creativity: Insights from music education research* (pp. 5–28). Surrey: Ashgate.

Chobert, J., François, C., Velay, J.-L., & Besson, M. (2014). Twelve months of active musical training in 8- to 10-year-old children enhances the preattentive processing of syllabic duration and voice onset time. *Cerebral Cortex, 24*(4), 956–967. doi: 10.1093/cercor/bhs377

Clarke, E., Dibben, N., & Pitts, S. (2012). *Music and mind in everyday life*. Oxford: Oxford University Press.

Clift, S., & Hancox, G. (2010). The significance of choral singing for sustaining psychological wellbeing: Findings from a survey of choristers in England, Australia and Germany. *Music Performance Research, 3*(1), 79–96.

Clift, S., Hancox, G., Morrison, I., Hess, B., Kreutz, G., & Stewart, D. (2010). Choral singing and psychological wellbeing: Quantitative and qualitative findings from English choirs in a cross-national survey. *Journal of Applied Arts & Health, 1*(1), 19–34.

Conway, C. M., Pisoni, D. B., & Kronenberger, W. G. (2009). The importance of sound for cognitive sequencing abilities: The auditory scaffolding hypothesis. *Current Directions in Psychological Science, 18*(5), 275–279.

Cross, I. (2001). Music, cognition, culture, and evolution. *Annals of the New York Academy of Sciences, 930*(1), 28–42.

Cross, I., & Morley, I. (2009). The evolution of music: Theories, definitions and the nature of the evidence. In *Communicative musicality: Exploring the basis of human companionship* (pp. 61–81). Oxford: Oxford University Press.

Crossick, G., & Kaszynska, P. (2016). *Understanding the value of arts & culture: The AHRC cultural value project*. London: Arts and Humanities Research Council.

DeNora, T. (2000). *Music in everyday life*. Cambridge: Cambridge University Press.

DiPietro, J. A. (2000). Baby and the brain: Advances in child development. *Annual Review of Public Health, 21*(1), 455–471.

Dunn, W. (1997). The impact of sensory processing abilities on the daily lives of young children and their families: A conceptual model. *Infants & Young Children, 9*(4), 23–35.

Evangelou, M., Sylva, K., Kyriacou, M., Wild, M., & Glenny, G. (2009). *Early years learning and development: Department for children, schools and families.* Research report DCSGF-RR176.

Fernald, A. (1989). Intonation and communicative intent in mothers' speech to infants: Is the melody the message? Child development, 60(6), 1497–1510.

Flohr, J. W. (2010). Best practices for young children's music education: Guidance from brain research. *General Music Today, 23*(2), 13–19.

Forrester, M. A. (2010). Emerging musicality during the pre-school years: A case study of one child. *Psychology of Music, 38*(2), 131–158. doi: 10.1177/0305735609339452

Francois, C., & Schön, D. (2011). Musical expertise boosts implicit learning of both musical and linguistic structures. *Cerebral Cortex, 21*(10), 2357–2365. doi: 10.1093/cercor/bhr022

François, C., Chobert, J., Besson, M., & Schön, D. (2013). Music training for the development of speech segmentation. *Cerebral Cortex, 23*(9), 2038–2043. doi: 10.1093/cercor/bhs180

Fujioka, T., Ross, B., Kakigi, R., Pantev, C., & Trainor, L. J. (2006). One year of musical training affects development of auditory cortical-evoked fields in young children. *Brain, 129*(10), 2593–2608.

Fujioka, T., Mourad, N., & Trainor, L. J. (2011). Development of auditory-specific brain rhythm in infants. *European Journal of Neuroscience, 33*(3), 521–529.

Gaser, C., & Schlaug, G. (2003). Brain structures differ between musicians and non-musicians. *The Journal of Neuroscience, 23*(27), 9240–9245.

Gromko, J. E. (2005). The effect of music instruction on phonemic awareness in beginning readers. *Journal of Research in Music Education, 53*(3), 199–209.

Gromko, J. E., & Poorman, A. S. (1998). The effect of music training on preschoolers' spatial-temporal task performance. *Journal of Research in Music Education, 46*(2), 173–181. doi: 10.2307/3345621

Habegger, L. (2010). Number concept and rhythmic response in early childhood. *Music Education Research, 12*(3), 269–280. doi: 10.1080/14613808.2010.504810

Hallam, S. (2010). The power of music: Its impact on the intellectual, social and personal development of children and young people. *International Journal of Music Education, 28*(3), 269–289.

Hallam, S. (2015). *The power of music: A research synthesis on the impact of actively making music on the intellectual, social and personal development of children and young people.* London: Music Education Council.

Hannon, E. E., & Trainor, L. J. (2007). Music acquisition: Effects of enculturation and formal training on development. *Trends in Cognitive Sciences, 11*(11), 466–472.

Hargreaves, D. J., & Marshall, N. A. (2003). Developing identities in music education. *Music Education Research, 5*(3), 263–273.

Holzman, L. (2009). *Vygotsky at work and play.* London and New York: Routledge.

Hyde, K. L., Lerch, J., Norton, A., Forgeard, M., Winner, E., Evans, A. C., & Schlaug, G. (2009). Musical training shapes structural brain development. *The Journal of Neuroscience, 29*(10), 3019–3025.

Johansson, B. B. (2006). Music and brain plasticity. *European Review, 14*(1), 49–64.

Kilroy, A., Garner, C., Parkinson, C., Kagan, C., & Senior, P. (2007). Towards transformation: Exploring the impact of culture, creativity and the arts of health and wellbeing. *A consultation report for the critical friends event.* Arts for Health, Manchester Metropolitan University, Manchester.

Kirschner, S., & Tomasello, M. (2009). Joint drumming: Social context facilitates synchronization in preschool children. *Journal of Experimental Child Psychology, 102*(3), 299–314. doi: 10.1016/j.jecp.2008.07.005

Kirschner, S., & Tomasello, M. (2010). Joint music making promotes prosocial behavior in 4-year-old children. *Evolution and Human Behavior, 31*(5), 354–364.

Lave, J., & Wenger, E. (1991). *Situated learning: Legitimate peripheral participation.* Cambridge: Cambridge University Press.

Lecanuet, J. P. (1996). Prenatal auditory experience. In I. Deliège & J. Sloboda (Eds.), *Musical beginnings: Origins and development of musical competence.* Oxford: Oxford University Press.

Lecanuet, J. P., & Schaal, B. (2002). Sensory performances in the human foetus: A brief summary of research. *Intellectica, 1*(34), 29–56.

Marshall, N. A., & Shibazaki, K. (2012). Instrument, gender and musical style associations in young children. *Psychology of Music, 40*(4), 494–507.

McIntosh, D. N., Miller, L. J., Shyu, V., & Hagerman, R. J. (1999). Sensory-modulation disruption, electrodermal responses, and functional behaviors. *Developmental Medicine & Child Neurology, 41*(9), 608–615.

Moritz, C., Yampolsky, S., Papadelis, G., Thomson, J., & Wolf, M. (2013). Links between early rhythm skills, musical training, and phonological awareness. *Reading & Writing, 26*(5), 739–769. doi: 10.1007/s11145-012-9389-0

Paavola, S., Lipponen, L., & Hakkarainen, K. (2004). Models of innovative knowledge communities and three metaphors of learning. *Review of Educational Research, 74*(4), 557–576.

Papoušek, M. (1996). Intuitive parenting: A hidden source of musical stimulation in infancy. In I. Deliège & J. Sloboda (Eds.), *Musical beginnings: Origins and development of musical competence.* New York: Oxford University Press.

Papoušek, M., & Papoušek, H. (1981). Musical elements in the infant's vocalization: Their significance for communication, cognition, and creativity. *Advances in Infancy Research, 1,* 163–224.

Parncutt, R. (2009). Prenatal development and the phylogeny and ontogeny of music. In S. Hallam, I. Cross, & M. Thaut (Eds.), *The Oxford handbook of music psychology* (pp. 219–228). Oxford: Oxford University Press.

Persellin, D. C. (1992). Responses to rhythm patterns when presented to children through auditory, visual, and kinesthetic modalities. *Journal of Research in Music Education, 40*(4), 306–315.

Piaget, J., & Inhelder, B. (1969). *The psychology of the child.* London: Routledge and Kegan Paul.

Pitt, J. (2014). *An exploratory study of the role of music with participants in children's centres.* (Unpublished doctoral thesis), University of Roehampton, London. http://hdl.handle.net/10142/321585

Pitt, J., & Hargreaves, D. J. (2016). Attitudes towards and perceptions of the rationale for parent – child group music making with young children. *Music Education Research,* 1–17.

Pitt, J., & Hargreaves, D. J. (2017). Exploring the rationale for group music activities for parents and young children: Parents' and practitioners' perspectives. *Research Studies in Music Education, 39*(2), 177–194. doi: 1321103X17706735

Polverini-Rey, R. A. (1992). *Intrauterine musical learning: The soothing effect on newborns of a lullaby learned prenatally.* (Doctoral dissertation). Los Angeles: California School of Professional Psychology.

Putkinen, V., Tervaniemi, M., & Huotilainen, M. (2013). Informal musical activities are linked to auditory discrimination and attention in 2–3-year-old children: An event-related potential study. *European Journal of Neuroscience, 37*(4), 654–661.

Rabinowitch, T. C., Cross, I., & Burnard, P. (2013). Long-term musical group interaction has a positive influence on empathy in children. *Psychology of Music, 41*(4), 484–498. doi: 10.1177/0305735612440609

Ritblatt, S., Longstreth, S., Hokoda, A., Cannon, B.-N., & Weston, J. (2013). Can music enhance school-readiness socioemotional skills? *Journal of Research in Childhood Education, 27*(3), 257–266. doi: 10.1080/02568543.2013.796333

Robson, S. (2012). *Developing thinking and understanding in young children: An introduction for students*. London: Routledge.

Rogoff, B. (1991). *Apprenticeship in thinking: Cognitive development in social context* (1st ed.). New York: Oxford University Press.

Rogoff, B. (2003). *The cultural nature of human development*. New York: Oxford University Press.

Särkämö, T., Tervaniemi, M., & Huotilainen, M. (2013). Music for the brain across life. *Sound-Perception-Performance Current Research in Systematic Musicology*, *1*, 181–194.

Sawyer, K. R. (2005). Music and conversation. In D. Miell, R. MacDonald, & D. J. Hargreaves (Eds.), *Musical communication* (pp. 45–60). Oxford: Oxford University Press.

Schellenberg, E. G., & Weiss, M. W. (2013). Music and cognitive abilities. In D. Deutsch (Ed.), *The psychology of music* (3rd ed., pp. 499–550). Amsterdam: Elsevier.

Schellenberg, G. E. (2005). "Music and cognitive abilities". *Current Directions in Psychological Science*, *14*(6), 317–320.

Schlaug, G. (2001). The brain of musicians. *Annals of the New York Academy of Sciences*, *930*(1), 281–299.

Schlaug, G., Forgeard, M., Zhu, L., Norton, A., Norton, A., & Winner, E. (2009). Training-induced neuroplasticity in young children. *Annals of the New York Academy of Sciences*, *1169*(1), 205–208.

Schlaug, G., Jäncke, L., Huang, Y., Staiger, J. F., & Steinmetz, H. (1995). Increased corpus callosum size in musicians. *Neuropsychologia*, *33*, 1047–1055.

Shahin, A., Roberts, L. E., & Trainor, L. J. (2004). Enhancement of auditory cortical development by musical experience in children. *Neuroreport*, *15*(12), 1917–1921.

Standley, J. M. (1998). Pre and perinatal growth and development: Implications of music benefits for premature infants. *International Journal of Music Education*, *os-31*(1), 1–13. doi: 10.1177/025576149803100101

Staricoff, R. L. (2004). *Arts in health: A review of the medical literature*. London: Arts Council England.

Steele, C. J., Bailey, J. A., Zatorre, R. J., & Penhune, V. B. (2013). Early musical training and white-matter plasticity in the corpus callosum: Evidence for a sensitive period. *The Journal of Neuroscience*, *33*(3), 1282–1290.

Strait, D. L., Parbery-Clark, A., O'Connell, S., & Kraus, N. (2013). Biological impact of preschool music classes on processing speech in noise. *Developmental Cognitive Neuroscience*, *6*, 51–60.

Thomson, N. R., Kennedy, E. A., & Kuebli, J. E. (2011). Attachment formation between deaf infants and their primary caregivers: Is being deaf a risk factor for insecure attachment? In D. Zand (Ed.), *Resilience in deaf children* (pp. 27–64). New York: Springer.

Tomlinson, M. M. (2012). Transformative music invention: Interpretive redesign through music dialogue in classroom practices. *Australian Journal of Music Education*, *1*, 42–56.

Tomlinson, M. M. (2015). Transmodal redesign in music and literacy: Diverse multimodal classrooms. *Journal of Early Childhood Literacy*, *15*(4), 533–567.

Trainor, L. J., Shahin, A., & Roberts, L. E. (2003). Effects of musical training on the auditory cortex in children. *Annals of the New York Academy of Sciences*, *999*(1), 506–513.

Trevarthen, C. (1979). Communication and cooperation in early infancy: A description of primary intersubjectivity. In M. Bullowa (Ed.), *Before speech: The beginning of interpersonal communication* (pp. 321–347). New York: Cambridge University Press.

Trevarthen, C., & Malloch, S. (2000). The dance of well-being: Defining the musical therapeutic effect. *Nordic Journal of Music Therapy*, *9*(2), 3–17.

Tronick, E. C., Als, H., & Brazelton, T. B. (1980). The infant's communicative competencies and the achievement of intersubjectivity. In M. R. Key (Ed.), *The relationship of verbal and non-verbal communication* (pp. 261–273). The Hague: Mouton.

Van Oers, B. (2010). Children's enculturation through play. *Engaging play* (pp. 195–209). Maidenhead: McGraw-Hill Open University Press.

Vygotsky, L. S. (1978). *Mind and society: The development of higher mental processes.* Cambridge, MA: Harvard University Press.

Wenger, E. (1998). *Communities of practice: Learning, meaning and identity.* New York: Cambridge University Press.

Wiggins, I., & Espeland, M. I. (2012). Learning contexts. In *The Oxford handbook of music education* (Vol. 1, p. 341). New York, Oxford: Oxford University Press.

Winnicott, D. W. (1941). The observation of infants in a set situation. *The International Journal of Psycho-Analysis, 22,* 229.

Winnicott, D. W. (1953). Transitional objects and transitional phenomena – a study of the first not-me possession. *The International Journal of Psycho-Analysis, 34,* 89–97.

Winnicott, D. W. (1971). *Playing and reality.* London: Tavistock Publications.

Wood, D. J., Bruner, J. S., & Ross, G. (1976). The role of tutoring in problem solving. *Journal of Child Psychiatry and Psychology, 17*(2), 89–100.

Woodward, S. C., & Guidozzi, F. (1992). Intrauterine rhythm and blues? *International Journal of Obstetrics and Gynaecology, 99*(10), 787–790.

3

COLLABORATIVE LEARNING IN MUSIC

This chapter takes the innate need for belonging and bonding as the starting point to explore the topic of collaboration – an important element for learning in music. Aspects of forming and being in groups are discussed, and a parent-child music group activity is examined.

IMAGE 3.1 Collaboration

Fruitful working in a group (as a facilitator or as a participant) requires a willingness to feel insecure and curious. All members affect the atmosphere and the process. An approach where dialogue and collaborative inquiry allow possibilities for working together directs the focus to group dynamics, removing the emphasis on managing behaviour, searching for a 'right solution' or applying ready-made strategies to solve problems. For the pedagogue, this means an emphasis on the understanding of group dynamics and sensitivity.

Bonding and belonging through music

There seems to be something primal and instinctive about the way we express ourselves and our connections with others through music. Musicality appears to be an essential part of our human 'being' that helps us coordinate both our intimate one-to-one relationships and our group social behaviour.

Walter Freeman (1997) points to the use of music by our ancestors for bonding beyond the nuclear family. Group music making seems to have its origins in our ancestry, and its value may be emotional as well as social. One only has to think of a sports event to be reminded of the power of communal singing of a familiar song, full of significance for the group. It establishes coherence and a sense of social bonding, as well as having a negative impact by reinforcing the boundary between those who belong and those who do not.

In music sessions we are dealing with emotions – our own as pedagogues and those of the learners. In music activities we are touched and affected in many ways (see e.g. Hallam, 2015). Collaborative learning in a group can be a focus for multiple emotions: peer-to-peer or a pedagogue with other group members (and in family music groups between parent-child), and these are intertwined with those feelings aroused by music. Although there is a wide range of research concerning music and emotions, it is not clear which musical content will cause which emotion – the individual and the context both influence this (Sloboda & Juslin, 2010). The emotional dimension of music teaching comprises several aspects. There is the emotional response to music, the emotional components experienced as a music pedagogue, and the group members' emotional reactions to being part of a group musical process.

Music enables cooperation and empathic relationships where creating and communicating music become part of learners' individual pathways of learning through collaboration (Burnard, Okuno, Boyack, Howell, Blair, & Giglio, 2017, p. 61). Hallam (2015) identifies participation in group music making as promoting feelings of togetherness, along with shared attention and intention. This, she suggests, can assist us in understanding the emotional state of others, a vital aspect in the development of empathy (p. 89). Emotional intelligence is a separate, more contested area that may be enhanced by active participation in music making. As we listen to and recognise the emotional components of music, our own emotional sensitivity may be enhanced (Hunter & Schellenberg, 2010).

In human mother-infant interactions, music occurs so readily that its function must assist the emotional coordination between them, promoting feelings of enjoyment and strengthening bonds. It may also play a part in soothing and regularising mother and child daily functions (Dissanayake, 2000, 2004, 2006, 2010). The surging, explosive feelings that are caused through repetition by mothers in their multimodal stimulation of their infants, Daniel Stern (1985) called 'vitality affect'. This 'vitality affect' may be thought of as a burst of energy that stimulates and sustains the interaction and leads to a shared feeling-state between the pair. Mothers' use of vocal and kinesic phrases in a series of repeated runs produced an episode of maintained engagement and was found to order the stimulus world for their infant interactions (Stern, Beebe, Jaffe, & Bennett, 1977). The multimodal quality of these interactions, combined with ritual community practices, may have helped our ancestors, and us, to cope with emotions caused by uncertain situations (see Mithen, 2005, as cited in Dissanayake, 2010, p. 25).

Alan Fogel (1993) believes that connections with other people are fundamental to the way individuals think and develop their sense of self-identity, and that it is through the 'micro-culture' of the parent-infant relationship that an infant learns the 'macro-culture' of the wider community (p. 13). From the very beginning, infants' musicality helps to shape the micro-culture that will inform the wider cultural community to which they belong. Active music making enhanced musical, communicative and social development in infants 6–12 months old (Gerry, Unrau, & Trainor, 2012). It was found that joint drumming facilitated synchronisation of body movement amongst groups of children aged 2 1/2- to 4 1/2-years-old (Kirschner & Tomasello, 2009). A subsequent study (Kirschner & Tomasello, 2010) showed that among a group of 4-year-olds who engaged in joint music making, their spontaneous cooperative and helpful behaviour increased. It appeared that sharing a common goal of moving or vocalising together in time had benefits that extended beyond the music activity and into behaviour in the classroom. It would seem that there are aspects of music that help us tune-in to others, and through sharing the same moment in time we feel more cooperative.

We are social beings from birth (Durkin, 1998); our relationships and their emotional connectedness are integral to our social behaviour. Howard Gardner in *Frames of Mind* speaks of 'personal intelligence' (one of the intelligences within his multiple intelligences theory) as being concerned with an ability to "access one's own feeling life", by discriminating and then synthesising feelings into symbolic codes, which assist in understanding and guiding behaviour. Personal intelligence also involves an ability to look outwards, "to notice and make distinctions with other individuals", to their moods, motivations, intentions and temperaments (Gardner, 1984, p. 253). These inward and outward dimensions of personal intelligence lead to understanding feeling and mood states in ourselves and others. They start to be acquired during the primary relationship of mother and child, in which musicality plays a strong part: "Emotions guide our actions, enable expression of our states to others, and allow us to interpret other people" (Clarke, Dibben, & Pitts, 2012, p. 82).

Belonging to the group, and the sense of ritual described by Victor Turner (see 1974, 1982, 1986, 2009) as occurring in group situations, plays a part in our cultural, social and emotional development. The unity of behaviour that occurs as part of a symbolic activity (e.g. a well-known folk dance or song with actions) creates a separate time and space where ritual and performance are made possible (see e.g. Pitt, 2014). In a group music activity, permission is given to share levels of intimacy and closeness that might not otherwise be possible. Christopher Small (1998) talks about the role of ritual, metaphor, art and emotion as inseparable parts of social interaction. He suggests that ritual – repeated actions that have lost their meaning – may have negative connotations in today's society. He highlights the positive position that ritual can occupy in group activities, as it articulates relationships and ways of being that can be ideal imaginings, combined with a sometimes imperfect reality (pp. 94–109).

Understanding the group as a learning environment

Bonding and belonging through music are fundamental to our human nature, which makes the group learning context a fruitful and interesting environment.

Group processes and activities that contain creative elements require particular attention in terms of creating a safe learning environment, to secure 'psychological safety' in the learning process (see e.g. Edmondson, 1999, 2004; Schein 1996). To feel safe means that we can somehow conceive of the tasks as not too challenging,

IMAGE 3.2 'The group photo'

the group is accepting of everyone as they are, and it trusts that the leader is competent to foster the process. When the group consists of people who are not acquainted with each other, these feelings of safety are weaker but grow stronger as the leader and the group members get to know each other, and the ways of working become more familiar. Trust and safety can be enhanced by activities using the names of the participants. A sense of togetherness can be built by focusing in the present moment and facilitating 'encounters' and interactions in the group, with movements and games.

The most common understanding of the phases of group behaviour was introduced by Bruce Tuckman (1965): Forming, Storming, Norming and Performing (Adjourning was added later – Tuckman & Jensen, 1977). Knowing this may help the pedagogue to focus on the possibilities and fruitful challenges in the different phases of a group. After the formation and creation of safety within the group, it is likely to enter a more turbulent storming phase (Tuckman, 1965). This does not have to be a dramatic event, but some critical junctions may occur. These junction points simply tell the members of the group that it is time to negotiate, to recheck and to discuss the group's functioning (for example, the purpose, working culture, the leader and their working practices, the group's motivation and engagement).

Wilfred Bion (1961) in his fundamental illustration about group dynamics suggested that groups are easier to understand if viewed as an outcome derived from emotionally driven aims. He suggested that every group functions at two levels simultaneously: one level focuses on the purpose of the group, trying to act at a rational level of behaviour (work group), the other, the 'basic assumption group', functions at a level of behaviour derived from tacit underlying assumptions. Bion identified three types of these: dependency, fight–flight and pairing (Bion, 1961); for example – in a students of teaching group, behaviours could be passive resistance to workshop activities, giggling, not listening to the instructions for activities, being over critical and analytical when the workshop activities call for emotional engagement. It can be useful if criticism and questioning can be guided towards a shared focus of inquiry (Nikkola & Löppönen, 2014; also Huhtinen-Hildén, 2012). This presents a challenge for the leader, although it offers beneficial experiential learning about group dynamics. When working with colleagues, indicators might be arriving late to meetings or concentrating on a mobile phone. This is not to say that criticism and questioning of the group's working together is unwelcome; indeed it is part of the process and can turn out to be a driving force for collaborative learning and creativity.

Exploring and approaching the functions of the group as a 'shared inquiry' in open dialogue, where positive and negative aspects are welcome, allow the group to use its capacity to develop a successful and well-functioning environment for working and learning. Some of the functions happen non-verbally, through actions, or in the creative process through artistic expression. The leader's role is to ensure that the dialogue includes all members of the group so as to enhance feelings of fairness.

Much creative working of the group is realised in this way as interaction in music takes a non-verbal form.

When supported well, the group becomes a system with its own norms, rules, working culture and internal management. At this stage it can be quite autonomous, and the leader's positions/tasks are very different from those needed when the group was in its infancy. Collaborative working takes into account all members of the group, respecting their different views and personalities.

In the turbulent 'storming' phase of the group, another direction is possible – a scapegoat is found. It could be the leader, a member of the group, or a particular circumstance, and as a result the working in the group becomes difficult or even impossible. Tiina Nikkola's (2011) research on teacher education programmes points to the necessity for pedagogues to be aware of these hidden and unconscious aspects that can prevent learning in a group.

The group process travels through different phases of challenge, storms or crises, and may arrive at a point where the working is collaborative and rewarding, with the group regulating and managing the process and enjoying flow in creativity. Understanding and being curious about group processes can help the leader to adjust their pedagogical approaches and will facilitate the interpretation of the ongoing dynamics. Our role as pedagogues is to focus on the potential of the group, finding the most successful tasks and ways to support the specific group by being present in that moment.

Group work needs, and even provokes, different roles from its members. Some take active, leadership roles whereas others follow. Some members take responsibility for the task, others may be concerned with keeping to time, while other members are concerned with the welfare of the group, resolving conflicts and caring about individual worries and concerns. Some members distract the group from its focus and function by disrupting, trying to steal the attention, making jokes or attacking others. As a group member, we are all part of these dynamics, and our roles are dependent on the roles of others; there is no neutral position (Rogoff, 2003, pp. 26–29). Etienne Wenger (1998) describes a negotiation that allows one to enter the community of practice in order to become an 'insider', which involves moving from the edges and a place of detachment and observation. Findings related to parent-child music group activities speak of a virtuous circle that is set up by the confident and dynamic atmosphere of an established group that enables newcomers to accelerate their assimilation into group activities (Youth Music, 2006, p. 31). "Outsiders are newcomers to the meaning system, with limited understanding of how practices fit together and how they developed from prior events" (Rogoff, 2003, p. 26). Issues of insiders and outsiders are connected to the fact that we are continually functioning in a socio-cultural context. Those on the edges may be seeking to understand a community's practices; it may be a new meaning system; they may be faced with the community's/group's conventions (we always stand on one leg as we sing hello, or we shake our heads when we dance like this).

As music pedagogues it is essential we reflect on our assumptions – what is acceptable music for a group of learners, and why do we think it is acceptable? How do we create a virtuous circle to include everyone in the creative process? Do we make assumptions about who are acceptable people, character-types or ways of learning? These questions highlight the importance of pedagogical awareness and actions that contribute to the formation of a community of practice in music group processes.

 Reflection and discussion

IMAGE 3.3 Encountering challenge

Group reflection: describe a challenging situation or event

In small groups, consider the challenging situation from different viewpoints:

- Practical scaffolds
- Structure and preparation of the session
- Ways to facilitate learning and interaction to include thoughts about pedagogical actions and choices.

Draw a flower with your challenging topic in the centre – make each petal an alternative approach, interpretation, view of the situation or solution.

Share the flower pictures and discuss your reflections. This way of working embraces the diversity of interpretations and possible pedagogical solutions to challenging situations. It draws our attention away from searching for 'right' solutions to focus on understanding the multi-faceted nature of group dynamics in the moment.

Early music activities as a form of collaborative learning and participation

In a music group for young children with their parents/carers, the non-verbal communicative competence shared by the group members is a means of participation. The sharing of the ritual culture of something as simple as an action song comprises formal structure, actual teaching and the need for imitative fidelity (Eckerdal & Merker, 2009, p. 251). By joining in with the symbolic actions, group members demonstrate a shared knowledge, meaning and understanding of the cultural tradition of that song, dance or activity, in that place and time. This could be seen as the development of a community of practice in which mutual engagement, shared repertoire and joint enterprise enable a shared understanding of what it is to 'be', in this case, a music group in this setting (see Wenger, 1998).

Vygotsky (1968) suggested that the essence of human growth is that children learn and develop by "performing a head taller than they are" (p. 102). Learning and development are social (joint, interpersonal, collective), with participants building 'zones' – the spaces between who they are and who they are becoming, at one and the same time (Holzman, 2009, p. 30). This could be applied to the music group above, in which self-assessment seemed to be part of the process of 'becoming' through performing the symbolic/ritualised actions with others.

Action songs can be viewed as the child's first introduction to active participation in human ritual (Eckerdal & Merker, 2009, p. 251). Clapping, lying down, jumping, moving side-to-side, holding hands, being lifted up or bounced rhythmically, performing specific actions to the song with hands – all these activities occur as part of a song, and participants perform them at particular moments within the song, in a sense ritually acting out the narrative of the lyrics. This ritual/symbolic element takes place because of the music – it provides the frame – creating a special, liminal environment (Boyce-Tillman, 2009), in which performance is accepted and enjoyed. Symbolic activities constitute "a formal framework providing both easily recognizable structural continuity and repeated occasions to celebrate progressively accumulating successes over developmental time" (Eckerdal & Merker, 2009, p. 253).

In a study of parent/carer-child group music making (Pitt, 2014), the music activities were seen to contain and support the group in their co-participation. It provided a safe framework for rehearsing a variety of social, cultural and symbolic activities. These were shared through the structured time of the music so that the group experienced a state of flow, which led to positive feelings and the building of self-esteem and confidence amongst group members. The musical-social-learning setting of the parent-child music making group allowed all participants (adult and child) to perform together, and the resultant group activity was greater than the sum of its parts (Pitt, 2014).

The Musical-Social-Learning model (Pitt, 2014, p. 310) shown in Figure 3.1 suggests that music is an inescapable environment that contains, supports and encourages the four other aspects of the group activity that simultaneously influence one another. The quality of the musical environment (if you are present in the

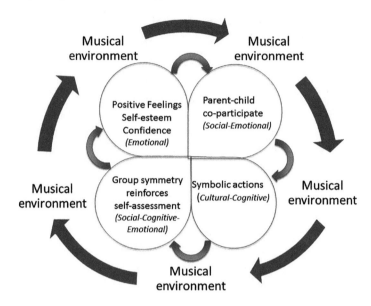

FIGURE 3.1   The Musical-Social-Learning Model (Pitt, 2014, p. 310)

room, you cannot escape the music) is shown by the encircling arrows at the outer edge of the diagram.

The inner figure shows the different elements observed as part of the group music making activity. They are interconnected and influence one another. Each piece in the central figure activates one or more domains of development and learning: social, emotional, cultural and cognitive. The way 'Parent-child co-participate' is both social and emotional. One-to-one interaction benefits parent-child bonding (Pitt, 2014). Furthermore, parents play an important role in their young children's music education (Street, Young, Tafuri, & Ilari, 2003; Street, 2006); co-participation facilitates active engagement and learning together. 'Symbolic actions' require memory skills to coordinate the actions of the song in the right place at the right time and to sing the song simultaneously – both cognitive functions. They represent a cultural interchange, which may convey subtle messages about cultural norms and expectations. The 'group symmetry' of interaction – sharing the same song at the same time – creates an emotional response, whereas the self-assessment – checking one's actions against the rest of the group – is essentially a cognitive one. The group sense of 'communitas', being together and participating in the song, is social. The final element of the figure represents emotional responses: the 'positive feelings, self-esteem and confidence' that result from the experience, feeding a desire to repeat it, thereby building skills and knowledge through the process (Pitt, 2014).

This view about early music activities reveals the potent learning potential of the group context which facilitates, for all participants, rich possibilities for learning about music, through music and in music.

Reflection and discussion

IMAGE 3.4 A childhood memory

1   Think about young children you know and find some adjectives to describe your thoughts about them. Using this list of words and the information in the text box below, reflect on how ideas about early childhood may affect music education.

The conceptualisation of children as learners from Western philosophical perspectives is still influencing our daily practice. Differing conceptions of childhood could exist in the minds of a gathering of pedagogues. These discourses can run through every teaching situation.

Heather Montgomery (2003) outlines the key discourses of childhood, a topic that has shaped the following section.

The evil and wild child

Thomas Hobbes (1588–1679) was an English philosopher who believed that children are born evil with unruly and wild behaviour that must be tamed by adults. This discourse was prevalent amongst Puritans of the time who advocated for sinful, ignorant children to be enlightened through discipline and moral education.

The child as a blank slate or empty vessel (tabula rasa)

The view proposed by John Locke (1632–1704) in his 'Essay Concerning Human Understanding' (1690) is of childhood as a time of 'becoming'. Childhood is seen as a precursor to being fully human and adult. Locke viewed children as being born with potential, and their experiences in life shaped and formed them. He felt education should develop a rational and reasoning mind. Children were not viewed as innately good or bad, but rather as a vessel to be filled with liquid or as a blank slate to be written on. Children, through correct guidance and experience, become a product of their environment. One can see in this discourse how parents may be viewed as being at fault and responsible for children's behaviour.

Innocent childhood (a romantic view)

This view is prevalent in Western culture. Children are viewed as naturally innocent, to be protected from the evils of adult life. Childhood should be a time of innocence and play, young children allowed to develop at their own pace in natural surroundings. Jean Jacques Rousseau (1712–1778), a French philosopher, published 'Emile or On Education' in 1762, which viewed childhood as a distinct phase that can be corrupted by adults who take away children's innocence. He implied that children are inherently good. Education of children should allow for individual progression and freedom to follow their own interests and pursuits.

Children as competent social actors

A dominant discourse about childhood comes from the United Nations, based on the notion that every person has the same human rights. The United Nations Convention on the Rights of the Child (1989) enshrined some universal rights for children, and almost every nation has signed the treaty. Children are regarded as the holders of rights, and the approach to pedagogy might focus on a critical view of the power relations inherent in teaching and a desire to empower the student through the pedagogical approaches selected.

(Montgomery, 2003, pp. 46–80)

References

Bion, W. R. (1961). *Experiences in groups*. London: Tavistock Publications.

Boyce-Tillman, J. (2009). The transformative qualities of a liminal space created by musicking. *Philosophy of Music Education Review*, 17(2), 184–202.

Burnard, P., Okuno, E., Boyack, J., Howell, G., Blair, D., & Giglio, M. (2017). Becoming performers: Creating participatory spaces collaboratively. In P. Burnard & R. Murphy (Eds.), *Teaching music creatively* (2nd ed., pp. 60–73). London: Routledge.

Clarke, E., Dibben, N., & Pitts, S. (2012). *Music and mind in everyday life*. Oxford: Oxford University Press.

Dissanayake, E. (2000). *Art and intimacy: How the arts began*. Seattle: University of Washington Press.

Dissanayake, E. (2004). Motherese is but one part of a ritualized, multimodal, temporally organized, affiliative interaction. *Behavioral and Brain Sciences*, 27(4), 512–513. doi: 10.1017/S0140525X0432011X

Dissanayake, E. (2006). Ritual and ritualization: Musical means of conveying and shaping emotion in humans and other animals. In S. Brown & U. Volgsten. (Eds.), *Music and manipulation: On the social uses and social control of music* (pp. 31–56). Oxford & New York: Berghahn Books.

Dissanayake, E. (2010). Root, leaf, blossom, or bole: Concerning the origin and adaptive function of music. In S. Malloch & C. Trevarthen (Eds.), *Communicative musicality: Exploring the basis of human companionship* (pp. 17–30). Oxford: Oxford University Press.

Durkin, K. (1998). Developmental social psychology. In W. S. Miles Hewstone & G. M. Stephenson (Eds.), *Introduction to social psychology* (pp. 46–73). Oxford: Blackwell Publishers Ltd.

Eckerdal, P., & Merker, B. (2009). "Music" and the "action song" in infant development: An interpretation. In S. Malloch & C. Trevarthen (Eds.), *Communicative musicality: Exploring the basis of human companionship* (pp. 241–262). New York, NY: Oxford University Press.

Edmondson, A. (1999). Psychological safety and learning behavior in work teams. *Administrative Science Quarterly, 44*(2), 350–383.

Edmondson, A. (2004). Psychological safety, trust and learning: A group-level lens. In R. M. Kramer & K. S. Cook (Eds.), *Trust and distrust in organizations: Dilemmas and approaches* (pp. 239–272). New York: Russell Sage Foundation.

Fogel, A. (1993). *Developing through relationships.* Chicago: University of Chicago Press.

Freeman, W. (1997). A neurobiological role of music in social bonding. In N. M. Wallin, B. Merker, & S. Brown (Eds.), *The origins of music* (pp. 411–424). Cambridge, MA: The MIT Press.

Gardner, H. (1984). *Frames of mind.* London: Fontana.

Gerry, D., Unrau, A., & Trainor, L. J. (2012). Active music classes in infancy enhance musical, communicative and social development. *Developmental Science, 15*(3), 398–407. doi: 10.1111/j.1467-7687.2012.01142.x

Hallam, S. (2015). *The power of music: A research synthesis on the impact of actively making music on the intellectual, social and personal development of children and young people.* London: Music Education Council.

Holzman, L. (2009). *Vygotsky at work and play.* London and New York: Routledge.

Huhtinen-Hildén, L. (2012). *Kohti sensitiivistä musiikin opettamista: Ammattitaidon ja opettajuuden rakentumisen polkuja [Towards sensitive music teaching: Pathways to becoming a professional music educator].* Jyväskylä: Jyväskylä Studies in Humanities 180. University of Jyväskylä.

Hunter, P. G., & Schellenberg, E. G. (2010). Music and emotion. In M. Jones, R. Fay, & A. Popper (Eds.), *Music perception* (pp. 129–164). New York: Springer.

Kirschner, S., & Tomasello, M. (2009). Joint drumming: Social context facilitates synchronization in preschool children. *Journal of Experimental Child Psychology, 102*(3), 299–314. doi: 10.1016/j.jecp.2008.07.005

Kirschner, S., & Tomasello, M. (2010). Joint music making promotes prosocial behavior in 4-year-old children. *Evolution and Human Behavior, 31*(5), 354–364. doi: 10.1016/j.evolhumbehav.2010.04.004

Mithen, S. (2005). *The singing Neanderthals: The origin of language, music, mind and body.* London: Weidenfeld and Nicolson.

Montgomery, H. (2003). Childhood in time and place. In M. Woodhead & H. Montgomery (Eds.), *Understanding childhood: An interdisciplinary approach* (Vol. 1, pp. 46–80). Milton Keynes: John Wiley and Sons Ltd. in association with The Open University.

Nikkola, T. (2011). *Oppimisen esteet ja mahdollisuudet ryhmässä: Syyllisyyden kehittyminen syntipukki-ilmiöksi opiskeluryhmässä ohjaajan tulkitsemana [Learning in a group: Obstacles and opportunities. A supervisor's interpretation of how guilt becomes scapegoating in a study group.].*

Jyväskylä Studies in Education, Psychology and Social Research, 422. Jyväskylä: University of Jyväskylä.

Nikkola, T., & Löppönen, T. (2014). *Oivalluksia ryhmästä – pintaa syvemmälle koulun ryhmäilmiöihin*. Helsinki: Kehittämiskeskus Opinkirjo ry.

Pitt, J. (2014). *An exploratory study of the role of music with participants in children's centres*. (Unpublished doctoral thesis), University of Roehampton, London. http://hdl.handle.net/10142/321585

Rogoff, B. (2003). *The cultural nature of human development*. New York: Oxford University Press.

Schein, E. H. (1996). Kurt Lewin's change theory in the field and in the classroom: Notes toward a model of managed learning. *Systems Practice, 9*(1), 27–47.

Sloboda, J. A., & Juslin, P. N. (2010). At the interface between the inner and outer world: Psychological perspectives. In P. N. Juslin & J. A. Sloboda (Eds.), *Handbook of music and emotion: Theory, research, applications* (pp. 73–97). Oxford: Oxford University Press.

Small, C. (1998). *Musicking: The meanings of performing and listening*. Middletown, CT: Wesleyan University Press.

Stern, D. N. (1985). *The interpersonal world of the infant: A view from psychoanalysis and developmental psychology*. New York: Basic Books.

Stern, D. N., Beebe, B., Jaffe, J., & Bennett, S. L. (1977). The infant's stimulus world during social interaction: A study of caregiver behaviors with particular reference to repetition and timing. *Studies in mother-infant interaction* (pp. 177–202). London: Academic Press Inc. Ltd.

Street, A. (2006). *The role of singing within mother-infant interactions*. (Unpublished Ph.D. thesis). London: University of Roehampton.

Street, A., Young, S., Tafuri, J., & Ilari, B. (2003). *Mothers' attitudes to singing to their infants*. Proceedings of the 5th ESCOM conference, Hanover University of Music and Drama, Germany.

Tuckman, B. W. (1965). Developmental sequence in small groups. In *Psychological Bulletin, 63*(6), 384.

Tuckman, B. W., & Jensen, M. A. C. (1977). Stages of small-group development revisited. *Group & Organization Studies, 2*(4), 419–427.

Turner, V. (1974). *Dramas, fields, and metaphors: Symbolic action in human society*. Ithaca and London: Cornell University Press.

Turner, V. (1982). *From ritual to theatre: The seriousness of human play*. New York: Performing Arts Journal Publications.

Turner, V. (1986). *The anthropology of performance*. New York: Performing Arts Journal Publications.

Turner, V. (2009). *The ritual process: Structure and anti-structure*. New Brunswick: Aldine Transaction.

Vygotsky, L. S. (1968). *Thought and language*. Cambridge, MA: MIT Press.

Wenger, E. (1998). *Communities of practice: Learning, meaning and identity*. New York: Cambridge University Press.

Youth Music. (2006). *Turning their ears on . . . : Keeping their ears open: Exploring the impact of musical activities on the development of pre-school age children; Summary of research project commissioned by youth music*. London: National Foundation for Youth Music.

4

PEDAGOGY – A SENSITIVE IMPROVISATORY PRACTICE

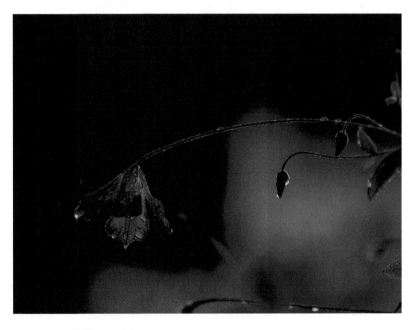

IMAGE 4.1 Being sensitive

This chapter focuses on pedagogical sensitivity in music practice. It explores the essential elements of professional practice that are more than the obvious and accepted skills and techniques of effective music teaching. It highlights the values and thinking behind the knowledge and skills through which we support learning. The likelihood of various emotions surfacing in creative and music activities needs to be taken into account. Custodero (2010) writes, "The ease in which music can be associated with strong feelings has implications for music learners, suggesting both much potential for personal growth and also a need to approach musical choices with caution and sensitivity" (p. 66). A dominant discourse in music teaching is concerned with learning outcomes. This has been the established way of expressing the professional pedagogical process, starting with careful planning. However, it can be problematic to focus on outcomes, as this approach might not meet the learners´ needs, foster their participation and allow for delicate initiatives in creative dialogue. On the other hand, a clear structure for the lesson is also important to create a framework for the learning process. These contrasting positions may be explained by the current vocabulary we are using and the thinking behind it.

Therefore, a new vocabulary may be needed to highlight those issues that encourage learner-centred practice. A challenge for many in music education is to develop a shared, mutually agreed-upon set of words and definitions that adequately express those learning dimensions that are open-ended, co-constructed, more difficult to assess and less visible in terms of achievement. Without this shared repertoire (Wenger, 1998), we rely on terms we are used to using as part of our professional practice. In order to foster learners' musical creativity, it is vital that the pedagogue can be viewed as the facilitator and not the one with the solution (Veloso & Carvalho, 2012). "At its most fundamental, it involves the posing, in multiple ways, of the question 'What if?' – and therefore involves the shift from 'What is this and what does it do?' to 'What can I do with this?'" (Craft, 2001, p. 54; Craft, Cremin, Burnard, & Chappell, 2007).

What if – instead of setting the goals for learning – we started using the idea of "opening possibilities for learning" (see Huhtinen-Hildén, 2017)? This would give us quite a different landscape. Rather than being concerned with what our learners will learn, or should achieve through different actions, we are interested in opening various possibilities for them to use this exploration for their own purposes and personal aims.

Teaching can be thought of as an improvisational profession (DeZutter, 2011), acknowledging that tension exists between teaching viewed from this lens and the planning-centric view of teaching (pp. 27–29). There is always a need to negotiate with unpredictable elements of professional practice and to be prepared to feel vulnerable (see Biesta, 2013; Van Manen, 1991, 2008). This means aiming for a delicate balance of structure and improvisation (see Sawyer, 2011, pp. 1–3).

Fascination and caring as cornerstones of pedagogy

Fascination as a guiding force for pedagogical decision-making is a revolutionary thought. Rather than having aims, targets, achievements, assessments and curriculum as definers of a 'quality' practice (although they still remain features of the work), a different force drives decision-making. The 'quality' discourse often dismisses the caring elements of teaching – which we might call 'loving kindness', 'professional love' (Page, 2011), 'pedagogical love' (Skinnari, 2007), or teaching as a 'caring profession' (Van Manen, 2008) – leading to a focus on achievement in education, denying perhaps what is equally important. This caring element is not a clear signifier of achievement, and therefore it is more difficult to assess. Associating education with care may position it with low status and importance. The affectionate, loving bond between pedagogue and learner is, however, essential to wellbeing and is a foundation for achieving what Plato and Aristotle defined as 'eudaimonia' or happiness – the primary human pursuit.

The notion of quality practice is ubiquitous in education – we do not question it as a concept. Gunilla Dahlberg, Peter Moss and Alan Pence (2007) argue that quality is a challenge to be achieved rather than a concept to be questioned (p. 3). They consider the term 'quality' as a product of enlightenment thinking that complements modernist constructions of children and education. It is not a neutral word but a socially-constructed notion, producing a quality-discourse that has measurable outcomes of achievement (p. 87). It is far more difficult to conceive of measurable indicators of 'loving kindness' in practice. How does a learner know that their pedagogue 'loves' them? Jools Page (2011) suggests that there is a certain taboo associated with using the term 'love' in connection with practitioners expressing feelings about the children they work with. She found that mothers in her study all wanted professionals to show what she called 'professional love' towards their children even though they may not have used the term (p. 320). Irrespective of the terms we use, the sensitive pedagogue sees "each child as the child needs to be seen through the lens of compassion and respect" (Littleton, 2015, p. 64).

Fascination as a cornerstone of pedagogy refers to an intense interest and attraction towards the shared adventure of learning in and through music coupled with the teacher's sensitive, caring and emotional involvement in the learning process. Caring and fascination go together to form "pedagogical thoughtfulness, a multifaceted and complex mindfulness toward children" (Van Manen, 1991, pp. 5–10). June Boyce-Tillman (2016) talks about searching for what lies beyond and the need for 'wonder' in our musical relationships with children.

Pedagogical sensitivity as a mode of professional knowing

Van Manen states that "the pedagogical dimension of teaching relies on forms of knowledge that are not always easily captured in conceptual and theoretical languages" (Van Manen, 2008). This dilemma comes into focus when dealing with the arts and artistic expression and experience as a learning environment. Pedagogical sensitivity (see Van Manen, 1986, 1991, 2008) is at the heart of learner-centred professional music practice and can be seen as a means to articulate the tacit dimension of professional knowing and actions.

The professional knowledge and skills that are visible, verbally easy to explain or otherwise obvious represent one level of expertise. There is also a large and vital level of expertise – the tacit professional knowledge and knowing – that steers our professional thinking and actions (see also Hakkarainen, Lonka, & Lipponen, 2005; Loughran, 2006; Toom, 2006, 2008). Donald Schön (1987) writes, "Whatever language we may employ, however, our descriptions of knowing–in–action are always constructions. They are always attempts to put into explicit, symbolic form a kind of intelligence that begins by being tacit and spontaneous. For knowing–in–action is dynamic and 'facts', 'procedures', 'rules' and 'theories' are static" (Schön, 1987, p. 25).

IMAGE 4.2   Sensitivity

The visible knowledge base might include features such as appropriate elements of music practice, clear use of instructions depending on the child's age or stage of development, modelling good use of the voice, and pitching of songs at a child-appropriate level. Less tangible skills and attributes (tacit knowing) might include an awareness of an individual's needs within the group, when to encourage participation and when to observe, and giving time and space for a child's musical response. This depends on being sensitive and aware of the 'sustained shared meaning' (Sylva, Melhuish, Sammons, Siraj-Blatchford, & Taggart, 2004) implicit in music. The adhesive that binds the different dimensions of music pedagogues' professional knowledge is 'pedagogical sensitivity' – synthesising the dynamics of the group, the pedagogue's actions and thinking in the moment, and music as a learning environment (Huhtinen-Hildén, 2012).

Figure 4.1 shows the intertwining of the music educator's professional knowledge and identity. This model is informed by Bereiter, 2002; Toom, 2006; and Tynjälä, 2007, 2008, 2011 – forming what Connelly and Clandinin (1995) call the professional knowledge landscape of the music educator. Pedagogical sensitivity is placed at the centre and ties the different forms of knowledge together, so it is usable in the pedagogical moment. Päivi Tynjälä's (2004, 2007, 2008) 'integrative pedagogics' is a principle based on the notion that theory, practice and self-regulation (key elements) should be integrated in any learning situation.

The figure also depicts 'Music-related knowledge', which might include the theoretical knowledge of music and the technical skills necessary to play an instrument.

FIGURE 4.1 The integrative model of professional knowledge and knowing needed in music teaching (Huhtinen-Hildén, 2012, p. 230)

'Knowledge related to teaching and interaction' comprises child development and preparing the learning environment. 'Self-regulative knowledge' could encompass meta–cognitive processes, such as being able to reflect on the teaching process as it happens. The way that the various pieces of the model work together and inform one another, or affect or influence professional knowledge and identity, is dynamic and dependent on the context and experiences.

Professional pedagogical sensitivity is something that can be developed. In a study investigating the formation process of professional knowledge and identity in becoming a professional music pedagogue, a participant explained, "I haven't thought for a long time now that you are born to be a teacher; it's more like an ongoing growing and developing process" (quote from a student of teaching, Huhtinen-Hildén, 2012, p. 123). A pedagogical moment can emerge as an art form, like a composition, and the music pedagogue can be seen as a 'pedagogical artist', facilitating and supporting the process (ibid., p. 122). In this view the participants are co-creators and the group an orchestra creating together.

There are elements to this professional knowing that can be compared to those found in a sensitive parent (see, e.g. Ainsworth, Blehar, Waters, & Wall, 1978; see also Arola, Paavola, & Körkkö, 2009; Kivijärvi, 2003). These include seeing the world through the child's eyes, to sense and to know things at a non-verbal level, and to interpret the child's messages, responding appropriately at the right time, depending on the child's age and developmental level.

Thinking about teaching as interaction and dialogue, with learning at the centre of the process, allows the possibility of including both the pedagogue's and the learner's potential for growth and change. This can be facilitated with the question, "How could I think, act and be as a pedagogue to enable learning, creativity and individually meaningful experiences for learners?" (Holm, 2013 adapted by Huhtinen-Hildén). The responses and pedagogical thinking in relation to this question can create a dialogic landscape for the learning situation.

Reflection as part of practice

Reflection is a term that is frequently used in relation to teaching; being a reflective pedagogue is an assumed characteristic of effective practice. What do we mean by reflection? What is reflective practice?

IMAGE 4.3 Reflection

Loughran (2006, p. 96) suggests starting with a problem – something to think about in relation to practice. He stresses that the problem does not necessarily need to be negative, but it does need to be recognised, in order to be a focus for drawing attention to the need for reflection. Schön (1983) talks of 'framing and reframing' the situation to firstly describe it and then to view it from different perspectives in order to understand what happened in the process. Seeing a problem through one frame is limiting, as only one set of possible solutions may be apparent. Viewing the problem through multiple frames reveals many possible pathways and solutions (Barnes, 1992, p. 17).

These notions are helpful for thinking about reflections on musical processes. The term 'problem' can be reconceptualised as 'an issue for inquiry' as part of the adventure in pedagogical thinking. The reflective, sensitive pedagogue lives with the presence of multiple lenses to reframe and enquire as a continual part of the pedagogical process: before the moment, in the moment, after the moment, with colleagues and alone. Van Manen (1991, pp. 98–99) describes the purpose of reflection in the educative process as enabling thinking about the meaning, purpose and significance of the experience; coming to decisions about possible alternative actions; and making choices based on this thinking.

Various positions of a pedagogue

In order to open up the possibilities for learning, the pedagogue uses different 'positions' (Langenhove & Harré, 1999). In a teaching situation, awareness of using 'the right tool for the job' guides the positioning in action. For example, if we want to teach a rhythmic pattern, the instructions must be clear, and learners are activated to concentrate (the pedagogue positions themselves as an activator, instructor, encourager, supporter, motivator or model). When the pedagogue facilitates the creation of a dance in a group, they position themselves differently. Initiative and ideas are encouraged, and the pedagogue acts as a facilitator, a project coordinator, a co-creator and an assistant rather than an instructor. In the first situation, learning can appear as 'concentrated working', while in the latter it may appear chaotic and messy with spontaneous expressions. Different situations require different pedagogical positions and choices.

In order to support all the learners in a group, the pedagogue is required to open up individual possibilities for learning, possibly at many skill levels simultaneously, which requires a teaching approach that challenges the pedagogue and calls for the flexibility to change positions.

> All the learners were invited to 'play their names' around the circle. The first few learners clapped the syllables of their name (the pedagogue's intention but not made explicit); the turn fell to Jason who expressed his name with a full body wiggle, without clapping the expected rhythm pattern. The pedagogue looked at Jason with confusion and responded by saying: "I think 'Jason' sounds more like this," and clapped the two syllables. Jason curled in on himself.

This (fictitious) example shows how underlying beliefs about practice can override in moments of uncertainty. The pedagogue was unable to be flexible in finding a position to support this unexpected interpretation of what 'playing your name' means and therefore missed the opportunity to open to a wider learning possibility, not just for Jason but for the whole group.

Each action calls for something in response, perhaps an 'improvisational pedagogical approach' (see Sawyer, 2011) that uses flexible positions – child-led or child-initiated, adult-led or initiated, supported or suggested. It can then be possible to open up possibilities for learning within the group, and the task in hand ('playing your name') can be flexibly interpreted. Positions are taken in many ways: by gestures, tone of voice, words chosen, so that the more creative and collaborative an approach, the more flexibly you need to use a variety of positions in the learning situation (e.g. as a project manager, creative assistant, co-musician, tutor). The different positions in pedagogical practice can be the tools for conveying a respectful attitude that supports the development of a competent learner through positive self-image as an important participant and an equal member of the ensemble. Sari Muhonen (2014) argues for collaborative, creative processes to enrich students' belief in their musical capability and agency. She also highlights the need for further research in this area.

Figure 4.2 illustrates a variety of positions and tasks a pedagogue may use to support learning within different learning processes.

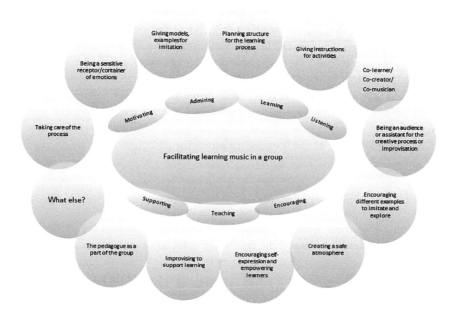

FIGURE 4.2   Facilitating learning music in a group

Reflection and discussion

1   Reflect on a teaching situation you found positive:
   - What were the pedagogue's actions, approaches or 'being' in this situation?
   - Share your reflections with others on the issues highlighted in this chapter concerning teacher knowledge and pedagogical sensitivity.
2   Think about the following tasks and positions of a pedagogue. What experiences do you remember that are related to them? What situations and concrete examples can you think of?
   - Teaching, supporting, encouraging, motivating, listening, learning and admiring
   - Giving models or examples for imitation
   - Giving instructions for activities
   - Taking care of the process
   - Planning the structure for the learning process
   - Being a co-learner
   - Being a co-creator
   - Being a co-musician
   - Being an audience member or assistant for the creative process or improvisation
   - Encouraging different examples to imitate and explore
   - Encouraging self-expression and empowering learners
   - Creating a safe atmosphere
   - Being a sensitive receptor or container of emotions
   - Improvising to support learning in various ways
   - Being part of the group
3   Thinking about yourself as a pedagogue, which of the items listed above do you find natural and easy, and which might you find more difficult or demanding? Share your thoughts in a small group.

References

Ainsworth, M. D. S., Blehar, M. C., Waters, E., & Wall, S. (1978). *Patterns of attachment: A psychological study of the strange situation*. Hillsdale, NJ: Erlbaum.

Arola, L., Paavola, L., & Körkkö, P. (2009). Äidin sensitiivisyys ja hoivapuheen perustaajuuden vaihtelu – yhteydet lapsen varhaisen kielen ja puheen kehitykseen. *Puhe ja kieli, 29* (3), 145–162.

Barnes, D. (1992). The significance of teachers' frames for teaching. In H. Munby & T. Russell (Eds.) *Teachers and teaching: From classroom to reflection* (pp. 9–32). London: Routledge.

Bereiter, C. (2002). *Education and mind in the knowledge age*. Mahwah, NJ: Lawrence Erlbaum Associates.

Biesta, G. J. (2013). *The beautiful risk of education*. London: Routledge.

Boyce-Tillman, J. (2016). *Experiencing music: Restoring the spiritual: Music as well-being*. Oxford: Peter Lang.

Connelly, F. M., & Clandinin, D. J. (1995). Teachers' professional knowledge landscapes: Secret, sacred, and cover stories. In D. J. Clandinin & F. M. Connelly. *Teachers' professional knowledge landscapes* (pp. 3–15). New York: Teachers College Press.

Craft, A. (2001). Little c creativity. In A. Craft, B. Jeffrey, & M. Leibling (Eds.), *Creativity in education* (pp. 45–61). London: Continuum.

Craft, A., Cremin, T., Burnard, P., & Chappell, K. (2007). Developing creative learning through possibility thinking with children aged 3–7. In A. Craft, T. Cremin, & P. Burnard (Eds.), *Creative learning 3–11 and how we document it*. London: Trentham.

Custodero, L. A. (2010). Meaning and experience: The musical learner. In H. F. Abeles & L. A. Custodero (Eds.), *Critical issues in music education: Contemporary theory and practice* (pp. 61–86). New York: Oxford University Press.

Dahlberg, G., Moss, P., & Pence, A. (2007). *Beyond quality in early childhood education and care: Languages of evaluation* (2nd ed.). London: Falmer Press.

DeZutter, S. (2011). Professional improvisation and teacher education: Opening the conversation. In R. K. Sawyer (Ed.), *Structure and improvisation in creative teaching* (pp. 27–50). Cambridge: Cambridge University Press.

Hakkarainen, K., Lonka, K., & Lipponen, L. (2005). *Tutkiva oppiminen: Järki, tunteet ja kulttuuri oppimisen sytyttäjinä*. Porvoo: WSOY.

Holm, P. (2013). *Voimavarakeskeisen työnohjauskoulutuksen 2013–2015 opetusmateriaali*. Unpublished.

Huhtinen-Hildén, L. (2012). *Kohti sensitiivistä musiikin opettamista: Ammattitaidon ja opettajuuden rakentumisen polkuja [Towards sensitive music teaching: Pathways to becoming a professional music educator]*. Jyväskylä Studies in Humanities 180. Jyväskylä: University of Jyväskylä.

Huhtinen-Hildén, L. (2017). Elävänä hetkessä: Suunnitelmallisuus ja pedagoginen improvisointi [Present in a moment: Systematic planning and pedagogical improvisation]. In A. Lindeberg-Piiroinen & I. Ruokonen (Eds.), *Musiikki varhaiskasvatuksessa – käsikirja [Music in early childhood education – a handbook.]* (pp. 389–411). Helsinki: Classicus.

Kivijärvi, M. (2003). Äidin sensitiivisyys varhaisessa vuorovaikutuksessa [Mother's sensitivity in early interaction]. In P. Niemelä, P. Siltala, & T. Tamminen (Eds.), *Äidin ja vauvan varhainen vuorovaikutus*. Juva: WSOY.

Langenhove, L., & Harré, R. (1999). Introducing positioning theory. In R. Harré & L. van Langenhove (Eds.), *Positioning theory: Moral contexts of intentional action* (pp. 14–31). Oxford: Blackwell Publishers Ltd.

Littleton, D. (2015). *When music goes to school: Perspectives on learning and teaching*. Lanham; Boulder; New York; London: Rowman & Littlefield.

Loughran, J. (2006). *Developing a pedagogy of teacher education: Understanding teaching and learning about teaching*. London: Routledge.

Muhonen, S. (2014). Songcrafting: A teacher's perspective of collaborative inquiry and creation of classroom practice. *International Journal of Music Education, 32*(2), 185–202.

Page, J. (2011). Do mothers want professional carers to love their babies? *Journal of Early Childhood Research, 9*(3), 310–323.

Sawyer, R. K. (2011). What makes good teachers great? The artful balance of structure and improvisation. In R. K. Sawyer (Ed.), *Structure and improvisation in creative teaching* (pp. 1–24). Cambridge: Cambridge University Press.

Schön, D. A. (1983). *The reflective practitioner: How professionals think in action* (Vol. 5126). New York: Basic Books.

Schön, D. A. (1987). *Educating the reflective practitioner: Toward a new design for teaching and learning in the professions.* San Francisco: Jossey-Bass.

Skinnari, S. (2007). *Pedagoginen rakkaus [Pedagogical love].* Juva: PS-kustannus.

Sylva, K., Melhuish, E., Sammons, P., Siraj-Blatchford, I., & Taggart, B. (2004). *The effective provision of pre-school education (EPPE) project: Final report: A longitudinal study funded by the DfES 1997–2004.* Institute of Education, University of London/Department for Education and Skills/Sure Start

Toom, A. (2006). *Tacit pedagogical knowing: At the core of teacher's professionality.* Helsinki: Helsinki University.

Toom, A. (2008). Hiljainen pedagoginen tietäminen opettajan työssä. In A. Toom, J. Onnismaa, & A. Kajanto (Eds.), *Hiljainen tieto: Tietämistä, toimimista ja taitavuutta* (pp. 163–186). Aikuiskasvatuksen 47. vuosikirja. Jyväskylä: Gummerus.

Tynjälä, P. (2004). Asiantuntijuus ja työkulttuurit opettajan ammatissa. *Kasvatus, 35*(2), 174–190.

Tynjälä, P. (2007). Integratiivinen pedagogiikka osaamisen kehittämisessä. In H. Kotila, A. Mutanen, & M. V. Volanen (Eds.), *Taidon tieto* (pp. 11–36). Helsinki: Edita.

Tynjälä, P. (2008). Perspectives into learning at the workplace. *Educational Research Review, 3,* 130–154.

Tynjälä, P. (2011). Asiantuntijuuden kehittämisen pedagogiikkaa. In K. Collin, S. Paloniemi, H. Rasku-Puttonen, & P. Tynjälä (Eds.), *Luovuus, oppiminen ja asiantuntijuus* (pp. 79–95). Helsinki: WSOY.

Van Manen, M. (1986). *The tone of teaching.* Richmond Hill, ON, Canada: Scholastic Press.

Van Manen, M. (1991). *The tact of teaching: The meaning of pedagogical thoughtfulness.* New York: State University of New York Press.

Van Manen, M. (2008). Pedagogical sensitivity and teachers practical knowing-in-action. *Peking University Education Review, 1*(1), 1–23.

Veloso, A. L., & Carvalho, S. (2012). Music composition as a way of learning: Emotions and the situated self: Musical creativity: Insights from music education research. In O. Odena (Ed.), *Musical creativity: Insights from music education research* (pp. 73–91). Surrey: Ashgate.

Wenger, E. (1998). *Communities of practice.* New York: Cambridge University Press.

5

PLANNING – PREPARING FOR NAVIGATION AND NEGOTIATION OF MUSIC LEARNING

IMAGE 5.1 Navigation

Previous chapters have discussed various discourses of learning and teaching and how they might affect pedagogical thinking and actions. This chapter focuses on navigation and negotiation in the learning process. How do I plan a session to support and scaffold learning? What motivates my pedagogical choices in the moment?

Recognising a successful teaching situation may be relatively simple – the 'flow' experience and the creative and positive atmosphere in the situation may be obvious clues. It can be more difficult to be aware of the underpinning pedagogical components that lead to this teaching situation being successful. This awareness could be important in deepening our pedagogical thinking and understanding.

This deeper, underpinning layer, harder to name, contributes to the added dimension that signifies good teaching. To the outsider it can appear a mysterious quality that only some teachers possess, marking them out as especially gifted. However, these deeper professional actions – presence, sensitivity and thinking – can be developed, understood and used deliberately by any pedagogue.

The underpinnings of pedagogical practice are often explained through a teaching method, also known as 'Grand Methods' in music education. Thomas A. Regelski (2004) suggests that we should be aware of a tendency to latch on to the technical notions presented in 'Grand Methods' (Kodály, Orff, Suzuki, Dalcroze) approaches without considering the socio-cultural contexts of the learners. This 'methodolatry' (Regelski, 2004, p. 7) can dominate practice and subjugate individual learning journeys. In any reflective music pedagogue's practice, there will probably be evidence of many threads and influences from the 'Grand Methods'. They are channelled through 'practical reasoning', which takes account of the fluid and ever-changing learning situations (see Regelski, 2012). Many of these pioneers of music education did not set out to build a method, but wanted to inspire an holistic approach to learning music. Cathy Benedict (2010, pp. 194–195) cautions music educators to look beneath the technical dimensions and search for the philosophical foundations to the 'Method'. Marja-Leena Juntunen and Heidi Westerlund (2011) present a way of thinking about 'Grand Methods' through narrative heuristics so that the approaches can be tested through the lens of reflection in practice (p. 8). In this way, the stories presented in the fundamental principles of the pioneers can be re-told through today's music education narratives. Re-telling these stories does not mean that we are stuck with the systems and structures that have been constructed around the pioneers' philosophies.

Thinking about the learning situation

Perceptions about the complex, multi-faceted nature of the learning space affect our pedagogical choices. As Loughran (2006, p. 45) mentions, we tend to focus on things we expect to see. Furthermore, we tend to see things we can handle and through lenses familiar to us. Unpicking and understanding the components, their interconnectivity and functionality, enhances our capacity to sense and capture the complexity of the teaching-learning situation. It is a system full of aims, emotions, elements and intentions. One way of approaching this system is illustrated in Figure 5.1. Every aspect in this system is interconnected – the pedagogue's knowledge, identity and sensitivity affect the approaches used in the situation. The learner, as well as the teacher, brings their feelings, values, temperament and experiences of learning to the situation, and these play a role in the process.

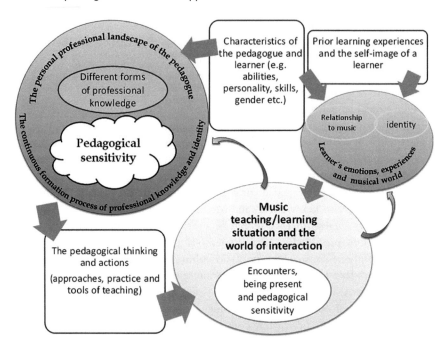

FIGURE 5.1 Dimensions and elements in a teaching situation (Huhtinen-Hildén, 2013, p. 170)

This figure illustrates the elements that form the landscape of a teaching situation that we navigate through. When looking at this figure, it is possible to understand the surprises we encounter in teaching situations – there are many elements that impact on the present moment mediated through the experiences, emotions and memories of all participants.

 Reflection and discussion

As a pedagogue:

- What makes me feel that I have succeeded?
- What am I afraid or ashamed of?
- What makes me angry?
- What would I like to learn more about?

Consider the various dimensions and elements in Figure 5.1 – how do the issues raised by your reflections impact on the different areas in the figure?

A map for navigation – preparing pathways for learning

Many teachers and pedagogues use lesson planning to define preparations they make prior to teaching/learning situations. By focusing differently on planning, it becomes possible to reconceptualise this as 'opening the possibilities for learning'. The multi-faceted planning that is needed to open learning possibilities for all the learners in a group, instead of using plans with clear, predetermined aims and targets, could be re-imagined as 'facilitating the journey', 'scaffolding possible learning pathways' or 'guiding the exploration'. Preparation for the journey remains of utmost importance; there may be several options or pathways to consider to support various learning possibilities, before the learning group comes together.

The metaphor of a map usefully describes the process of preparing for the teaching situation with options in mind. A map is needed to enable us to navigate (see Wenger, 1998) in the pedagogical situation. In order for this to happen, the leader has had to consider several possible pathways beforehand. Just like planning a group journey, there are many things to think about in advance. You will have considered the needs of the group and appropriate places to visit based on their needs and wishes. You will also have thought about suitable modes of transport for the group and will be adequately prepared for the different weather conditions, with snacks to hand, sun-cream, aspirin, umbrella etc. You will have studied the maps and read the guide-books. These plans are the preparation that allows for spontaneity to meet the needs of the group in each moment of the adventure. Without this preparation, the trip would most likely be chaotic; it might be a success, or you could miss all the sights and get lost.

As in this metaphorical example of the journey, opening possibilities for learning includes many aspects that are prepared for and thought about in advance. Pedagogical learning situations need framework and structure. Sometimes improvisation or creativity is misunderstood as being without guidelines, instructions or structure. This may cause chaotic freedom, which seldom enhances creativity. Creative learning can be viewed as generating original work, as opposed to reproducing the ideas of others (see Craft, 2005). Structures and scaffolds provide space for creativity, improvisation and skills development. On the other hand, an inflexible structure, or following the leader's instructions alone, will not lead to creative freedom or flow. The delicate balance between freedom and structure is hard to describe yet important to aim for (see Sawyer, 2011).

The following section presents various ways of scaffolding learning.

Physical and practical scaffolds for learning

- **Preparing the physical space for learning**:
  - Different groups need different physical scaffolds; learners may experience an environment through movement within it and exploration of it with

their senses. It is useful to study the room from this perspective to ensure that everything is arranged in order to support the attention and learning possibilities for the group activity.

- Ensure that all the instruments and other resources are readily accessible to the pedagogue when needed.
- Thoughtful preparation of suitable seating arrangements within the space for the group and their mobility needs is required: chairs, floor, pillows, carpet – taking into account the possibility of moving in the space.
- For those working with young children, or the easily distracted, it is vital to be aware of doors, tempting instruments, toys or interesting things that grab the attention. These should be hidden or moved, if possible. Maintaining concentration and interest in musical activities amidst competing distractions can be impossible, even for the most diligent learner. Finding innovative ways to screen-off distractions or remove stimulating, colourful images from walls can influence learners' attention on the task in hand. An example of creating a pop-up space with easily transportable wrap-around screens can be found in Margareta Burrell's (2015) work. She found that the screens turned an ordinary room into an imaginative environment, which helped to sustain attention and focus.
- **Rituals for starting and ending the session**:
  These can clearly demarcate the space for music-making adventures – ritual greeting and goodbye songs can form bridges to help the 'crossing over the threshold' from one space to the other. The opening and closing rituals clearly mark the time allocated for the session. These rituals are of benefit to all learning groups, not just children.
- **Pictures to make the structure of the session visible:**
  For some groups, it can be helpful to provide a visible scaffold (visual timetable) for the structure of the session. This can be achieved by using pictures similar to PECS (Picture Exchange Communication System). These can support self-regulation for some learners, helping them to concentrate in the present moment.

I experimented with this in a lecture in higher education; I had pictures to illustrate different phases of the session (small-group discussions, PowerPoint, workshop). I found that it helped me as a teacher as I was relaxed about allocating the timing of the phases of the session because I could see what was to come. The pictures helped keep me to time. In discussions afterwards, the students of teaching also found that the visual symbols gave a clear structure. Students fond of structure enjoyed the visual clues and the visible reminder.

Constructing the abstract dimensions or elements in the learning environment

- When preparing a 'landscape to explore', the following questions can help shape the learning situation:
  - What kinds of possibilities are there for learning and experiencing music in the session?
  - What are the possibilities for learning in and through music?
  - What different approaches and elements of music practice am I using: listening, playing, singing, moving, visual elements, self-expression, improvisation, arts-integration?
  - What is meaningful for this group?
  - How will the session allow for different types of engagement and activity levels: listening, relaxation, concentration, a balance of cognitive demand and being in the moment?
  - How do I move through the different parts or actions to form a continuum that ties together the different elements of the session?

This preparation of a landscape for exploration can be thought of as an artistic process, seeing the learning situation as a composition, or a pedagogical artwork.

Tuning your pedagogical senses: opening yourself to dialogic working

The written map for navigating the learning situation is only the first step in the process. It is also important to imagine how the map will be used in action. Training our pedagogical thinking-in-action is part of professional preparation. This involves prior visualisation and thinking through the different pathways, pedagogical choices or possible experiences and reactions of the learners. Being thoroughly prepared beforehand frees the mind and allows better concentration and presence to be available for the group creative process. When working with music we are affected emotionally; preparation also includes tuning ourselves towards the emotions that might arise in the pedagogical process, both for the pedagogue as well as the learners.

 Reflection and discussion

1   How do I prepare/tune myself to be present in the situation?
2   Thinking metaphorically about the group of learners, and the leader, as an ensemble:
  - How do I make sure I am warmed-up to play with them?
  - How can we be in tune with each other?

Pedagogical improvisation

When the map is prepared, it is possible to identify the various pathways and focus on what it is to 'navigate' in the learning situation rather than following a recipe or a set of instructions. Although preparation for the learning journey is vital for fruitful learning, of equal worth is 'pedagogical improvisation' (Donmoyer, 1983; see also Ben-Horin, 2016; Holdhus et al., 2016). This can be described as adjusting to the needs of a pedagogical moment, changing and taking new turns in the pathway, in collaboration with the learners. Rigidly following the plan may miss the delicate initiatives or unspoken information in the actual teaching situation. Being flexible in the use of the map and aiming for a balance of structure and improvisation (Sawyer, 2011) is something that can be developed, but needs time and effort. This is essential especially

IMAGE 5.2 Finding your way is not always easy

at the beginning of a pedagogue's career. With experience and practice, navigation-in-action gets easier. A comforting thought may be that pedagogical improvisation is the most advanced level of a music pedagogue's expertise. It can be developed by continually challenging our thoughts, values and perceptions of learning and teaching in music education.

Leading/guiding with gestures, music and intensity

The pedagogue can support learning, experiences and working in music in many ways. Some pedagogical actions are non-verbal in nature, the use of body language: gestures, and facial expressions, are powerful tools in facilitating the group process in music. There is no reason to start an activity by saying, "Now we are starting the activity". The group – no matter what age – are much more alert if the activity starts with the leader making positive eye contact with the group and a pulse with her feet, for example. This draws the participants into the action and lets the instructions find their way without language getting in the way. Remembering too that our body posture conveys more information than words.

There are moments in the activities where words (either spoken or sung) can be useful tools. It is pertinent to remember that in every group there may be someone who – for different reasons – is distracted by lengthy instructions, for whom just one or two words will be enough. This can be seen when the group becomes restless and concentration declines.

- Make sure you have the attention of everyone when giving instructions,
- Give just one short instruction at a time. Divide longer or more complicated tasks into manageable steps and give instructions that are timed to support the task (not too early and not too late).
- Lead the activity by movement whenever you can (for example, convey "stop playing- sign" by raising your claves in the air).

Feedback is a central scaffold for maintaining interest, focus and motivation. Immediate and activity-targeted feedback is much more effective than restrictions. It is good to keep in mind that where we give our attention, strengthens and directs the focus of the activity; for example, instead of saying, "Don't play so loudly", it is more effective to say, "Can you find very quiet sounds with your instrument?"

Some critical aspects to consider when preparing and navigating pathways in learning

1   What are my pedagogical intentions in different moments and what choices do I make?

2 Have I thought of possibilities for learning in, through and about music?
3 Does my plan allow for different ways to explore and learn music (singing, playing, moving)?
4 Have I thought of the various possible opportunities afforded by each element to be worked with in the session? E.g., teaching a song – the same song can be used for its rhythmic, melodic, playing, moving, action game potential.
5 Does the prepared map for the process open pathways to creativity, learning and artistic experience for all participants?
6 How do I create and maintain the intensity of interest and engagement through the whole learning situation? How do I move from one part (or action) to the next while maintaining that intensity?
7 What kind of pathways for pedagogical improvisation can I imagine, and what kind of actions might these require of the pedagogue?

(see Huhtinen-Hildén, 2017)

Reflecting on pedagogical situations

There was a group of 4-year-olds in a music activity with rhythmical elements, structure in music and the use of the body to experience certain rhythmical patterns before singing or playing. This included composing a dance together. The dance had been carefully taught – step by step, adding challenge from easy to more demanding. It had been partly co-constructed; there was a section that had been composed through improvisatory preparation; the children had contributed to this part of the process. Lily was particularly enjoying the complex rhythm of part C in the dance. She used that rhythm later on in the session while playing the instruments and improvising a solo section. Steven, a rather shy and scared boy, was, for the first time, brave enough to take part in a circle dance. He had been apprehensive at the beginning of the year and gradually become more confident. The thrill of sharing the co-constructed dance – its structure, rhythm and ability to hold his fellow dancers' hands – made the whole boy shine with happiness.

We can see that the pedagogue has planned the actions required to form a dance in a collaborative process and thought carefully about giving instructions to the children in the different parts of the process. And yet the pedagogue cannot define exactly what each member of the group should learn or gain from this situation. She can, knowing the children well, have expectations and even hopes for different children. She knows that Lily is very interested in learning to play an instrument and therefore expects that she might be enthusiastic about the challenge of the rhythm in the process. She also knows how important social courage is for Steven: active participation will be a huge step for him and support the development of his self-regulation skills.

Underpinning the situation above are the pedagogue's expectations and thinking related to the individual learner's needs and the support needed. If the aim for the group activity had been to assess visible audible skills – as shown by Lily – there may have been little space for encouraging the gestures and attention given to form the safe scaffolds for the social support that Steven needed in order to meet his learning needs, which were more in the social and emotional domain. The reverse is also true. There may be an overriding emphasis in some early childhood music practice on meeting social and emotional needs, thereby losing sight of building a beneficial learning environment in music. The group musical process is a complex, multi-layered context for learning. What is most needed from the pedagogue is a sensitivity towards the context, the learners, the interaction and the pedagogue's own emotions, values and thoughts, all framed by the desire to open the possibilities for learning in an open and flexibly negotiated process of co-construction. The aims are not fixed but built on a conceptual understanding based on musical inspiration with an awareness of the potential for flow experience, "teaching to the possible" (Custodero, 2005, p. 205). The pedagogue learns also from the learner in the process of supporting their learning. It is dialogue – the learner feeds the pedagogue's process of knowing how best to feed the learner or the group of learners. There is a mutual inquiry, fascination and shared growth. As Van Manen (1991, p. 13) beautifully crystallises the approach of a learner-centred pedagogue, "Pedagogy is a fascination with the growth of the other".

The pedagogue navigates between structure and pedagogical improvisation. Each pathway can lead in a different direction. None is right or wrong, better or worse. What is essential is that the pedagogue has the group in mind when preparing and is also open to unpredictable and unexpected creative impulses of the group process. The pedagogue also sets goals for her own actions and employs her sensitive approach to support learning. In our example of Lily and Steven:

- For Lily – To feed her engine with interesting musical, rhythmical experiences and challenges.
- For Steven – To position herself to support him with physical scaffolding by being near him to encourage him to take part if she senses that he is ready to join with the group. She facilitates the situation so that it is safe for him and the others.
- She tries to talk less and listen more.
- She challenges herself to be sensitive to the emotions in action; they might indicate some information for her in her choices for action.

To explore the pedagogical thinking behind music teaching allows us to reflect on music teaching across the music education landscape. Allowing for musical play as process, not product or outcome, in early childhood settings may depend on the way that music is positioned in early years practice. This may be influenced by several factors. One may be an individual practitioner's personal attitudes and conceptions of music teaching (Addessi & Carugati, 2010; Berger & Cooper, 2003; Kim & Kemple, 2011; Young, 2003a), as there are limited models offered as part of their training. Another factor may be the confusion about 'learning through play' that may inhibit adult-led activities that include musical elements. Incorporating free-flow musical play in settings as recommended in recent years by research and music specialists (Berger & Cooper, 2003; Evans, 2007; Moorhead & Pond, 1941; Young, 2003b, 2007; Young, Street, & Davies, 2006) has meant that models of 'circle-time' music – where the whole group participates together – may be regarded by some as out of date, or inappropriate practice, and yet it has been a model frequently adopted in settings. The confusion about 'learning through play' and free-flowing activities that practitioners reported in the UK's Tickell Review (2011) of the Early Years Foundation Stage (EYFS) may mean that music-based activities are reduced as few appropriate models of free-flow, child-initiated music exist, and the previous 'circle-time' music may no longer occur as it is felt to be too adult-led.

The notion of process and product in terms of musical activities can be applied to thinking about young children's emerging singing. This can be approached from different viewpoints. Children's singing could be conceived of as replicating accurately known musical material (e.g. pitching accurately something that you recognise or have offered the child yourself). Or the idea of children's singing could include acknowledgement of the improvisational vocalisations of the child exploring her voice and interpreting her mood and playing with sounds.

Interestingly, a 1940s seminal research study (Moorhead & Pond, 1941) encourages us to focus on exploratory and free-flowing vocal learning. Gladys Moorhead and Donald Pond found that physical movement and speech were interlinked with musical play (the speech becoming musical in form). They found that to separate musical learning from other learning was impossible, and that experimentation and repetition of action-patterns eventually gave rise to their coordination into meaningful ideas. They found that invented chants featured as part of children's play. These were based on a repeated recitation note with melodic inflections for emphasis. Chants were different from the song-singing, which occurred frequently when children were moving; these songs were typically experiments with melody, often the same words repeated each time with a different melody, representing a free and flexible approach akin to plainsong (Moorhead & Pond, 1941, pp. 12–13). David Hargreaves (1986) describes these early 'outline' or spontaneous songs as similar to the 'tadpole-man' type drawings that Piaget suggests occur in the pre-operational second stage of development. Moorhead and Pond noted that adults' recognition of children's musical products was subject to an arbitrary standard of their own, and that they may reject most of what might be considered children's real music (Flohr, 2010; Moorhead & Pond, 1941, p. 4). Children needed the freedom to pursue their own interests, to experiment and repeat in order to produce their own music. Rhythmic vocal communication seemed to accompany group socialisation around a common play activity. Moorhead and Pond's research focused on the need for adults to be sensitive to a child's urge for expression and growth and to then provide help in acquiring the technical skills needed.

Accuracy in pitch reproduction may be less significant to the child than to an adult monitoring their singing. Children's free drawing attempts do not seek to accurately reproduce another's work – to imitate another's drawing is a different task altogether – and so it may also be with children's free vocal play as distinct from joining in with and recreating a known song.

 Reflection and discussion

Reflection to build the pedagogue's positive self-esteem with a group of students of teaching

This can be a very powerful reflection when all the students have had their turn in teaching, and their situations have been analysed. It helps the group to focus on the positive aspects – things we have learned or that we are good at (too often we focus on things we need to learn or can't do yet). It is vital that the group either knows each other well or has discussed in some detail the pedagogical thoughts and actions of individual members.

In groups of three:

> Two of the group discuss together the third member's practice and pedagogical thoughts (without looking at the third member of the group), sharing only the positive aspects of their development as a pedagogue (pedagogical actions and thinking).

They change roles so that each member has this experience. What is essential in this exercise is the differentiation between listening and talking. There is no need to react to positive feedback as the third member of the group.

Analysing a teaching/learning situation

The pedagogical situations are complex systems, and therefore it is beneficial to organise the reflections and observations. The framework shown in Figure 5.2 (Huhtinen-Hildén, 2017) provides a structure for the analysis of pedagogical approaches and strategies.

If this framework is being used to include the pedagogue as part of the reflection process (e.g. with higher education students or a continuous education group), remember to share the in-action thoughts of the pedagogue, e.g. "Is this part too long, should I encourage Steven to join in more or would it be better to let him come to me, oh bother, I've left the Lycra at home, what can I use here . . .?" This can add much to the reflective process when used in conjunction with the framework (Figure 5.2). It is a central part of thinking aloud about the teaching process and understanding the underlying thoughts that affect pedagogical choices (see Loughran, 2006, pp. 47–48). This pondering, shared in the context of reflection, contributes to the development of the personal professional landscape.

**Observing and analysing a session through different lenses
(Huhtinen-Hildén 2017)**

1. Focus on the learner's experiences, possibilities for learning and interaction in the session

- Pathways in learning: what possibilities for learning and experiencing music does this situation enable?
- What did you notice about the interaction and group dynamics?
- If you participated yourself: what did you feel or experience?

2. Focus on the pedagogue's actions, choices and presence

- How did the pedagogue use different positions during the session? (e.g. leading activities, giving instructions, maintaining engagement/intensity, providing scaffolds, encouraging, listening, inspiring, co-creating, being part of the ensemble, supporting, observing - dialogue)
- How did the approaches affect the motivation, activity, agency and participation of learners?
- Dialogue and group dynamics:
  - How did the teacher enable dialogic learning?
  - What did you notice about speech, gestures, facial expression, body language, initiatives of the pedagogue and learners?
  - What kind of pedagogical choices were used? What kinds of possibilities for learning did these open for the learners?
  - How did the pedagogue act in relation to a) supporting and leading the structure of the session and b) pedagogical improvisation?

3. Focus on the process: development of the process and structure of the session

- How did the process start, what happened next, how did it develop?
- How did the process move from one part to the next?
- What elements of music practice were used and how?
- e.g. singing, exploring voice, playing instruments, listening, movement, dance, creating, composing, improvising, visual arts, drama, stories, poems, story-crafting
- How did the prepared map and structure a) enable pathways for learning that were initiated by the teacher b) open up possibilities for learner-initiated improvisation and creative working? (leading, directing, structuring - improvising, creating, innovating in dialogic process)
- What kind of artistic, pedagogical, interactive, holistic piece of art did the session build?

FIGURE 5.2 Observing and analysing a session through different lenses (Huhtinen-Hildén, 2017)

Reflection and discussion

Examples for using the framework for analysis

Group reflection 1

In small groups – each group using a different lens from the observation/reflection framework:

1 The first focuses on the learner's experiences, possibilities for learning, and interaction in the group,
2 the second on the pedagogical choices,
3 the third with a focus on the process.

Each group discusses the shared session through their lens and then these different views are shared and discussed.

Group reflection 2

In small groups: using one of the lenses as a focus, the first group begins a reflective discussion about the session through that lens, and the other two groups listen. Next, group two follows with their reflective discussion of the session, and they add their reflections to the issues raised in group one's discussion while the other two groups listen. Finally, group three discusses the session and the topics raised during the other two groups' discussions.

References

Addessi, A., & Carugati, F. (2010). Social representations of the 'musical child': An empirical investigation on implicit musical knowledge in higher teacher education. *Music Education Research, 12*(3), 311–330. doi: 10.1080/14613808.2010.505645

Benedict, C. (2010). Methods and approaches. In H. F. Abeles & L. A. Custodero (Eds.), *Critical issues in music education: Contemporary theory and practice* (pp. 194–214). New York: Oxford University Press.

Ben-Horin, O. (2016). Towards a professionalization of pedagogical improvisation in teacher education. *Cogent Education, 3*(1), 1248186.

Berger, A., & Cooper, S. (2003). Musical play: A case study of pre-school children and parents. *Journal of Research in Music Education, 51*(2), 151–165.

Burrell, M. (2015). *Pantomimus: Amazing music space.* Paper presented at CFMAE-MERYC2015 Conference, Tallinn, Estonia, 5th–9th May, 2015.

Craft, A. (2005). *Creativity in schools: Tensions and dilemmas.* London: Routledge.

Custodero, L. A. (2005). Observable indicators of flow experience: A developmental perspective on musical engagement in young children from infancy to school age. *Music Education Research, 7*(2), 185–209.

Donmoyer, R. (1983). Pedagogical improvisation. *Educational Leadership, 40,* 39–43.

Evans, N. (2007). *Tuning into children: A training handbook to deepen early years practitioners' and musicians' understanding of young children and their music making*. London: Youth Music.

Flohr, J. W. (2010). Best practices for young children's music education: Guidance from brain research. *General Music Today, 23*(2), 13–19. doi: 10.1177/1048371309352344

Hargreaves, D. J. (1986). *The developmental psychology of music*. Cambridge: Cambridge University Press.

Holdhus, K., Høisæter, S., Mæland, K., Vangsnes, V., Engelsen, K. S., Espeland, M., & Espeland, Å. (2016). Improvisation in teaching and education–roots and applications. *Cogent Education, 3*(1), 1204142.

Huhtinen-Hildén, L. (2013). Herkät tuntosarvet musiikin opettamisessa. [Sensitive antennae in music teaching]. In P. Jordan-Kilkki, E. Kauppinen, & E. Viitasalo-Korolainen (Eds.), *Musiikkipedagogin käsikirja. Vuorovaikutus ja kohtaaminen opetuksessa. Oppaat ja käsikirjat 2012:2* (pp. 159–174). Helsinki: Opetushallitus.

Huhtinen-Hildén, L. (2017). Elävänä hetkessä. Suunnitelmallisuus ja pedagoginen improvisointi. [Present in a moment: Systematic planning and pedagogical improvisation]. In A. Lindeberg-Piiroinen & I. Ruokonen (Eds.), *Musiikki varhaiskasvatuksessa – käsikirja [Music in early childhood education – a handbook]* (pp. 389–411). Helsinki: Classicus.

Juntunen, M.-L., & Westerlund, H. (2011). The legacy of music education methods in teacher education: The metanarrative of Dalcroze eurhythmics as a case. *Research Studies in Music Education, 33*(1), 47–58. doi: 10.1177/1321103X11404653

Kim, H. K., & Kemple, K. M. (2011). Is music an active developmental tool or simply a supplement? Early childhood preservice teachers' beliefs about music. *Journal of Early Childhood Teacher Education, 32*(2), 135–147.

Loughran, J. (2006). *Developing a pedagogy of teacher education: Understanding teaching and learning about teaching*. London: Routledge.

Moorhead, G. E., & Pond, D. (1941). *Music of young children: II general observations*. Santa Barbara, CA: Pillsbury Foundation for Advancement of Music Education.

Regelski, T. A. (2004). Social theory, and music and music education as praxis. *Action, Criticism and Theory for Music Education, 3*(3), 2–42.

Regelski, T. A. (2012). Musicianism and the ethics of school music. *Action, Criticism, and Theory for Music Education, 11*(1), 7–42.

Sawyer, R. K. (Ed.). (2011). *Structure and improvisation in creative teaching*. New York: Cambridge University Press.

Tickell, C. (2011). *The early years: Foundations for life, health and learning*. An Independent Report on the Early Years Foundation Stage: Her Majesty's Government.

Van Manen, M. (1991). *The tact of teaching: The meaning of pedagogical thoughtfulness*. London, Ontario: Althouse Press.

Wenger, E. (1998). *Communities of practice*. New York: Cambridge University Press.

Young, S. (2003a). *Music with the under-fours*. London and New York: RoutledgeFalmer.

Young, S. (2003b). The interpersonal dimension: A potential source of musical creativity for young children? *Musicae Scientiae, Special Issue 10th Anniversary Conference Issue*, 175–191.

Young, S. (2007). Early childhood music education in England: Changes, choices, and challenges. *Arts Education Policy Review, 109*(2), 19–26.

Young, S., Street, A., & Davies, E. (2006). *Music one-to-one report*. Exeter: Youth Music. http://education.exeter.ac.uk/music-one2one/

COLOURFUL MEMORIES OF LEARNING IN MUSIC

IMAGE 6.1   Exploring the kantele

IMAGE 6.2   The castle of Sleeping Beauty

IMAGE 6.3 The castle of The Pavane

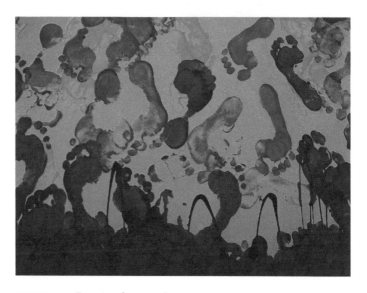

IMAGE 6.4 Dancing feet in red

IMAGE 6.5 Dancing feet in blue

IMAGE 6.6 Following sunbeams

IMAGE 6.7 One sea for sailing on

IMAGE 6.8 Buttons – source for inspiration

IMAGE 6.9 A sound basket

IMAGE 6.10 Steps for the dance

IMAGE 6.11 Painting the stone A

IMAGE 6.12 Painting the stone B

IMAGE 6.13 Graphical notation A

IMAGE 6.14 Graphical notation B

IMAGE 6.15 Graphical notation C

IMAGE 6.16 Graphical notation D

IMAGE 6.17 Scarves for movement

IMAGE 6.18 Secretive fish

IMAGE 6.19 Who wore these?

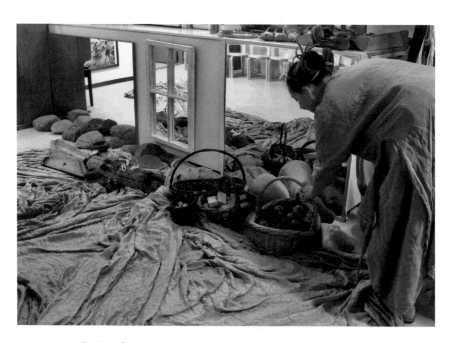

IMAGE 6.20 Setting the scene

PART II

Reflecting on learner-centred music education practice

INTRODUCTION TO PART II

The perspectives introduced in Part I of this book are now brought into the practical world with material to explore various aspects of learner-centred pedagogy. This material is shaped around themes:

*   The group as an orchestra, team and learning environment
*   Music, emotions and interaction
*   Voice and body as first instruments
*   Making music visible and tangible
*   Improvising and learning music with instruments
*   Creating learning environments through imagination
*   The music pedagogue as a creative instrument

This material has mainly been developed through work with students of music teaching, continuing professional development courses and conference workshops, and can be used in a number of ways:

*   The activities can be adapted to suit your music education or community music practice.
*   A workshop process can be used as a starting point for reflection and discussion with colleagues at network events and meetings.
*   As a course of study with a group of students of music teaching, continuing professional development courses, music therapy courses and community music studies.

We encourage you to experiment with the material, and develop your own ideas and pathways for learning music. Attending workshops, exploring the Internet and sharing with colleagues all offer wonderful opportunities to inspire you and develop your unique perspective.

Through these practical experiences, reflective thinking and practice are combined with theoretical notions (see Tynjälä 2004, 2007, 2008) so that you can embody the theory and the practice simultaneously within your own reflective practice framework.

How to use Part II

Themes

The themes presented comprise creative process workshops that include a beginning, a middle and an ending and offer the whole trajectory of a creative learning process. Each theme also includes parts of a process for experimentation and integration into existing practice.

> We have created imaginary pedagogues and their learners to offer different perspectives and voices to our dialogue with you, the reader. The fictional experiences are based on real-life practice. Their voices are marked by a speech bubble.

Working with the materials

Each theme has an introductory section explaining the rationale, followed by the practical elements associated with the theme as presented through workshops, pathways and examples.

Workshops

These are whole processes, journeys that include several pathways. These adventures consist of tuning the group, pathways and closing sections. There are longer and shorter workshops, each consisting of a different number of pathways that you can combine according to the needs of your learning group and the time available. Some workshops could take a few hours; others can last several days.

To start using the workshop material, you might like to choose whichever of the pathways within the workshop best suits your group and purposes – modifying them to fit your context. You can then add and develop the material from this starting point.

Pathways

Pathways form part of the whole journey of the workshop. They are working processes that utilise the thematic material, working to explore and experience the ideas in different ways and then sharing or reflecting together. They stand alone as small units to use with learners.

Examples

An example is one activity found within a pathway that can be integrated into a longer series of activities or tried on its own.

The approach in Part II promotes and fosters a view of music education practice through multiple perspectives. The aim is to encourage exploration and facilitate pedagogues to create their own artistic "sound-meals" (Glennie, 2016) with a group of participants.

References

Glennie, E. (2016). *Shaping the way teachers teach the young.* Keynote Address (25th July, 2016): 32nd ISME World Conference, Glasgow, 24–29 July, 2016.

Tynjälä, P. (2004). Asiantuntijuus ja työkulttuurit opettajan ammatissa. *Kasvatus, 35*(2), 174–190.

Tynjälä, P. (2007). Integratiivinen pedagogiikka osaamisen kehittämisessä. In H. Kotila, A. Mutanen, & M. V. Volanen (Eds.), *Taidon tieto* (pp. 11–36). Helsinki: Edita.

Tynjälä, P. (2008). Perspectives into learning at the workplace. *Educational Research Review, 3,* 130–154.

Theme 1

THE GROUP AS AN ORCHESTRA, TEAM AND LEARNING ENVIRONMENT

In this theme, the group as a learning environment is approached through the metaphor of an instrument, a multi-faceted creative system. This instrument has to be tuned and cared for. Making music in a group can build an environment where learning takes place. This applies to music groups for children, children and their parents, and groups of student music pedagogues. Working with music groups provides pedagogues with an opportunity to explore various group processes and experiences. This theme can be seen through two lenses, the first sees pedagogues opening possibilities for learning in different group contexts, the other sees them as a member of a group (student/colleague/teacher).

By reflecting on the experiences that emerge in group work, pedagogical thinking about learning, as part of a collaborative process, can be developed. Experiential learning plays a vital role in facilitating creative working in a group. Understanding our own experiences as a group member, we get insight into the possible experiences of others in a group. We are all part of different groups and group processes (see Bion 1961; Tuckman, 1965) throughout our life, which give multiple opportunities to explore groups and their dynamics.

Working with groups in music can be approached with curiosity and interest in group dynamics. This helps to focus on the collaborative process and dialogue, rather than being distracted by possible challenges and a search for 'right solutions' or trying to apply ready-made strategies to 'solve problems'. For the pedagogue, this means prioritising *the understanding of group dynamics* and being sensitive to the interaction over 'group management', as highlighted in Chapter 3. Fruitful working in a group (as either a leader or a participant) always requires a willingness to be unsettled or curious, and ready to take a risk (Biesta, 2013); all members affect the atmosphere and the process. Therefore, adopting a spirit of shared inquiry and dialogue forms a fruitful landscape for exploration.

IMAGE 8.1   Swimming together

The process of creating and making music in a group requires feelings of safety and togetherness. Building these from the beginning, when the group is forming, is a principal aim for the pedagogue (see e.g. Edmondson, 1999, 2004; Schein 1996). It is useful to remember that working with creative inputs can make us vulnerable, because we are sharing something of ourselves, even if at an unconscious level.

Starting the shared adventure – forming a group

At the beginning of the adventure – the shared journey of collaborative learning – it is important to build a safe and creative atmosphere where everyone feels accepted as they are. This needs preparation, active working and facilitation by the pedagogue. The feeling of being accepted and part of the group needs to be built carefully. The group always consists of different personalities, energy levels and temperaments. Everyone needs to feel "This is something for me" and "I am an important member of this group". Diversity needs to be embraced with actions that take account of the needs of each participant. One person may need time to adjust; another might be ready for interaction. Self-expression is different for extroverts compared with introverts: where one feels safe, the other might be challenged to the limit of their expressive capacity.

When starting a journey, you form a special group with a shared target or purpose. Every member of that expedition brings their expectations, and sometimes fears, to the group process. Getting to know these can be a vital starting point for collaborative working. For a group of students of teaching, these might include fears, misbeliefs, excitement, passion, motivations and aspirations about becoming a music pedagogue. It is valuable to explore these to help expand the understanding of the profession. Members benefit from experiencing different views, which add to the facets for reflection. It is possible to share non-verbally: everyone shares what feels comfortable and participates in ways that feel suitable. Creativity – when used carefully – offers a wonderful, safe environment, an alternative space in which an individual can choose their level of sharing.

Getting to know each other

Receiving and giving acceptance

Sharing formal personal information may not prove to be the most successful way to create a safe and relaxed atmosphere when forming a group. In the example 'Instrument and Player', an alternative means of introduction is given – sharing information and receiving it from another group member. Being either an instrument or a player moves participants to a safe environment, leaving behind their expectations and fears. It creates a sense of freedom and feelings of acceptance – maybe more so than would be possible by sharing names and study backgrounds. Working in pairs instead of a large circle can reduce nervousness.

Example: 'Instrument and Player'

Music suggestion: Guem Percussions: Le chant du monde (Balance and conversation)
This activity enhances feelings of acceptance and activation through the tactile sense.

- Choose (or be given) a partner; one of you is an imaginary instrument that the other plays (the instrument doesn't have to make sounds or respond in any way; it just experiences being played).
    - It is vital to listen to each other (non-verbally, through hands, eyes and movements) – what kind of instrument is this, and how does it want to be played?
- After the activity, reflect how this felt, first in pairs, and then with the whole group.

Names

At the beginning of the group session, activities using the names of participants can enhance trust and safety. There are many games for learning names in a group. Below are two well-known examples. You may know others or wish to develop these examples further.

Example: learning names through a game in a group

Using wool

Sitting in a circle throw a ball of wool (or string) across the circle. The first person says their name as they throw it to someone else while keeping hold of the end. The second person repeats the process, and so on. When everyone has had a turn, there is a tangled mesh of wool across the circle. Now the activity is reversed; the muddle in the middle of the circle is unravelled when the last person names the person who threw the wool to them and passes it back to them, and so on.

Throwing a ball or a bean bag with the group standing in a circle

One person starts by saying their name and something they like, which starts with the same letter as their name (e.g. Sam, singing). They throw the ball and the person catching it repeats the process. When everyone has had a go, reverse the process so that each person throws the ball to the person who threw it to them, calling out the thing the recipients said they liked (rather than their name).

Example: learning names with a song

There are many lovely songs to introduce names in a group. Here are two examples.

MUSIC 8.1

This song has a strong pulse, which you can feel by tapping your knees, or clapping for the 'Kilele' section. During the 'awo, awo' section, touch your head gently with both hands. Establish the pattern by repeating 'Kilele, Kilele, awo, awo' as many times as you need to feel the pattern is coming naturally for the group. The next step is to add each person's name in place of 'awo, awo'. This is a good song for using with a large group of learners as a new name is added every other bar.

You can find different ways to keep the beat – the song works well while moving (e.g. stamping feet and gently touching heads).

Whisper Song

MUSIC 8.2 published with permission from the composer

2   whisper your favourite colour, then I'll know. Speaking very gently, then our friendship can grow because . . .

3   whisper your favourite food,

4   whisper your favourite song,

5   whisper your favourite toy.

Add your own verses.

1   Jos haluat kuiskata nimesi mulle, olisin iloinen. Aivan hiljaa puhumalla tutustuu parhaiten, sillä aivan hiljaa puhumalla tutustuu parhaiten.

2   Jos haluat kuiskata lempivärisi, olisin iloinen. Aivan hiljaa puhumalla tutustuu parhaiten, sillä aivan hiljaa puhumalla tutustuu parhaiten.

     . . . mieliruokasi . . .

     . . . lempilaulusi . . .

     . . . salaisuuden . . .

- Sing this song gently, either sitting in a circle (each participant whispers their name at the end of the song), or by walking gently in the space whispering names (or favourite foods etc.) to each other.
- Sing the song while walking in the room. When the song stops, find a friend and share your favourite thing with them. Repeat.

Pathway: names with movement

There are many activities for introducing names with rhythm or movement; here are a few.

The group is standing in a circle. Allow your feet to make the pulse (right foot step – left foot side, left foot step – right foot side) with a slow tempo. Working around the circle in turn:

- Say your name, and the group repeats it. Fill the rests by clapping your hands (Laura, clap, clap, LAURA, CLAP, CLAP). It is important to use the exact rhythm of the spoken name, which may be syncopated.
- Say your name and accompany that with a movement (the group repeats).
- Do your movement and add a sound to it (the sound replaces saying your name, the group repeats).
- Each member of the group chooses their own path by picking one of these three options.
- Develop your own version of the 'name-rhythm circle', for example:
  - name – rhythm ostinato – repetition of the name – rhythm ostinato
  - use different steps for the beat like swinging forward and back (e.g. right foot steps front, step back with the left, right foot steps back, step front with the left)

Expectations and orientation towards the expedition

Example: forming a group through pictures

It is sometimes easier to talk about yourself with new people when you have something else as a focal point (e.g. Workshop: stones p. 85). You can use postcards or similar to facilitate introductions in a group.

- Pick a postcard and tell others why you selected it. Share your name and your expectations or thoughts about the course/session/topic.

Example: making expectations visible

This activity can be used to explore the expectations of the course or task. You can prepare statements about the course topic or another topic of interest to the group.

The group is standing in the space. The participants listen to the statements and, according to what they think about them, they move to the right place in the line as follows:

- When you hear a statement and you
  - agree with it: you stand in one end of the line.
  - disagree with it: you stand in the opposite end of the line.
  - don't know whether you agree or disagree: you stand in the middle.

For example, the statements with a group of students of teaching, on the topic of teaching, could be:

- Starting with the movement game made a relaxed feeling in the group.
- I like to sit in a circle and not move at the start.
- I like to start with a musical activity rather than talking.
- Hearing how others feel before starting musical activities creates a safe atmosphere.
- I feel slightly nervous about being part of the group activities.

 Reflection and discussion

1   Thinking about the beginnings of sessions you have seen or experienced, list some favourite activities or songs and share them in the group.

Group as an instrument – tuning and focusing for activity

The metaphor of 'group as an instrument' makes it easy to grasp the notion of the need for tuning the instrument. When a group is gathered together and getting ready to start a session, it is useful to be aware of the different expectations, energy levels and personalities. In order to create a fruitful collaborative atmosphere, there is a need to enhance the senses of acceptance, safety, and being and feeling free to contribute to the current task/purpose of the group.

With music, movement and the search for the same pulse, it is possible to facilitate the formation of a safe atmosphere. With movements and a shared focus, we tune our individual bodies and the focus of our concentration to the group dynamics and the present moment. Starting a session is an important phase. If handled with care, speaking metaphorically, it tunes the orchestra to play the same score with the same vision of the piece. This is a far deeper issue than simply 'doing a warm-up activity'.

To tune the mind and body to the present moment, to attune the group to work together with the current topic and to waking up the senses, you need to build the beginning carefully. By facilitating 'encounters' and interaction in the group with movements and games as well as enhancing focus in the present moment, the sense of togetherness can be fostered.

Example: train and rope

This activity helps to bring a group of learners together and move as a system from one place to another, either in our imagination or physical location. Some learners are uneasy about close physical contact; using a long piece of rope, a sense of 'group' can be established without the need to hold hands. The rope is flexible; it can move in a straight line or a circle; it can snake and wander. You can move outdoors; you can move from inside to outside and back again. It enables an imaginative and physical journey.

The rope can guide the group into a mindful state when it walks into a spiral while singing a repetitive melody – moving gradually inwards until the spiral is formed. The leader then turns and moves in the opposite direction, slowly unravelling the spiral.

> *I have found the idea of climbing aboard a train to be useful when using the rope, especially if there is a whistle available to start the imaginary move to a liminal space. If children are playing outside, you can blow the whistle and invite them to join the journey. Once the train is ready to depart (you can decide this together), the train driver sets off. The driver can be the pedagogue, but once the idea of moving together is established, other learners can lead the group. Invite train sounds from the group as it leaves the station. Where are you going? What will you need for the journey? These questions can help us move into the inner realm of fantasy as a group, and holding the rope we also move together as a system in the outer physical space. Questions about what we might see on the way to the destination can inspire the singing of known songs, e.g. Old MacDonald – when we pass a farm. Once we have arrived at our destination, the rope can be helpful for a circle song as it visibly provides the shape of a circle, allowing the group to be together without physical touch. I have used a thick piece of boating rope, long enough for up to 20 children and their parents to comfortably find their place. I have used vocal exploration as a warm up – making train sounds helps you enter the world of the train. There is a wide repertoire of songs about trains that can be included; Villa Lobos' composition "The Little Train of the Caipira", has been a great inspiration in this theme.*

Example: sharing your favourite things

Sing a song while walking in the space. When the song stops, find a friend and share a favourite thing. Repeat.

Searching

Markku Kaikkonen
(trans. JP & LH-H)

```
Search-ing  here  and    search-ing  there. My    song has gone to    hi – de.    Look-ing  all  a –
Kier     rän, käyn ja     kat - se - len  ja     lau - lu - a - ni    et - sin.    Mis - tä  sen  nyt

round            who        knows   what      I     might     find
löytä           nen, ja      mis –   tä      sen    nyt      keksin.
```

MUSIC 8.3 published with permission from the composer

2   Searching here and searching there. My rhythm has gone to hide . . .
3   Searching here and searching there. My friend has gone to hide . . .

Form a circle.

- Say a favourite thing to someone in the circle, focusing only on this person.
- Repeat, but add a movement when saying the favourite thing.
- You can also use this activity to form groups. Find favourite things that go together; they can be alike or complementary. This is a useful way of grouping people for creative working in smaller groups.

Example: entering the room with a song and a circle dance

A beginning song can start outside the room.

- Start by playing a steady pulse on a djembe.
- Add simple steps for this rhythm.
- Start singing your chosen beginning song (example: Jaa dan duui p. 213).
- The group enters the room together.
- Form a circle; the process now continues from this point either by learning steps for the dance, learning harmony for the song, or any other direction you and your group choose.

> I have used a song (with adapted lyrics) with groups of children with com-
> munication difficulties and their parents to create a feeling of acceptance
> and welcome, "Love is like a circle" (tune: Puff the Magic Dragon), "Love is like a
> circle, a circle big and round, and when you see a circle no ending can be found. Love
> is very special, it goes on eternally, forever and forever there's love for you and me."
> (adapted by J. Pitt). I used a rope to facilitate this activity.

💭 Reflection and discussion

1   Think about a welcoming and safe beginning to a session that you have experienced.
   - What was the beginning like?
   - What activities/instructions/words/gestures did the session begin with?
   - How did the leader act, and how did you feel?
   - How did the other group members react?

Discuss in a small group the elements that supported the formation of this positive experience. Make a list of these elements and approaches.

Instrument in tune – time to play! – facilitating trust and creating psychological safety

After the session has started, it is time to lead, follow and co-create further working together. The pedagogue can use different positions to open possibilities for learning (see Figure 4.2 p. 50). This needs careful preparation before the session and reflection-in-action to consider possible pedagogical choices in the learning situation.

When the process is well prepared, you have scaffolds ready for pedagogical improvisation in the moment, and you can focus on facilitating a flow experience in the group. Questions to assist preparation could be:

- How can I build a sense of community?
- How can I create ways to allow positive feedback – verbal and nonverbal?
- What are the ways to facilitate freedom for self-expression in the group?
- How can emotions be accommodated as part of the process?
- When are clear instructions needed and why?
- When are open-ended choices and the freedom for possibilities needed, and how are they facilitated?
- What could facilitate an atmosphere for learning that is warm, supportive and non-judgmental?

Pathway: sculptures or installations as a visible result of collaboration

- Ask the group to stand in a line, organised by birthday, in alphabetical order (by their name or their mother's), the size of their favourite animal etc. This needs negotiation and interaction to help participants focus on collaboration.
- Divide the big group from this line into smaller groups of up to five people.
- Give each group something with which they can create a piece of art. This could be thread, plasticine, matches, clay, spaghetti and marshmallows or objects found in the room.
- The groups are asked to make a sculpture or installation with their materials.
- Each small group then
    - reflects on their feelings about group work,
    - writes a name for their artwork on a piece of paper.
- Organise an exhibition. Each small group views all the sculptures.
- Reflect and share feelings.
- If you choose to do this activity in silence, reflect on the role/intention of non-verbal communication compared with collaboration with words.
- After the process reflect on:
    - how the group worked (if you tried both approaches, compare them)
    - what are my strengths in group work, where do I need support, where can I support others?

Pathway: learning machine

The idea of the group forming a machine, in which everyone plays a part, is useful for creating a sense of togetherness. It allows every member to find a suitable way to be involved in the activity. The notion of a machine is flexible, including both real machines and imaginary ones.[1] The idea of a machine removes thoughts of "Can I do this?", even if the activity covers musical elements like sounds, rhythm ostinatos etc.

1   In a pair create a sentence that describes a fruitful atmosphere for learning.
2   Form groups of four people and create a 'Learning Machine' based on these sentences or ideas.
3   Share or perform the machines.
4   When the activity leader touches one part of the machine, this part can speak, and we can hear their sounds or thoughts about learning!

   You can also vary this activity by changing the focus (words, sounds, sung words, rhythm ostinatos etc.).

 Reflection and discussion

1   Think about a flow experience in a group process you have been part of: what happened in the situation? What feelings did you have? What were the roles of the facilitator and the group?
   •   Discuss in a small group which elements made this a positive experience. List these elements and approaches.
2   Think about a challenging experience in a group and use the reflective discussion described in Chapter 3 p. 36.

Reflecting thoughts and feelings and ending the process

Thinking about a session as a musical composition with a beginning, middle and end is a helpful model for the group process. The beginning and ending rituals mark the phases of the process and can become fixed points to anchor the group.

   When a participant reflects and shares something about their experience from the process, the group benefits. This can be achieved by asking, "Can you say in a few words what you will take with you from this session?" Non-verbal and artistic expressions offer alternatives to speaking, for example with a movement, sound or poem.

   If the ending is more significant – for example at the end of a study year – it is necessary to allow time for the emotions arising from the ending of the group process and the inevitable separation from the fellow group members to be expressed. These emotions can make participants vulnerable, and it is important to let the group live together through this phase.

Example: goodbye circle

Using a small sensory object, e.g. a colour changing egg, dim the lights and sing a calming song with a goodbye theme. Each learner holds the object in turn and can share something with the group. If you have a garland of lights, these could be placed in the centre of the group as a focal point.

Example: living sculptures

- Form a living sculpture of the group. Ask everyone to think about what they will take from the session and in silence form a 3-D tableau guided by their thoughts. One person starts, and the rest of the group add to the sculpture one-by-one, taking different positions to form a collaborative piece of art.
- Each part of the sculpture can 'think aloud'. The leader can indicate the turn to 'think aloud' by putting a hand on their shoulder. This is a common activity in both drama and music education practice that many pedagogues have found to be a useful way of closing a session and sharing experiences.

 Reflection and discussion

1   Think about the closing of sessions you have been part of. List some of your favourite closing activities or songs and share them in the group.

Workshop: stones – very different from each other – each one with a story to tell

You need: at least two stones for each group member (different shapes, colours and sizes).

IMAGE 8.2   Stones inspiring us to play

Tuning the group

Sitting in a circle: the group gets to know each other with introductions and by sharing expectations.

- Choose a stone and get acquainted with it: what it looks like and how it feels in your hand. Say why you chose this stone from all the others. You can also share your name, your expectations and your feelings towards the topic of the session.
    - With eyes closed, start moving the stones from hand to hand round the circle. Try to picture whose stone you have in your hand as you touch different stones. This continues until the stones return to their owners.

Pathway: moving with a stone

Music suggestion: Maria Kalaniemi: Napoleon, Lappfjärd

- Find ways to move with the stone: it can be held in the hand, the foot, on the top of the head etc. The shape of the stone might suggest places for it to be positioned and inspire different movements.
- Stones start to wander in the room. Find different ways for the stone to encounter others; this could involve sharing stones amongst the group.

Pathway: playing with the stones

- Take another stone and listen to the sounds the two make together; with this exploration a rhythmic ostinato is formed.
- Share and play together each participant's ostinato.
- Forming an orchestra – all the ostinatos playing together: one starts, then the other ostinatos are added in free order.
- One participant is a conductor experimenting with the sound material. Solos, tutti-parts, rests, dynamics, tempi can all be employed.

> I used this material with a group of musicians to explore ways of conducting. This seemed to help them become aware of the importance of body gesture and language in leading or giving instructions in a group music activity.

Pathway: moving rhythms and composing

- Change the ostinato formed with your stones to be played with body percussion and moving in the space (hands, feet, mouth).

- When you hear the word 'stones', you play your rhythm with the stones, when you hear 'body' called out, you move and play with body percussion; hearing 'stop', you stop moving and play the rhythm in your mind. These three different parts can be changed in free order; the leader is the conductor using the words 'stones', 'body' and 'stop'.
- In small groups make a composition with this material to be shared with the rest of the group.

A safe environment for improvisation can be formed by limiting the options for the creative process. This removes the initial feelings of 'where to start'.

 I have experimented with painting bigger stones with water (see pictures 6.11 and 6.12). This is a wonderful way to avoid thinking about creating a product or end result because when the stones dry, the painting vanishes. This is a good tool for active music listening: painting something (e.g. brown paper) with water frees your mind from the result but still gives you the focus.

Reflection and discussion

A. **Discuss the experiences in small groups**
  1 Having explored the pedagogical ideas in this workshop, what are your thoughts on the following?
    - Enhancing feelings of acceptance and activation.
    - Facilitating trust and creative working in a collaborative process.
    - Learning to play an instrument.
    - How was the process constructed, what suited this group, what else could have been explored?
    - What else you found significant in this process.
  2 How could you apply these ideas and approaches with children or family music groups?
    - What could be done differently in the learning session and why?
    - What aspects would be similar?
B. **You can also use the guidelines for observing a lesson in Chapter 5, p. 66, and reflect on the process in three groups, each focusing on a different aspect:**
  1 Process.
  2 Participants' view: what were the possibilities for learning?
  3 Pedagogue's actions and choices.

Note

1 There is a wonderful, hilarious series of children's picture books in Finnish where two strange boys named Tatu and Patu have all kinds of adventures. In one of these (Aino Havukainen & Sami Toivonen: *Tatu, Patu ja oudot kojeet*, transl. *Tatu, Patu and the strange machines*) they invent fantastical machines, e.g. a machine for mornings (aamutoimiautomaatti). This has been a useful book for stimulating the creative invention of machines – for adults and children alike.

References

Biesta, G. J. (2013). *The beautiful risk of education*. Abingdon, UK: Routledge.

Bion, W. R. (1961). *Experiences in groups*. London: Tavistock Publications.

Edmondson, A. (1999). Psychological safety and learning behavior in work teams. *Administrative Science Quarterly, 44*(2), 350–383.

Edmondson, A. (2004). Psychological safety, trust and learning: A group-level Lens. In R. M. Kramer & K. S. Cook (Eds.), *Trust and distrust in organizations: Dilemmas and approaches* (pp. 239–272). New York: Russell Sage Foundation.

Schein, E. H. (1996). Kurt Lewin's change theory in the field and in the classroom: Notes toward a model of managed learning. *Systems Practice, 9*(1), 27–47.

Tuckman, B. W. (1965). Developmental sequence in small groups. *Psychological Bulletin, 63*(6), 384.

Theme 2
MUSIC, EMOTIONS AND INTERACTION

Music and the artistic imaginative world are multi-faceted – offering opportunities to encounter genuine emotions at the heart of our being. They permit an exploration and reflection upon different emotions from a distance. The liminal space that music affords, creates an environment where risk-taking and stepping outside normal behaviour are encouraged as part of entry into another world, where

IMAGE 9.1 Music permits exploration and reflection on emotions from a distance

greater possibilities are available (see Kurkela, 1993, pp. 48–59). This can build self-esteem and self-knowledge and can facilitate working through our feelings. These aspects make the music learning situation a powerful adventure in life. To be able to gain deeper understanding of this aspect of teaching music, it is beneficial for the pedagogue to reflect on their own feelings as a learner in a group. This opens the possibility to empathise with other learners.

 Reflection and discussion

1   Think about a significant experience in music that you had as a child:
    *   What emotions were related to that experience?
    *   Were other people involved? If so, what was their significance?
    *   Has that experience and those emotions played a role later in your life?
2   What kinds of experiences have you had of 'communicative musicality' (Trevarthen & Malloch, 2000, and see Chapter 2 of this book) – musicality as an inbuilt psychobiological capacity?
    *   What have these experiences meant to you?

Exploring emotions

Pathway: music, emotion and imagination

You need: mats to lie on the floor and six different recorded music examples.

*   Lie down. Close your eyes. Relax by concentrating on what you hear from within the room, from outside the room, back in the room, then inside your body. Concentrate on your breathing and the present moment.
*   Let your thoughts wander. Listen to sections (about two minutes each) of the six pieces of music without interruption.
*   After listening, focus slowly on the present moment, the room and gently wake up your body by moving your feet, then your legs, your hands and slowly come to a sitting position.
*   Internally reflect on the thoughts and emotions that listening to the music prompted in you. Share any images, thoughts or emotions from the listening process with the group. Discuss the similarities, differences and the importance of your different experiences.

Music suggestions

Maria Kalaniemi: Napoleon
Philip Glass: The poet acts

Nature sounds: Rain or wave sounds

Kalevi Aho: Symphony No. 7 ("Insect Symphony"). Part: The parasitic hymenopter and its larva

Vincent Youmans: Tea for two (instrumental version for example from Stephane Grappelli)

Wolfgang Amadeus Mozart: Clarinet Concerto A Major K 622. Adagio

Example: pictures to facilitate discussion about music and emotions

You need: a variety of art pictures or postcards and some recorded music examples. How to talk about music or work with feelings by using pictures.

1   Listen to a piece of music and choose one picture that you feel suits the music.
   • Share your thoughts with the group. Why did you choose that picture?
   • This is also a useful way to discuss music – you do not need special vocabulary – you can talk about the picture as a metaphor for the music.
   • Pictures can facilitate talking about emotions – at whatever level feels comfortable to the participant: from talking about the colour in a picture to personal feelings.
2   Pick a postcard. What kind of music or soundscape would suit the picture? This music can then be:
   • Improvised by a musician based on the described sound world.
   • Improvised by the group, who follow the instructions from the person who chose the postcard.
   • Chosen from the recorded music examples.
3   Listen to three different music examples.
   • Pick a postcard for each piece of music.
   • Share your reasons with the group.
   • Compare and reflect on each other's cards and thoughts.
4   Look at one picture while listening to different music examples.
   • How does looking at the picture change with different music?
      • Are there contradictory effects?
      • Does the music make the feelings in the picture stronger?
      • Does the music change the 'message'?
      • Does the music pick up a detail in the picture?
      • Do you notice anything else?

Pathway: being frightened and getting courage

Sharing a story by Max Velthuijs: Frog is frightened

One option for sharing a story with a group of adults is to turn it into a play (the story written as dialogue). Prepare this before the session by writing lines for the actors. In the session, just improvise and act (no rehearsal required!). The story below is an example; there are lots of great storybooks to work with.

This story is about friendship. Frog, Duck and Pig hear some scary noises at night. They comfort one another together in Pig's bed. Their fourth friend, Hare, gets concerned the next morning when he does not find Frog at home, nor anyone at Duck's house. He runs through the forest to Pig's house and wakes them all up with a fright as he arrives in a rush at the window. They then discuss all the different ways that they have felt frightened and begin to understand that everyone is frightened at some time or other. They reassure each other that they don't need to be afraid as they have each other's friendship (Velthuijs, 1994).

What other things could the animals be afraid of?

- Think about something to be afraid of and a sound to describe that fear.
- Where would the animals get courage from to cope with their fear? Think of a movement to show this.
- Sing the song, "Are you afraid of what you hear?", and play the 'fear sounds' within the middle two bars of the song. In part B ("No, no I'm not afraid of sounds I hear") use the 'courage movement' while singing.

Are you afraid of what you hear?

Hannele Huovi (trans. JP & L H-H)   Soili Perkiö

MUSIC 9.1   published with permission from the composer & lyricist

Create a scary sound or chord with a tuned instrument (e.g. a five-stringed kantele, ukulele and guitar)

Workshop: music as a source of comfort and safety

You need: pentatonic pitched instruments, selection of percussion instruments, torches for each participant, a darkened space, white paper, a piece of dark fabric/bedsheet.

In Tove Jansson's, *Moominvalley in November* (1970/1971), Fillyjonk is afraid and concerned with life in many ways. She appears to be a complex character – conventional, but also frantic and wild – based both on control and lack of it. The researcher Sirke Happonen (2007) says of Fillyjonk, "She is a refined lady who loves cleaning, but also a shock-haired dare-devil who flings herself into a storm, ecstatic about her own annihilation" (Happonen, 2007, p. 55). Fillyjonk has made strict rules in order to control her fears, a strategy that has not always been successful. She provides a fruitful character with whom to empathise and reflect on our own fears and worries.

Tuning: Read the excerpt below to understand Fillyjonk's night time experiences.

> *It was late in the autumn and the evenings were very dark. Fillyjonk had never liked night time. There's nothing worse than looking into complete darkness, it is like walking straight out into eternity and not having anybody with you. That's why she put out the bucket of rubbish on the kitchen steps double quick and shut the door tight again, that's what she'd always done.*
>
> *But tonight Fillyjonk stood on the steps and listened to the darkness. Snufkin was playing in his tent, a beautiful, vague tune. Fillyjonk was musical, although neither she nor anybody else realized it. She listened breathlessly. She forgot all the awful things; tall and thin, she was silhouetted against the lighted kitchen, an easy prey to all the lurking dangers of the night. But nothing happened. When the melody was finished she gave a deep sigh, put down the bucket and went back into the house.*
>
> (©**Tove Jansson, 1970/1971, p. 93 (in the English translation). Moomin Characters ™)**

Pathway: comforting tunes

> *"Snufkin was playing in his tent, a beautiful, vague tune."*
> *(Jansson, 1970/1971, p. 93)*

- What kind of music would make us forget all the awful, frightening things?
- Create a small tune in a group using a pentatonic scale for pitched percussion (prepare the instruments for c- or d-pentatonic scale – removing the other keys makes it easy for playing); un-pitched percussion and voices are also effective.
- Version for a large group
  - Each member plays or sings one bar, the next one continues. Select some of the co-created material to form part A of a larger piece.
  - Part A forms the refrain – Using rondo form (ABACAD), the B, C and D sections are for solo improvised melodies from individual participants, with A played together.
- Version for a small group
  - Once the larger group is confident working together in this way, create compositions in smaller groups either using material composed in the larger circle or something new.
- Share these comforting tunes and discuss what you found comforting in them.

Pathway: rehearsing being afraid

- Discuss in a group the things that Fillyjonk might be afraid of.
- Divide the group in half. One half starts by playing sounds for one of the fears (discuss first how it might sound). The other half starts playing the comforting tune and the sounds of the fear slowly fade away.
- Share and reflect.
- The group can be divided into three, with one part forming an audience. Their role is to observe and reflect on the process.

When working with this workshop material, it is imperative that the pedagogue doesn't suggest topics for fears. By focusing on the fears of Fillyjonk and not our own, it is possible to be detached from the fearful thing. It is also essential that the safe or comforting aspect is considered first and established as a haven to return to during the working processes. Even if it is a play for participants, it can feel real and important and needs to be approached as such.

IMAGE 9.2 Where do you get courage?

Pathway: Fillyjonk and the darkness

- Think about where you get courage.
- Find and prepare a safe place in the room, where you can go at any time.
- The group is divided in two. One half has instruments and spreads out in the space. The other half explores "the walk in the darkness" by walking in the space with their eyes shut. When they approach a stationary instrumentalist, the latter plays (the closer, the louder!)
- Share feelings in a group.

Pathway: real darkness

Preparing for real darkness needs to be built safely over time. The group needs to be familiar with each other and the leader; otherwise a safe atmosphere cannot be guaranteed. When the group know each other well, exciting and new music can be used, and suggestions for pieces welcomed.

You need: torches or flashlights for each participant. A darkened space.

Music suggestions

Jukka Koskinen: String quartet
André Jolivet: Serenade pour deux guitares
- *Preludio e canzona*
- *Allegro trepidante*
- *Andante malinconico*
David Hudson: Didgeralia (Rhythms with percussion & didgeridoo)
Conversations between didgeridoo and drum can be found in these pieces of music:
- *Conversation part one*
- *Conversation part two*

Make the space as dark as you can manage. The participants sit in a circle. Each participant has a torch.

- Listen to the music.
- Switch your torch on and off as you like, to explore the darkness while listening to the music.

The dance of two lights in the dark.

- Perform a duet of two torches dancing on the wall.
- Two volunteers perform this improvisatory dance with their torches while the whole group listens to the music. Use the same music as in the previous activity.

The lights feel lonely and would like to have company.

- Repeat as above, but instead of shining the lights on the wall, point them to the floor.
- Improvise a dance with the lights.

Moving in the darkness.

- Move with the music in the space with your torch.
- Point to a part of your body and dance with the light illuminating that part of your body – legs, arms, toes, face. Let the lit part lead the movement.
- The group can be divided into two parts – one being the audience.

Pathway: sounds of the night

Sounds of the night

Markku Kaikkonen (trans. JP & L H-H)

MUSIC 9.2   published with permission from the composer

You need: a selection of instruments.

- Invite the participants to find an instrument that captures the feeling of the night for them.
- Teach the song.
- Form a rondo: part A is the song, other B and C etc. parts are improvised (using dorian mode accompanied with the Dm7, G/D chords).

Closing: the lights reveal creatures in the dark

You need: white paper, a piece of dark fabric/bedsheet and recorded music (use the same music as in the previous activity).

- Tear different shapes to create creatures while listening to the music. Place them on the fabric.
- Think about the special abilities of these creatures and where they get their courage from – what is their secret?
- When the music stops, share these secrets.
- To conclude, wrap the creatures in the fabric to use another session.

Lullaby

- Sing a lullaby suggested by the participants for their creatures.

 Reflection and discussion

1   Discuss the power and responsibility of the pedagogue in this process.
2   Think about this process and its different aspects. What possibilities does this kind of working open for participants?
3   Discuss and reflect about the role of recorded music in this process, e.g. how might the experience of the torch dance change with different kinds of music?
4   What is frightening music for you? Why? Share, compare similarities and differences in experience.
5   Do you remember any lullabies from childhood?

Pathway: music as a safe place

Read the following text to facilitate reflective discussion about music and emotions.

Fillyjonk playing

Actually, Fillyjonk was neither happy nor upset and not a little bit tired. It was as though everything had come to a standstill, and she went on listening. Snufkin had left his mouth-organ on the table, she picked it up, held it in her paw and waited. There was only the rain outside. She raised the mouth-organ and blew into it, she moved it backwards and forwards listening to the sound. She sat down at the kitchen table. How did it go? Toodledi, toodledoo . . . It was difficult to get it right, she tried and tried again, moved very carefully from one note to the next and found the right one, the next came of its own accord. The tune slipped past her, but then came back. Obviously one had to feel for it, not search here and there. Toodledoo, toodledi, a whole string of notes came, each undeniably in the right place.

Toodledidee tune

Jessica Pitt

MUSIC 9.3

Hour after hour Fillyjonk sat at the kitchen table playing the mouth-organ, tentatively but with great devotion. The notes began to resemble tunes and the tunes became music. She played Snufkin's songs and she played her own; she couldn't be got at, nothing could make her feel unsafe now. She didn't worry whether the others could hear her or not. Outside in the garden all was quiet, all the creepy-crawly things had disappeared, and it was an ordinary dark autumn night with a rising wind.

(©Tove Jansson, 1970/1971, pp. 133–134 (in the English translation). Moomin Characters™)

Music and emotions

Think about the meanings of music for Fillyjonk.

* What is it about listening to music that can make everything else feel like it is standing still?
* What is it for you to 'feel for music' rather than 'search for it'?

Reflect on the ways in which music can help control and cope with anxiety. Think about this in relation to the use of music by a mother in proto-musical interactions of communicative musicality that coordinate emotional states in themselves and their infants (Dissanayake, 2008, p. 172).

Musicality and its innate nature of human being

Malloch and Trevarthen (2009) define musicality as the

> expression of our human desire for cultural learning, our innate skill for moving, remembering and planning in sympathy with others that makes our appreciation and production of an endless variety of dramatic temporal narratives possible – whether those narratives consist of specific cultural forms of music, dance, poetry or ceremony, whether they are the universal narratives of a mother and her baby quietly conversing with another; whether it is the wordless emotional and motivational narrative that sits beneath a conversation between two or more adults or between a teacher and a class.
>
> *(pp. 4–5)*

The English version of Janssons's, 'Moominvalley in November', includes a mistranslation: it says Fillyjonk "wasn't musical". In the original Swedish, Fillyjonk "was musical" – and this is the version used here. Malloch and Trevarthen's notion of 'communicative musicality' (Trevarthen & Malloch, 2000), where musicality is seen as an underlying capacity of human communication, challenges traditional ideas of what it is to be 'musical'.

Reflection and discussion

1   Who decides whether one is musical or not, and what influences this decision?

2   What if we adopt the lens of communicative musicality to reflect on situations where being musical or non-musical are decided? What changes and why?

Let this small discovery of Fillyjonk's musical capacity influence your thoughts.

References

Dissanayake, E. (2008). If music is the food of love, what about survival and reproductive success? *Musicae Scientiae, 12*(1, suppl.), 169–195.

Happonen, S. (2007). The Fillyjonk at the window: Aesthetics of movement and gaze in Tove Jansson's illustrations and texts. In K. McLoughlin & M. Lidström Brock (Eds.), *Tove Jansson rediscovered* (pp. 54–74). NewCastle: Cambridge Scholars Publishing.

Jansson, T. (1970). *Sent I November.* Helsinki: Schildts & Södeström. English translation *Moominvalley in November.* (1971). Ernest Benn Ltd.

Kurkela, K. (1993). *Mielen maisemat ja musiikki: Musiikin esittämisen ja luovan asenteen psykodynamiikka.* Helsinki: Sibelius Academy.

Malloch, S., & Trevarthen, C. (2009). Musicality: Communicating the vitality and interests of life. In S. Malloch & C. Trevarthen (Eds.), *Communicative musicality: Exploring the basis of human companionship* (pp. 3–11). New York: Oxford University Press.

Trevarthen, C., & Malloch, S. (2000). The dance of well-being: Defining the musical therapeutic effect. *Nordic Journal of Music Therapy, 9*(2), 3–17.

Velthuijs, M. (1994). *Frog is frightened.* London: Andersen Press.

Theme 3

VOICE AND BODY AS FIRST INSTRUMENTS

In this chapter, we think about ourselves as musical instruments, including the amazing human voice and the body in which it is housed. The starting point for music making comes from what is inside us. The voice and the body are our first musical instruments, and playing with these should form a solid foundation for all music learning. Music is experienced and felt in the body and voice; the fundamental instruments work together and are consciously experienced as musical tools and expressers of music and emotion, which can be transferred to instrumental playing.

IMAGE 10.1   Exploring possibilities of the voice

Voice

The beginning of this section focuses on the theoretical background to the voice and singing, followed by an approach to the topic from the perspective of the pedagogue and their actions: sharing songs with others and encouraging people to explore the possibilities of their voices and the enjoyment of singing together.

Evolutionary aspects

Ellen Dissanayake (2000) describes the evolutionary changes that took place in order for humans to walk upright. Infants were born in increasingly immature and helpless states due to the production of an increasingly larger-brained infant and a necessary narrowing of the pelvis because of walking on two legs rather than four (Morgan (1995), as cited in Dissanayake, 2000). Dissanayake (2000) found that parent and infant maintained "communicative ('protoconversational'[1]) sequences that careful analyses have shown to be exquisitely patterned over time" (p. 15). These "rhythmic-modal capacities" are crucial to mutuality between mother and infant but also, she argues, "create and sustain other ties of intimacy" amongst humans (p. 20). In addition, as children develop, their own vocal anatomy and physiology changes so that different vocal behaviours become possible (Welch, 2006a, p. 325).

Early vocal behaviour may include rhythmic patterns, which might not constitute a musical structure, but are a mode of communicating emotional content. Patricia Eckerdal and Bjorn Merker (2009) would describe this as "over and above the basic repertoire of non-verbal vocal expressiveness" (p. 243). Infant-directed speech (Fernald, 1992; Papoušek, 1996; Trainor, Austin, & Desjardins, 2000; Trevarthen, 2000) allows emotional information to be shared mutually between parent and child. Parents' previous musical experiences (Custodero, Britto, & Brooks-Gunn, 2003; Ilari, 2005) and gender may affect their singing practices too. This provides part of the complex communicative background for the development of ritual culture to which song and dance belong (Eckerdal & Merker, 2009, p. 246; Merker, 2001).

The development of young children's singing voices has been approached from many perspectives. It has been perceived to develop through different stages (Rutkowski, 1990, 2013) and also as a characteristic of a young child's creative playful abilities with an improvisational character, which can be difficult to assess in a testing situation (Gudmundsdottir & Cohen, 2015).

Bruno Nettl argues that it is not straightforward to assume that there are universals of, and among musics, in every culture and society. Thinking of the world's musics as evolving from a limited range of pitches is one option; another is that early human music moved around a glissando-like vocal range, what he describes as being "like emotional speech" (Nettl, 2000, p. 471).

Stephanie Stadler Elmer (2011) considers that it is essentially a human characteristic to organise sounds and signs in order to regulate inter- and intrapersonal psychological processes and that singing is a universal, socio-cultural expression of human development that has its origins in playfulness. Music making is "rooted in repetitive and varied playing with sounds, all irrational but structured and full of affective and symbolic meanings for the creators sharing these experiences" (p. 26). Spontaneous singing was considered by Jon Bjørkvold to be linked to language development and a need to express thoughts, feelings and a sense of identity (Bjørkvold, 1992). Young children have been found to sing on their own in moments of solitude, suggesting that it serves a purpose of emotional regulation (Trehub & Gudmundsdottir, 2015).

Our evolution has included the development of song and singing for a variety of purposes; it supports infant-parent interaction in the first months of life and onwards, thus helping to sustain attention between the dyad, which assists with the nurture and bonding that is so vital for survival.

Song may also be useful in our developing need to speak together to express thoughts and feelings through language and then to experience through playfulness, a ritualised community bonding in song and dance, as an element of sexual attraction and reproduction (Miller, 2001).

Perspectives on the development of singing

Children's early vocalisations begin with rhythmic babbling (Dolata, Davis, & MacNeilage, 2008) and spontaneous songs mentioned by Helmut Moog (1976), David Hargreaves (1986), Graham Welch (2006a) and Margaret Barrett (2006) that develop into pot-pourri songs, where snippets of learned songs appear in different places and formats. These may be serving a cognitive, emotional or social purpose for the child. Hargreaves (1986) described these snippets as akin to 'tadpole-man' drawings, and they may constitute an important part of children's real music in early childhood that may be dismissed or ignored by adult teachers or observers, as they do not conform to adult notions of singing or copying a song correctly. These seemingly random snippets of songs may be part of thinking, remembering or play processes (Dean, 2011) that are developmentally helpful or therapeutic for self-regulation of mood state. Accuracy in pitch reproduction may be less important to the child than to any adult monitoring their singing. Children's free drawing attempts are clearly not seeking to accurately reproduce another's work, to imitate another's drawing is a different task altogether, so it may be with children's free vocal play as distinct from joining in with recreating a known song.

A longitudinal, ethnographic study (Barrett, 2006) explored the ways in which young children's (4–5 years old) invented songs showed examples of mutuality and belonging, finding and making meaning, developing competence and elaborating (Barrett, 2006). Barrett argues that group music making, with a focus on ensemble performance, is a good vehicle for achieving many extra-musical developmental aims. However, invented song-making has the key role of encouraging elaboration, which allows music to be a creative practice rather than a recreative one (Barrett, 2006).

When spontaneous singing and sound exploration are encouraged and valued as a regular part of young children's play, they can become more prominent and overt aspects of creativity (Gluschankof & Kenney, 2011; Moorhead & Pond, 1941; Niland, 2009; Smithrim, 1997; Young, 2005, 2008). Amanda Niland (2006) found that allowing children to pursue their interests over time and including children's contributions to specially composed songs led to a sense of ownership of the musical material that was sustained and became embedded in the setting for at least two years after the event.

Barrett acknowledges that children's creative endeavour gives children agency and a sense of their own musical culture. Children's original music making is rarely regarded in the same way as children's visual art. In her case study of a 4-year-old's (Charli) invented songs, she makes a strong case for music as a creative rather than recreative process, finding that Charli gained much social, emotional and cultural capital from the creative process and products of her own invented song-making. This relied on fostering and valuing children's musical agency as songwriters in early childhood settings (Barrett, 2006).

 Reflection and discussion

1   Find some of the many clips on the Internet of infants vocalising with their mother, father or carer. Watch and reflect on:
  - The pitch ranges and patterns of the melodies you observe.
  - The body language and eye contact.
  - The timing of responses between the pair.
  - Who leads and who follows, and how and when do the roles change?
  - How is the 'space' to express invited, negotiated and shared?

The socio-cultural aspects of singing

Welch (2006b) sees enculturation and generative skill development as significant in the changes in singing behaviour that occur as a child ages. A young child is a member of several social groups, and each may influence individual musical behaviour and development. He suggests the family can have a key role, and parents' enjoyment and participation in music can have a strong impact on the musical environment for young children. Barbara Rogoff – an educator whose research interests include both anthropology and psychology perspectives – suggests that "humans develop through their changing participation in the socio-cultural activities of their communities, which also change" (Rogoff, 2003, p. 11). This implies that family and community practices can influence our cultural and artistic experiences, and our involvement in these practices also contributes to the way that these practices change and evolve. It is a dynamic process.

Action songs – described by Eckerdal & Merker (2009) as "schematized sequences of obligatory bodily action" (p. 250) – are frequently used in music making with young children and their parents. These might include knee bouncing, clapping or finger games that are applied in a predictable sequence that allows the child to interact in a predetermined manner with their carer. The purpose of these songs in children's development is ambiguous. Often regarded as useful in teaching language skills (Goswami & Bryant, 1990), the language of many of these songs seems ill-suited to the task: it is often archaic or nonsensical. The musical purpose does not seem to be a priority either, as metrical and melodic errors do not seem to matter in rendition. What does appear to matter is the person-to-person interactive component. Eckerdal and Merker (2009) found that the purpose of action songs was to encourage the child to actively participate – adults often praising the child's efforts to join in. They suggest that this participation represents entry into the ritual level of human culture – clapping, for example, is a ritual sign of approval. Following the 'rules' is not learning for life but just learning for the confines of the action song.

Jessica Pitt's (2014) research suggested that the non-verbal communicative competence displayed through the sharing of action songs by parents/carers, young children and the music pedagogue was a ritualised 'coming together' with a shared meaning and understanding of the cultural traditions implied in that song, in that place and at that time. It helped nurture a sense of belonging amongst group members. She found that there was symmetry in the group's interaction because the song and its actions guided the learning group through the shared musical event (Pitt, 2014). It was communicative in its nature as the familiar song communicates information about culture, the melody communicates information about the musical traditions, and the actions narrate the meaning of the words that assist with their understanding. The shared affect experienced as part of the group symmetry (Fogel, 2000) may enhance positive emotional responses to the experience.

Example: exploring your voice

You need: soap bubbles. The group moves freely in the space.

1   One person blows bubbles, and the rest of the group makes sounds with their voice and mouth while looking at the bubbles. Pick one bubble and follow it with your voice until the bubble disappears.
2   Walk in the space and breathe calmly. Let your breath out with a sound. Explore a different sound for each breath.

Example: warming up voice, body and the group

You need: different sizes of balls with varying bouncing heights. The group is in a circle.

1   Throw a ball to someone in the circle and say your name. Repeat around the circle.
2   Repeat the same activity with an imaginary ball, this time you say the name of the person receiving the ball; include different-sized imaginary balls, making sure that the movement of throwing shows clearly what size of a ball you have and to whom it is thrown.
3   Accompany the movement of different balls (either real or imaginary) with sounds from your voice and mouth.

Example: sun beams

You need: a picture of a sun beam, ribbons, tape or something that can be laid on the floor to represent sun beams (see as an example, "Following sunbeams" image 6.6).

•   Follow the beams on the picture with your finger and sing a long note with one breath.
•   When you change to follow another beam, choose another pitch.
•   Sing as you walk along the sunbeams, breathing in at the centre and singing as you move out along the sunbeam.

Pathway: nature sounds

This exercise warms up the voice and the body in preparation for singing.
   You need: a poem or part of a story that describes movement in the natural world (e.g. wind blowing through trees or flowers).

1   Read the poem or part of the story to the group.
2   Explore the ways the wind is moving the trees or flowers by:
   •   Bending forward and backwards.
   •   Reaching up to the sun and the clouds.
   •   Swaying from side-to-side.
   •   Stretching the neck from side-to-side.
   •   Moving in the space, breathing out with a sound of the wind.
   •   Exploring different ways that the wind can sound: short and direct, long and flowing.
   •   Continuing to walk freely, vocalising glissandi with 'rrrrr'.
   •   Chewing with 'mmm' on different pitches – one pitch for each out-breath.
   •   Walk in the space and sing with an open vowel: oo, aah, ee, ay with one pitch per out-breath.

3   Create a composition 'Nature Sounds' using both the movements and sounds that has just been explored.
    •   Pick your favourite movement and sound.
    •   Prepare a choir, with one person conducting.
    •   Let the movements of the conductor create the sounds – with no verbal discussion or instructions!
    •   Explore this with two choirs and two conductors, performing at the same time.

Pedagogical dimensions of working with songs

Music pedagogues have a great opportunity to create positive early experiences of songs and singing, using the rich variety of song repertoire available, that can be carried throughout our lives. It is not uncommon at a first meeting of a family music group for some parents to admit a reluctance to sing. Some recount experiences from school where it was made clear to them that they were not good enough singers to join the choir. The pedagogue needs to handle the situation sensitively to develop trust and a relaxed atmosphere, where parents can explore their voices alongside their children.

Choosing songs for music education practice opens doors into the world of music. Songs that include a variety of musical elements offer a rich palette to use to encourage listening, to explore the voice and to develop perception of musical elements such as pitch, form, pulse and dynamics. Some songs are meant for children to be able to sing themselves, and some songs can be sung by adults for children (and be accompanied by a game or movement).

There is a risk the pedagogue may unintentionally imply that singing ability is either equivalent to musicality or valued over 'the feeling for singing' (for example by admiring a child singing perfectly in tune). Singing at pitch requires a combination of muscular control, perception of pitch, self-regulation and social development (being in a group and able to sing with others). When exploring your voice and playing creatively with this element of music practice, singing should not be thought of as either an achievement or a performance.

Singing to and with young children is a universal pastime. It forms the basis of much early childhood music education. Nursery rhymes and lullabies are the established repertoire for many nursery settings and parent-child music groups. When choosing songs for children to sing, the melodic framework, as well as the pitch intervals in the melody, have to be taken into account. Songs with a limited melodic framework and easy melody are immediately accessible. Fascinating words, or an important song like 'Happy Birthday', can capture a child's attention and encourage them to try to join in. Infants are already musically discerning, with preferences for certain aspects (some prefer rhythmical songs, some like challenges such as jumps in the melody). The lyrics or story can tempt the singer into the musical structure of the song or its arrangement.

A small baby is already developing their voice as a vehicle for self-expression. Singing is part of the normal phase for language development and babbling. Playing with the possibilities of your voice is a vital part of self-expression. A child's first attempts at singing a song can take place early in life, and sometimes the songs are hard to identify. Even professional early childhood music pedagogues reveal that they have not always noticed their own child's first attempts at a particular song until they have managed to produce enough of it to be recognisable. This means that there are far more attempts at singing songs and joining in than we can identify, demonstrating that all babbling and gurgling is important exploration of the voice. Attuning our awareness to young children's vocalisations and singing attempts can help us to support this rich expression of melodic and musical use of voice and sounds.

World of songs

There are all kinds of songs: songs for action, songs for relaxation, songs that facilitate young children's singing and those that facilitate listening. There are songs that help a child to develop their body-image or bring joy by rehearsing newly-learned motor skills of walking, galloping and crawling. There are songs that feature different musical elements: songs in minor and major keys, with different rhythms, time signatures and in different scales. Some songs engage certain age groups: "Stop" (see p. 211) might work well with under-2-year-olds whereas older children might prefer more complex lyrics. Other songs offer more challenge and the opportunity to work on musical aspects.

Simple songs that can be easily adapted to different learning situations offer flexibility for musical exploration (e.g. songs can be sung higher or lower, faster or slower, quieter or louder etc.). Songs can also convey different cultural aspects – they may belong to a particular season or tradition. By choosing different arrangements of recorded songs, you can explore different genres in music, thus broadening the musical experience. Songs can also be made for certain purposes in the learning/teaching processes (see as an example "Snowflake Song" p. 210); in order to be useful, they do not always need to be great compositions. Songs created together in a group can sometimes be the most useful and meaningful. Some song examples can be found at the back of this book.

 Reflection and discussion

1   Using either the song examples at the back of this book, or from another book, analyse the list of songs from different viewpoints.

- What scales and melodic structures do the songs have?
- What tempi and rhythmic elements do they introduce?
- Is there a song that could be added to open a musical possibility that has not been explored?

> 2   Repertoire
>   Reflect on songs that you know and would like to use in your own practice.
>   • List 10 songs and analyse them based on aspects explored in this chapter.
>   • Look at your list and think whether there are some features missing? E.g. major/minor keys, different tempi, varied melodic range of the pieces, songs with challenges and songs that are easy to sing.
>   • What needs to be added to make your list more varied and rich musically or pedagogically?

Teaching a song – many variations

When you have chosen a song, think about how you could 'dive into' it. There are many ways to learn the song and make its elements familiar. One approach is echo singing (the teacher sings first and the group repeats); another is to sing the song and let the participants join in gradually as they begin to learn the song.

'Call and Response' teaching suits songs that have short phrases and an easy and symmetrical form. The challenge is leading this approach; clear signs for listening and responding are needed – e.g. putting your hand behind your ear as a sign for listening and then inviting with open hands for the participants to repeat (with young children, the leader may have to sing for both).

For many songs, joining in gradually is a useful approach and can be facilitated in many ways:

• Starting with the words. Learn the words in a rhythm and then add the melody.
• Starting with the actions/movements/game before learning the melody.
• Using pictures to learn the words of a song is especially good for songs with many verses (also supporting the speech with signs is a good way to teach songs, especially for those children that may need special help in the group).
• Using drawing to help remember the song through the narrative of the lyrics.
• Drawing the shape of melody in the air. Using a 'singing hand' can help participants notice the shape of the melody, especially if there is a jump in the melodic line.
• Singing with the beat while clapping, walking etc.
• Singing the melody first without words.

The pedagogue can introduce the song by singing it in the background while other activities are in progress. This enables participants to become acquainted with the 'big picture' of the song. One way to do this is by listening to the song at the

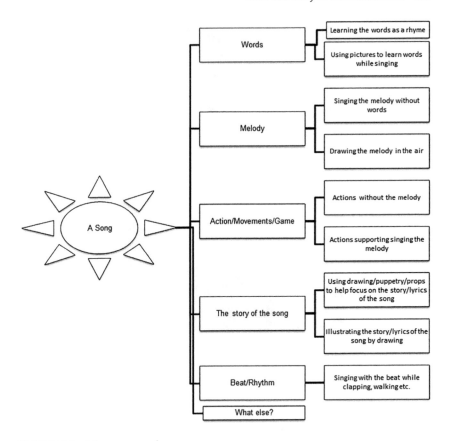

FIGURE 10.1 Many ways to learn a song

end of a session while engaged in a calming activity such as lying under a piece of garden fleece wafted over the group. This helps to maintain focus and attention. The song can be taught explicitly in a subsequent session.

Soili Perkiö describes dimensions of song like this: "I perceive songs as 'puzzlesongs' and 'flowersongs'. Puzzlesongs can be approached through elements or fragments of the song. This simply adds to the pleasure – what will the picture reveal when the fragments have been gathered together? Flowersongs are as delicate as a rose. Dividing the song into pieces would be the same as giving a flower away, petal by petal, followed by the stalk and leaves. By doing this you're never able to recreate the beauty of the flower!" (S. Perkiö, personal communication, October 11, 2017).

Starting to teach a song: short checklist

1   Plan well and have a plan B (and C) ready – be flexible in your thinking!
2   Prepare any material or instrument you may need.
3   Warm up your instruments: voice, body and the group dynamics!

IMAGE 10.2   A song can be like a flower

4   Model a calm, relaxed but focused atmosphere.

5   Sing in a key that is suitable for the group. It is a common mistake to use keys that are too low, expecting children to join in. If you have a low voice, first sing the song to the children in a comfortable key for you and then move the song into a more appropriate key for children to sing.

6   Sing the song at a slow tempo for a few rounds. You can increase the tempo when the song is more familiar.

7   Talk as little as possible and let the actions (game, singing, moving etc.) lead.

8   If verbal instructions are needed, give them clearly and concisely, one instruction at a time.

9   Use your body movement to instruct whenever possible.

10   Time your instructions to keep the activity flowing.

11   Be focused and goal-orientated. Don't expect the group to know the song already. Develop the learning situation incrementally, gradually getting more challenging. In a safe learning environment, the level of challenge is optimal – not too easy nor too difficult.

12   When you move to the next activity or phase, be clear and give time to adjust.

13   Repetition of the material should include a variety of ways to sing or develop the activities, so that the group feels they're making progress even though they're repeating material.

There are many benefits to be gained from working in multiple ways with one song. A session need only include one or two songs to focus on different musical aspects. Working in depth with dancing and playing, the process of using the song might go beyond anything that is achievable in one session alone.

Reflection and discussion

1   Teaching a song (to a group of students of teaching or colleagues).
    • Bring with you a song to share with the group (a song you like and easy enough to teach by heart).
    • Think about how you would introduce the song. There are lots of ways.
    • How can we learn the song best – with the lyrics, the melody, or the movements first?
    • After sharing the songs with the group, discuss:
       What were the strengths of these pedagogical choices in teaching the song? What other choices were there?
       What feelings did you have while learning a song, and what pedagogical observations do you have?
       How did the short checklist (p. 109) work in this example, and what points could be developed?

2   From a song to a process.
    Choose a song you like.
    • What are the musical elements of this song?
    • What possibilities for learning does this song offer?
    • How will you teach this song? Will you start with the lyrics, the rhythm or some other starting point?
    • How can different elements of music practice (movement, dance, visual elements, drama) facilitate learning this song and its musical elements?
    • Draw a map of the possible pedagogical pathways this song offers the group learning process.

3   Your voice as your pedagogical instrument.
    This last exercise is vital to us, as pedagogues need to connect to the inner experience of singing and our voices as a part of ourselves. The voice is deeply connected to our self-esteem and sense of worth. Negative comments about one's voice can be deeply hurtful. The exploration of one's voice helps to re-establish oneself as part of the learning group, and not as a separate, cognitive facilitator, divorced from the feeling side of using one's voice. Rena Upitis (2017) encourages all teachers to experience music and other arts with their whole being, to capture the essence of artistic work. There can be a tendency for musically-trained singers to become absorbed in the technical aspects of producing a good tone, in

the right way, and a sort of detachment from the true vocal instrument can occur. These technical, production aspects of singing can preoccupy those singers who are not musically trained, but think that this is what is needed. This approach can also influence the way that we facilitate learning songs and singing with people we work with. Upitis (2017) suggests that the true power lies in the teacher's engagement with their whole being if the art practice is to be truly transformational.

For this you need a quiet place to be alone.
- How do you feel about your voice? What colour is it? What shape does it remind you of? Using watercolour paints, relax your shoulders, close your eyes, breathe calmly and think of a lovely sunny day on a beach or in your favourite place. Allow your voice to come out with different sounds. After a while, paint the sound of your voice.
- Share and reflect on this activity with the group in the next session. Compliment each other on the sound of your voices (both singing and speaking).

Note: If you use your voice for much of your working day, vocal lessons are recommended to preserve your vocal cords and to understand healthy ways to use your voice.

The sound of movement – the body as a musical instrument

This section focuses on the body, movement and the important role they both play in supporting our internal musicality. Our body can be seen "as the vehicle of being in the world" (Merleau-Ponty, 1962, p. 82) and is the first instrument through which we experience the temporally organised, rhythmical world into which we are born (see e.g. Pouthas, 1996). The foetus experiences the rhythms of a mother's heartbeat, her walking, speaking, singing and dancing, and her experiences of day and night. These all convey to the foetus the temporal organisation they will join. When observing a young child moving to the rhythm of music, it is possible to see how the body is our first instrument for interpreting sound sensations. The embodiment of "being conscious of the world through the medium of the body" (Merleau-Ponty, 1962, p. 82) has influenced music education practice. Although we are bodily creatures throughout our lives, as adults we tend to forget this – there is no age-limit to working with movement.

The best-known music educators who worked with movement are Emile-Jacques Dalcroze and Carl Orff. Their pedagogical approaches are based on experiential learning, the process, and creativity. Interaction within groups of learners and the learner´s own intentions in the learning process are also strongly emphasised (see e.g. Bachmann, 1991; Benedict, 2010; Greenhead, Habron, & Mathieu, 2016; Frazee, 2006; Juntunen, 2004; Juntunen, Perkiö, & Simola-Isaksson, 2010; Niewbrandt Wedin, 2011; Saliba, 1991).

Playing an instrument is often regarded as 'real music making', and valued more highly than learning music with our bodies as musical instruments. Adults are sometimes too focused on the cognitive and analytical aspects of learning and 'knowing' about music. Reconnecting with the bodily form of knowing by experiencing music with movement is also needed. It is important the pedagogue reconnects with their creative and musical body in order to nourish and respect this instrument in their learners.

The following examples address:

- My body – a unique instrument.
- Exploring and learning music through movement.
- The group – a moving and sounding instrument.
- Self-expression – listening to music through your body – creativity through movement.
- Dance Form – a rich source for learning music.

My body – a unique instrument

To remind ourselves of the primal need to feel accepted and treasured, activities that involve touch immediately connect us to ourselves and the present moment (for example, 'Instrument and Player', Theme 1, p. 76). A parent's playful and instinctive touching, moving and playing with their baby's body, through songs and rhymes (e.g. 'This little piggy' or the Finnish rhyme 'Konkkis, Konkkis, koira metsään menee'), non-verbally communicates: 'your body is acceptable and you are worthwhile and valued as a whole being'.

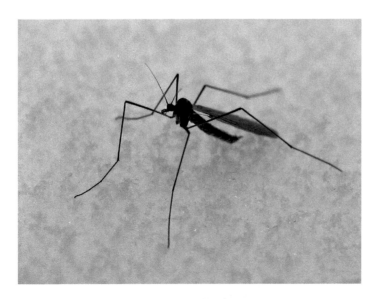

IMAGE 10.3   Body – our personal and unique instrument

Example: body – a moving instrument

Music: Benjamin Britten: Simple Symphony, Op 4: 2 Playful pizzicato

The music starts with a very quiet pizzicato. Move your body to the music. How do your movements change as the piece progresses?

Example: bodily conversations

In pairs, explore musical and bodily conversations inspired by David Hudson's music. One person moves as the didgeridoo is playing, and the other when the drum plays.

Music: David Hudson: Didgeralia (Rhythms with percussion & didgeridoo)

- *Conversations between didgeridoo and drum can be found in 'Conversation part one' and 'Conversation part two'.*

 Reflection and discussion

1   Your body is an important professional tool for communication, expression and sensation. You actually express more with your body than with your words. Reflect on this by painting a picture of yourself – drawing an outline and painting with colours that reflect your emotions.

Workshop: fish

You need: some pictures of the sea, a fish prop/puppet, plasticine, Lycra, serviettes and thread, a selection of instruments, dark coloured paper, brushes and cups of water, bowls of water, different containers and sand.

IMAGE 10.4   Secrets of the sea

Tuning with the song

- Begin by singing the two-phrase song continually. Encourage the participants to join in. A fish prop (e.g. puppet, soft toy) can be moved amongst the group (see an example in picture 6.18).
- Once the group is settled and attuned to one another through the imaginative experience, invite participants to share their memories of the sea.

Secrets of the Sea
(This song harmonises with 'Secretive Fish')

Laura Huhtinen-Hildén

MUSIC 10.1   published with permission from the composer

Pathway: sea paintings

You need: some pictures of the sea (e.g. Monet's seascapes, 'The Rock Needle and Porte D'aval Etretat' and 'Rocks at Port Coton, The Lion Rock'), or create your own. (For inspiration, see an example in picture 6.7).

The group is looking at the paintings and improvising sounds.

- Imagine what sounds could be 'heard' from the painting (e.g. waves, wind, seagulls)
- Share the ideas and sounds; the group imitates the sounds together.
- Allow these sounds to develop and create a sound landscape and add singing the "Secrets of the sea".

"Secretive fish" can be sung on top of these ostinati. This can be taught either to a small group while others are constantly producing the sound landscape and singing "Secrets of the sea", or it can be taught separately and added step by step to the musical material.

Secretive Fish

Hannele Huovi (trans. JP & L H-H)

Soili Perkiö

MUSIC 10.2   published with permission from the composer & the lyricist

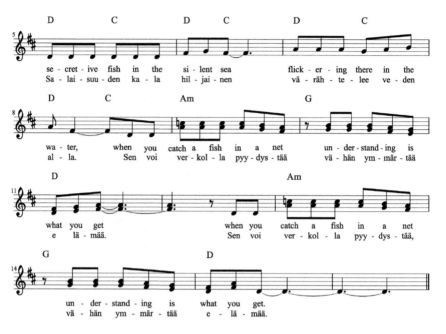

MUSIC 10.2   (Continued)

Pathway: dance of the waves

- Create a movement to each sound you found in the pictures in the Pathway above.
- Combine these to make a dance of the waves.

Pathway: fish and frogs

- On the seashore, there are frogs jumping. Explore how they jump into the water.
    - *Eppelin peppelin peurun meurun, kipulin kapulin kiurun kaurun, kiveltä veteen, pulskis! (This is a Finnish nonsense rhyme about jumping – ending in 'from the stone to the water, Splash!')*
- Fish and frogs/ABA (fast-slow-fast)
    Music: Edward Grieg: Holberg Suite, op. 40. 5th movement, Rigaudon.
    - Fish and frogs are moving in turn. Part A is the jumping of the frogs (the movement can be facilitated by the rhyme 'eppelin peppelin'. B is the slower and smoother movement of the secretive fish, after which the faster A frog theme repeats. Participants move to the music as frogs and fish.

Pathway: finding friends for the fish and frog

- Create creatures that live in the sea or on the seashore, e.g. using playdough or Plasticine.
- Relatives for secretive fish can be made of thin, almost transparent serviettes and thread. Scrunch up the serviette to make a fish-like shape, make the tail by tying the serviette with thread (about two-thirds down the body). Don't cut the thread but make a loop to hold the fish from the tail thread.

IMAGE 10.5 Relatives of Secretive fish

You can nurture your imagination with music by listening to Miguel Castro: Cadence of Waters

- When the creatures are ready, place them on top of Lycra to listen to the sounds of the waves.
- If you made a fish, repeat the dance of fish and frogs by moving with your own fish in the space (*Grieg: Holberg Suite, op. 40. 5th movement, Rigaudon*).
  - Experiment by repeating this dance with instruments. The beat in part A (frogs) can be played with rhythm instruments, and the middle part B can be danced with the fish.

Pathway: sounds of the seashore

- What did the creatures or fish hear? Refer to the pathway above, listening to the "Cadence of Waters" or using your imagination. Paint with water on dark coloured paper.
- Before the painting dries, use it as a graphical score, play it with instruments according to the preference of the group.
  - Bowls of water and cups, or different containers and sand, can make interesting instruments.

Closing with the song: secrets we have seen, secrets of the sea

Return to the mood of the beginning of the workshop by singing the opening melody, changing the line 'Secrets we shall see' to 'Secrets we have seen'.

> *We used this workshop process with children between 4 months and 4-years-old and their parents/carers in a museum. We used the song, "Secrets of the sea", to travel within the space and also to move from one idea to another. Once established, the song gave a framework for wonderful improvisational harmonies and counter melodies that filled the beautiful acoustic of the museum. We can never look at the paintings of the sea that were used in the workshop without hearing and feeling "Secrets of the sea".*

Reflection and discussion

1   Merleau-Ponty (1962) suggests that our bodies can be seen "as the vehicle of being in the world" (p. 82). Discuss and reflect on your experiences of the workshop in light of this thought.

Exploring and learning music through movement

The following examples focus on opening possibilities for learning about the elements of music.

Example: beat/pulse

Beat and pulse can be experienced with every movement activity. Experiment with a circle dance with improvised movements or moving freely with ribbons. Some music to experiment with:

Music suggestions

Antonio Vivaldi: Sinfonia in G, RV 149 (1) Andante. Bobby McFerrin version
Bombino: Tenere (The desert, my home), Agadez Album, 2011
Whirl-Y-Reel 1 Afro Celt Sound System – Sound Magic Vol 1
JPP (Järvelän Pikkupelimannit): Retu-matin polokka

> In a parent/carer and baby group, I noticed a baby bouncing on an adult's lap with excitement. I encouraged this, using "Whirl-Y-Reel" and inviting the adults to tap the pulse on their baby's legs while bouncing to the beat.

Pathway: tempo

You need: coloured ribbons.

Music: Edward Grieg: Holberg Suite, op. 40. 5th movement, Rigaudon

ABA-form (fast-slow-fast)
Each participant has a coloured ribbon(s).

- Move freely to the music with the ribbons.
- Choose whether to be in a fast-moving group or a slow-moving group.
- Move freely when you hear your group's music (fast or slow). Watch the ribbons and movements of the other group. Change over to experience the different tempo.

> When I used this with my 4-year-olds, I found that having one coloured ribbon for the fast movers and another colour for the slow movers helped those children whose aural discrimination was less well developed. The visual clue helped them to become aware of what was happening in the music and for them to begin to discriminate.

> *Using this activity helped the children realise that there are different ways of feeling. Through the reflection on the experiences, some learners spoke about the fast movement suiting them because they feel active, and others found the slow movements suited how they were feeling that day.*

Pathway: timbre

You need: coloured ribbons

Pjotr Tšaikovski: The Nutcracker Suite, op. 71 a. Chinese dance

The group is divided into two, and each participant has a coloured ribbon(s).

- One half listens for the flute, moving when they hear it and the other half listens for the pizzicato strings and moves similarly.
- This call and response activity can be developed: with pairs, other props (e.g. claves), different creatures . . .

The group is divided into four, and each small group has distinctive coloured ribbons.

- The groups move when they hear their instrument: bassoon, flute, violin, clarinet.

> *In order for this activity to be meaningful for my family music group, I chose the theme of animals to represent the instrumental parts in the music. When we heard the flute part, we moved as birds. We slowly found other animals for other instruments and built the auditory discrimination deeper each time.*

> *Once my group was familiar with moving with ribbons, we decided to use percussion instruments for the various movements: djembe (for the bassoon), maracas (pizzicato), rainstick (flute) and guiro (clarinet). We played our movements on the instruments with the music and then we removed the recorded music and played the structure of the piece with the percussion instruments.*

Example: form and structure

Form and structure can be found in all compositions, see "The Sleeping Beauty's Pavane" in Theme 4 and the "Holberg Suite" here as examples. Folk and children's songs are also a good source for simple structure and form.

> Caroubel's "Gavotte" in Mr Arbeau's School of Dancing, Vol 2 was a fantastic resource. Its high energy inspired the group to dance together. There were clear solo sections with drum that could be used for tapping partners'/babies' shoulders. After dancing the piece, we then added drums and used the circle dance and drumming together. It became a joyful shared musical event!

Pathway: melody line

You need: strips of crepe paper or scarves

Music: Antonio Vivaldi:Violin Concerto in D, Opus 11. No.1 (1). Largo

- The first time the music is played:
- Work in pairs, with one sitting on a chair and the other gently playing the pizzicato accompaniment on their partner's body according to how their partner would like to be played. Halfway through the piece, change roles.
- The second time, the music is played:
    - Working in the same pair. One person lies on the floor, and the other draws the melody line on their partner's body, first with one hand and then the other.
    - Swap roles.
    - The basic principle of one person 'playing the other' can be used with a partner standing, or being moved in the space, leading or being led. When leading, concentrate on the melody line; the partner being led has their eyes closed.
- Sit facing a partner. Make a duet with one moving with the pizzicato line and the other with the melody.
- Scarves or strips of crepe paper are given to half the group. They move in the space, painting the melody line in the air with the scarf or paper strip. The pizzicato line group moves with small steps to the rhythm, and no arm movements. Change roles by handing over a scarf or paper strip.

> I used this piece of music with my music activity group for the elderly and their caregivers. The elderly participants appreciated being able to take turns as equals in playing the pizzicato and the melody. I took the inspiration for the process from the rain that morning; this became our guiding image. There was a great sense of togetherness and sharing.

> My class of 5-year-olds was lying on the floor with their eyes closed as we listened to the music. Using the water theme we had been exploring, I had a houseplant spray filled with water. I sprayed a little in the air above the face of each child as they listened to the piece. After that, in pairs, we played raindrops with our fingers on each other's backs and used watercolours to paint the melody line as we listened to the music several times.

The group – a moving and sounding instrument

Participating in a group movement activity can be empowering, giving permission to everyone to participate and experience music at the point that is most appropriate for them.

This way of experiencing and interpreting music also offers opportunities for rich, non-verbal interaction, both musically and socially. It supports social development in children's groups by enriching early interaction between parents and their children as well as nourishing self-expression and a sense of all-age togetherness.

Pathway: listening to music with your body

You need: a large piece of garden fleece, elastic tape.

Music: Johann Sebastian Bach: Cello Suite No. 1 in G, BWV 1007

Listen to the whole suite. The group listens throughout the movement activity.

1   Prelude: the whole group stands and holds a large (5–6m) rectangle of garden fleece. Feeling the music of the Prelude, slowly move the fleece to the music (no speech needed).
2   Allemande: in pairs, with a piece of elastic tape (0.5 metre), move together to the music, either with the ribbon slack or tight, close together or far apart, led by one or both alternating.
3   Courante: one of the pair paints to the music using the arms or whole body of their partner. Change roles without speaking – use body language to indicate the change-over.
4   Sarabande: in pairs, one 'plays' the other – as in the 'Instrument and Player' example, p. 76.
5   Minuet 1 & 2: two pairs work together. Make a diamond shape and face towards the leader. The leader moves to the music, and the other three mimic them. When the leader wants to pass on the lead, they face the person they choose, and so it continues.
6   Gigue: the whole group, no matter how large, forms an amoeba shape, bodies touching and close, not in a circle but an ever-changing shape, flowing and moving to the music.

Example: movement as conductor

You need: a selection of instruments, scarves.

•   The whole group has instruments (un-tuned or tuned percussion or an instrument they play).

- One person is given a scarf. They lead the group playing by moving the scarf in the air. The movement becomes a living and moving score for the players to interpret.
- The activity is repeated in pairs. The conductor makes their movement, they then stop and wait for the interpretation from their partner who plays an instrument. This process can be reversed. The instrument partner offers a phrase and the scarf partner turns it into a movement.
- Try this without a break, the conductor continues with the next movement while the player is repeating the previous one.

Pathway: body – a sounding instrument

You need: umbrella.

Exploration of our bodies as a group instrument can be facilitated with the use of a conductor. A parasol or umbrella can be a helpful visual sign.

Thinking of a rainstorm:

- Make your quietest possible body sound (a one finger clap or rubbing finger nails together).
- Slowly make louder sounds (e.g. one finger clap, two finger clap, three finger clap, whole hand clapping. Patting the chest progressing to the knees and stamping feet).

The umbrella is introduced, and a conductor is invited from the group. Umbrella shut = silence. As the conductor starts to open the umbrella, the rainstorm begins. The crescendo continues until the umbrella is open and the conductor can shelter underneath.

The conductor now starts to close the umbrella; the group matches their playing to the diminuendo until it is firmly closed, and the improvised piece is complete. The conductor can choose to open and close the umbrella to explore dynamics. The least confident participant can be encouraged to lead the group as it can be an empowering and exciting experience that helps to build their self-esteem.

Once the conducting role is established, the umbrella can be used to conduct instruments in a similar way. The opening and closing of the umbrella resemble crescendo and diminuendo marks in musical notation.

> *I found that I could extend this activity by opening large golf umbrellas to create a listening space for small groups of children. I used "The Storm" from "The Tempest" by Sibelius.*

Pathway: voice and body join in dance

This movement activity can be used with a canon. An example of an African song 'Nanuma' is on page 212.

The group moves in the space with bare feet.

- Start moving as a group and listen to the sound of the feet.
- Listen to your own feet and let them form a rhythm ostinato (led by the beat on a drum).
- With the ostinati formed and continuing, the leader introduces the song.
- Gather in a circle and perform each ostinato, in turn, solo and then tutti while singing the song.
- Divide into smaller groups. Create a dance that combines ostinati chosen by the group.
- Practise while singing in canon.
- Share dances while singing in canon.

> From an art supplies shop I found a roll of thick paper and gave each group a piece large enough for five people to dance on. Paint was added to the paper as the group wished, and they danced their dance on the paper with the paint. (A great outdoor activity!) I then presented this painting (see the pictures 6.4 and 6.5) to another group and asked them to make a dance from the picture.

Pathway: moving stories

You need: paints or crayons and paper

Music: J.S. Bach: The Brandenburg Concertos: Concerto No. 6 BWV 1051 in B Flat major. Allegro.

Form and Structure: walking music – painting music.

- Part A – listen to the music and walk in the space.
- Part B – paint the music in the air.
- Listen again – walk for Part A, and find a partner for Part B and improvise movements together.
- Each participant has some paints or crayons and paper. Listen again, and this time paint or draw for part B.
- In small groups, use the drawings to create a story for the music. Perform the story in mime for the whole group. The paintings can be used as graphical notation for the story to help remember it.

Workshop: cars

Movement activities can be encouraged by imagining the rush hour through cars.

Tuning: starting the engine

Participants select an imaginary car; start the engine and begin to move in the space.

Pathway: rush hour

- Explore the space and experiment with the speed of the car. The leader identifies one particular car's movements and follows with musical accompaniment. The group discovers which car is being followed and join that movement.

Music suggestions

George Gershwin: An American in Paris
Apocalyptica plays Metallica: Enter sandman

- Whilst listening to the music, move in the space experiencing various car journeys – different roads, bends, problems with the engine etc. – according to how they interpret the music.

Pathway: different cars

- The group writes words about cars, driving and traffic.
- Divide these words between small groups as material to write a poem.
- Small groups compose a sound and movement performance to the poem.

Closing: arrival at the destination

- Lie down; you have arrived and the engine is turned off. Think about where you are.
- Discuss and share your thoughts and reflections on the process.

> With small children, I have found that using a stop-go sign (red on one side, green on the other) can be a fun introduction to conducting. The concepts of 'stop' and 'go' can be introduced when the group is playing with toy cars while listening to recorded music. Later, when the group are playing instruments, the stop/go sign can be used by one of the children to control the group's playing. I have found that the shyest and least able children benefit from having the power – it seems to build their self-esteem and confidence. The stop/go sign can be used in many instrument-playing and group situations.

Reflection and discussion

1   Collect songs about cars and driving and compositions that have a transport or urban theme. Share and discuss how you would use them.

Self-expression: "listening to music through your body" – creativity through movement

IMAGE 10.6   Listening

The previous section focused on group movement activities. This section concentrates on self-expression through movement.

Example: painting music in the air

Music suggestions

Sergei Rachmaninov: Piano Trio in D minor, Op. 32: III Elegia
Wolfgang Amadeus Mozart: Piano Concerto No. 21, KV 467 (Elvira madigan). Andante

- Imagine that your hands are two giant brushes to paint in the air as the music inspires you.
- Now explore your feet being the brushes.
- Could your whole body become one giant brush? How does the movement change?

Example: moving emotions

You need: a selection of instruments.

• Find movements for being:
  • Angry
  • Happy
  • Sad
  • Friendly
  • Frustrated
• What kind of music would suit these different feelings? (This can be impro-
  vised with one or more instruments).
• Share how you felt expressing the different movements.

> *I asked the teenagers in my class to bring a piece of music that was
> meaningful for them. We listened to each piece and selected a picture
> that suited the music for us, from a range available. We shared the emotions or
> thoughts stirred by the music and pictures. This helped to find words to express
> thoughts and feelings.*

Dance form – a rich source for learning music

Western classical music, as well as music from other cultural traditions, provides a
rich source of dance material for learning in music. They offer an opportunity for
adventures in culture, tradition, music and history. The dance form allows exploration of musical elements as well as the structure of the dance.

An inspirational approach to music learning can be the creation of dance movements within a group. Even if you do not know the original steps to the dance, you
can create your own for, or with, your group of learners. Online resources can help
find dance moves to modify and alter to suit your group.

Using dances

• Teaching the dance – a step by step process – from easy to more difficult.
  • When we begin to move, vulnerabilities may become obvious. Creating a
    safe atmosphere is crucial.
  • Start at the easiest level and add challenge to what is successfully learned.
    This calls for sensitivity and awareness; sometimes you need to give differ-
    ent tasks to different learners, to ensure everyone is challenged at the right
    level for them.
  • Interpreting the group dynamics, in the moment, maintains involvement
    and wellbeing for every learner (e.g. giggling and restlessness can signify
    people aren't feeling safe in the learning process).

- Speak only when needed. Use key words like 'steps' or 'circle' or 'centre' instead of long explanations, which can lead to loss of attention.
- Wherever possible, use gesture and body language rather than speech.
- Give key words or signs at the appropriate time for the steps of the dance.
- Use the same music several times but vary the way you dance to it.

Pedagogical aspects

- When you teach movements in a circle, only some of the group are in a position to mirror you. For the more complicated parts of the dance, place the whole group in front of you so they can mirror your movements.
- Practise the difficult parts of the dance separately and then link them to the easier parts.
- Creating a short story can help the group to remember the dance movements and structure. It also creates a reason to throw yourself into a fantasy world and a sense of liberation to explore the features of the different dance movements.

 Reflection and discussion

1   Think about the dance steps or traditional dances that you know:
- Teach the dance to the group.
- Focus on the process of introducing the dance steps little by little.
- Reflect (from the participants' point of view) on the amount and quality of verbal support in the teaching process that is needed as well as the timing of the instructions.
2   Find other dances to increase your repertoire. How can these dances be taught in a group?

Pathway: towards a dance

The pedagogical aim of this process is to use minimal verbal instructions and to explore how this affects group learning of music.

Music: Leoš Janáček: Suite for strings. 3rd movement, Andante con moto

Sit in a circle.

- Use the underlying rhythmic ostinato in the music – 'ta, ta, te-te, ta' – to wake up hands using the rhythm pattern
- Move this rhythmic activity to the legs (first sitting, then moving in the space).
- While the group is moving:
  - Find a partner – share the rhythm with each other's hands.
  - Find a different partner to clap the rhythm with.
  - Ask the group to invent different ways to use the rhythm.

IMAGE 10.7   Rhythm wall

- Keep the rhythm in your feet and form a circle. Introduce the steps or first part of the dance – Part A. Use one rhythm pattern to move to the centre of the circle and repeat it moving backwards. Hum the melody of Part A to accompany this.
- Part B. Move one way with the circle to the rhythm and then back the other way, using the phrasing in the music to guide you. Don't stop the flow; just simply take the hands of people standing on either side of you and start moving the circle. Large, clear movements will be easier to follow than spoken instructions.
- Part B has a surprise towards the end. Walk into the circle for 2 bars and when you hear a 'shh-movement', lean towards the centre of the circle and back again. Listen out for the closing, 'ta, ta, te-te, ta', in the music to close the dance. Part B is repeated.

> Jaakko (6 years old) found it difficult to find the pattern with his feet. I extended practising of the 'ta, ta, te-te, ta', pattern by placing some plastic feet on the floor to show the rhythm pattern (see picture 6.10). With the music playing, the group moved round the circle so that everyone had a turn walking on the plastic feet. This made the pattern concrete and visible.

> *I helped my parent and toddler music group to remember the dance moves by devising a story for the dance that fit a wider theme that we were working with – small ghosts. The dance was their morning dance, when the small ghosts were tiptoeing home and reminding each other to be silent (shhh!). I used the dance some months later when our theme was kittens.*

Reflection and discussion

1   Reflect on giving instructions for movement and dance:
  - What non-verbal ways are there to maintain the attention of the group?
  - What impact does using limited verbal instructions have on the experiences of the group?

Pathway: moving art pictures, pictures as starting points for a dance

You need: about 40 art postcards (different artists, colours and themes), selection of instruments.

Exploring movements

- Find a postcard that inspires you to move.
- Explore these movements in the space in silence (the whole group moves at the same time).
- Share your movements (participants demonstrate their movements, and the rest of the group imitates them).
- Improvise music to suit each movement.

Which movement?

- The group moves again, in silence. An instrumentalist chooses one movement and improvises music. The rest of the group guess whose movement has been accompanied and join in that movement.

Dancing Prokofjev

Music: Sergei Prokofjev: A summer day, Op. 65. No. 10 Marche

- Adapt your own movement to fit the music without losing its character (the movements can be developed as the participants work with the music. The whole group experiments in their own way at the same time).

Compose a small dance using postcards

The group is divided into smaller groups (4–5 people).

- Compose a small dance using movements inspired by the pictures. Each group has 4–5 movements.
- The cards can be used as a 'score' to represent the structure of the dance.
- Share dances and 'scores' with the group.

 Reflection and discussion

1 How did you feel when your own material was used to form a dance?
2 How would you facilitate and lead this kind of process with a group of children?

Note

1 See Bateson (1975).

References

Bachmann, M.-L. (1991). *Dalcroze today: An education through and into music.* Oxford: Oxford University Press.

Barrett, M. S. (2006). Inventing songs, inventing worlds: The "genesis" of creative thought and activity in young children's lives. *International Journal of Early Years Education, 14*(3).

Bateson, M. C. (1975). Mother-infant exchanges: The epigenesis of conversational interaction. *Annals of the New York Academy of Sciences, 263*(1), 101–113.

Benedict, C. (2010). Methods and approaches. In H. F. Abeles & L. A. Custodero (Eds.), *Critical issues in music education: Contemporary theory and practice* (pp. 194–214). New York: Oxford University Press.

Bjørkvold, J. R. (1992). *The muse within: Creativity and communication, song and play from childhood through maturity.* New York: Harper Collins Publishers.

Custodero, L. A., Britto, P. R., & Brooks-Gunn, J. (2003). Musical lives: A collective portrait of American parents and their young children. *Journal of Applied Developmental Psychology, 24*(5), 553–572. doi: 10.1016/j.appdev.2003.08.005

Dean, B. (2011). Oscar's music: A descriptive study of one three-year-old's spontaneous music making at home. In S. Young (Ed.), *Proceedings of the 5th conference of the European network of music educators and researchers of young children.* (pp. 59–68). Helsinki, Finland, 8–11 June, 2011. Unpublished conference proceedings.

Dissanayake, E. (2000). *Art and intimacy: How the arts began.* Seattle: University of Washington Press.

Dolata, J. K., Davis, B. L., & MacNeilage, P. F. (2008). Characteristics of the rhythmic organization of vocal babbling: Implications for an amodal linguistic rhythm. *Infant Behavior and Development, 31*(3), 422–431.

Eckerdal, P., & Merker, B. (2009). "Music" and the "action song" in infant development: An interpretation. In S. Malloch & C. Trevarthen (Eds.), *Communicative musicality: Exploring the basis of human companionship* (pp. 241–262). New York, NY, US: Oxford University Press.

Fernald, A. (1992). Meaningful melodies in mothers' speech to infants. In H. Papoušek, U. Jürgens, & M. Papoušek (Eds.), *Nonverbal vocal communication: Comparative and developmental approaches* (pp. 262–282). New York, NY and Paris, France: Cambridge University Press, Editions de la Maison des Sciences de l'Homme.

Fogel, A. (2000). Beyond individuals: A relational-historical approach to theory and research on communication. In M. L. Genta (Ed.), *Mother-infant communication* (pp. 123–161). Rome: Carocci.

Frazee, J. (2006). *Orff schulwerk today: Nurturing musical expression and understanding*. New York: Schott.

Gluschankof, C., & Kenney, S. H. (2011). Music literacy in an Israeli Kindergarten. *General Music Today, 25*(1), 45–49. doi: 10.1177/1048371311414880

Goswami, U., & Bryant, P. (1990). *Phonological skills and learning to read*. London: Lawrence Erlbaum.

Greenhead, K., Habron, J., & Mathieu, L. (2016). Dalcroze eurhythmics: Bridging the gap between the academic and practical through creative teaching and learning. In E. Haddon & P. Burnard (Eds.), *Creative teaching for creative learning in higher music education* (pp. 221–226). Oxford, UK: Routledge.

Gudmundsdottir, H. R., & Cohen, A. J. (2015). Advancing interdisciplinary research in singing through the AIRS test battery of singing skills. *Musicae Scientiae, 19*(3), 234–237.

Hargreaves, D. J. (1986). *The developmental psychology of music*. Cambridge: Cambridge University Press.

Ilari, B. (2005). On musical parenting of young children: Musical beliefs and behaviors of mothers and infants. *Early Child Development and Care, 175*(7/8), 647–660. doi: 10.1080/0300443042000302573

Juntunen, M.-L. (2004). *Embodiment in Dalcroze eurhythmics*. (Doctoral thesis). Acta Universitatis Oulu-ensis. Scientiae Rerun Socialium E73. http://herkules.oulu.fi/isbn9514274024/

Juntunen, M.-L., Perkiö, S., & Simola-Isaksson, I. (2010). *Musiikkia liikkuen. Musiikkiliikunnan käsikirja 1*. Helsinki: WSOYpro.

Merker, B. (2001). Synchronous chorusing and human origins. In N. L. Wallin, B. Merker, & S. Brown (Eds.), 2000. *The origins of music*. Cambridge, MA: MIT Press. ISBN 0-262-23206-5

Merleau-Ponty, M. (1962). *Phenomenology of perception*. London: Routledge.

Miller, G. F. (2001). Evolution of human music through sexual selection. In N. L. Wallin, B. Merker, & S. Brown (Eds.), *The origins of music*. Cambridge, MA: MIT Press.

Moog, H. (1976). *The musical experience of the pre-school child*. London: Schott.

Moorhead, G. E., & Pond, D. (1941). *Music of young children: II general observations*. Santa Barbara, CA: Pillsbury Foundation for Advancement of Music Education.

Morgan, E. (1995). *The Descent of the Child: Human Evolution from a New Perspective*. Oxford: Oxford University Press.

Nettl, B. (2000). An ethnomusicologist contemplates universals in musical sound and musical culture. In N. L. Wallin, B. Merker, & S. Brown (Eds.), *The origins of music* (pp. 463–472). Cambridge, MA: MIT Press.

Niewbrandt Wedin, E. (2011). *Spela med hela kroppen. Rytmik och motorik undervisningen*. Stockholm: Gehrmans musikförlag.

Niland, A. (2006). *An exploration of young children's engagement with musical experiences*. Paper presentation for ISME Early Childhood Music Education Commission Seminar, Taipei, Taiwan, 9–14 July, 2006.

Niland, A. (2009). The power of musical play: The value of play-based, child-centered curriculum in early childhood music education. *General Music Today, 23*(1), 17–21. doi: 10.1177/1048371309335625

Papoušek, M. (1996). Intuitive parenting: A hidden source of musical stimulation in infancy. In I. Deliège & J. Sloboda (Eds.), *Musical beginnings: Origins and development of musical competence.* New York: Oxford University Press.

Pitt, J. (2014). *An exploratory study of the role of music with participants in children's centres.* (Unpublished doctoral thesis), University of Roehampton, London. http://hdl.handle.net/10142/321585

Pouthas, V. (1996). The development of the perception of time and temporal regulation of action in infants and children. In I. Deliège & J. Sloboda (Eds.), *Musical beginnings: Origins and development of musical competence* (pp. 115–141). Oxford: Oxford University Press.

Rogoff, B. (2003). *The cultural nature of human development.* New York: Oxford University Press.

Rutkowski, J. (1990). The measurement and evaluation of children's singing voice development. *The Quarterly, 1*(1–2), 81–95.

Rutkowski, J. (2013). The nature of children's singing voices: Characteristics and assessment. *The Phenomenon of Singing, 1,* 201–209.

Saliba, K. (1991). *Accent on Orff: An introductory approach.* Englewood Cliffs, New Jersey: Prentice Hall.

Smithrim, K. L. (1997). Free musical play in early childhood. *Canadian Journal of Research in Music Education, 38*(4), 17–24.

Stadler Elmer, S. S. (2011). Human singing: Towards a developmental theory. *Psychomusicology: Music, Mind and Brain, 21*(1–2), 13–30. http://dx.doi.org/10.1037/h0094001

Trainor, L. J., Austin, C. M., & Desjardins, R. N. (2000). Is infant-directed speech prosody a result of the vocal expression of emotion? *Psychological Science, 11*(3), 188–195.

Trehub, S. E., & Gudmundsdottir, H. R. (2015). Mothers as singing mentors for infants. In G. Welch, D. Howard, & J. Nix (Eds.), *The Oxford handbook of singing.* Oxford: Oxford University Press.

Trevarthen, C. (2000). Musicality and the intrinsic motive pulse: Evidence from human psychobiology and infant communication. *Musicae Scientiae, Special Issue 1999–2000,* 155–215.

Upitis, R. (2017). Celebrating children's invented notations. In P. Burnard & R. Murphy (Eds.), *Teaching music creatively* (2nd ed., pp. 118–134). London: Routledge.

Welch, G. (2006a). Singing and vocal development. In G. McPherson (Ed.), *The child as musician* (pp. 311–329). Oxford: Oxford University Press.

Welch, G. (2006b). The musical development and education of young children. In B. Spodek & O. N. Saracho (Eds.), *Handbook of research on the education of young children* (2nd ed.). Mahwah, New Jersey: Lawrence Erlbaum Associates, Inc.

Young, S. (2005). Musical communication between adults and young children. In D. M. Miell, R. A. MacDonald, & D. J. Hargreaves (Eds.), *Musical communication* (pp. 281–299). New York: Oxford University Press.

Young, S. (2008). Collaboration between 3- and 4-year-olds in self-initiated play on instruments. *International Journal of Educational Research, 47*(1), 3–10.

Theme 4

MAKING MUSIC VISIBLE AND TANGIBLE

Respecting every learner's artistic capacity and ideas are a vital part of the participatory learning process and can be a complex dimension of music pedagogy. Working with rich and varied compositions can widen the musical experience. Children or beginners have the potential to benefit and learn from what may be considered 'complicated music'. This can be enabled by regarding the intangible elements of the music as playthings to connect with and add to.

This theme explores using compositions in music education and provokes thinking about the pedagogical aims and theoretical background to the learning process.

Music as a world of imagination, creativity and play

The world of imagination and play that 'composed music' offers has the potential to be diminished and instrumentalised for learning purposes (e.g. identifying 'ta te-te' rhythm patterns). The art, mystery and ambiguity that complex music presents can be lost in the teaching and learning process.

This figure shows the layers that may exist in a beginner, or young child musician. What we often plan for, and respond to, in our music activities is represented by the visible part of the plant. Without suitable nurture, support and sensitivity, the lower layers (the root system) – important aspects of embodied musicality – may fade and die. All that would remain is the rote learning and demonstration of simple recall activities.

Might a reason why learners of music give up be because it does not feed their inner artistic world? This can happen at any point on the learning journey, from a young child to a professional music student.

What is clear from Figure 11.1 is the power that a music pedagogue has over an individual's musical experiences.

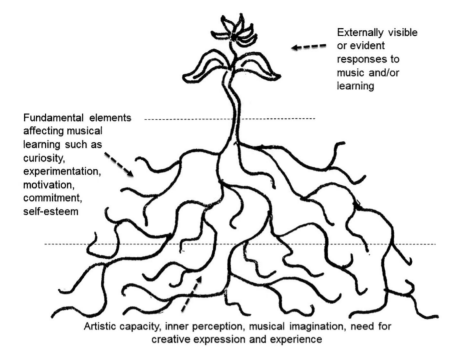

Externally visible or evident responses to music and/or learning

Fundamental elements affecting musical learning such as curiosity, experimentation, motivation, commitment, self-esteem

Artistic capacity, inner perception, musical imagination, need for creative expression and experience

FIGURE 11.1   Layers of musical learning and experiences

Nurturing the inner artist – diving into music/composition together

Merleau-Ponty (1962) says: "The world is not what I think, but what I live through" (pp. 16–17). If we substitute 'music' for 'the world' in this quotation, we can envisage music as something that must be embodied in experience. If music is seen as 'a world', then the role of the pedagogue is to open doors or negotiate the pathways within it.

This negotiation process includes the following components: the composer of the chosen piece of music, the fundamental artistic capacities that each participant possesses, and the knowledge base of both participants and pedagogue. Using these, the pedagogue scaffolds the process, taking prompts from the music, to play with and co-construct a composition.

This theme reflects participation and learning in music through creating and contributing in diverse ways: composing stories, dance and group improvisations with instruments.

Rather than thinking about what learners should be learning, we could ask ourselves how we can open the doors or widen the landscape to this world. This calls for a sensitive pedagogical approach; the questions in Figure 11.2 may help with this.

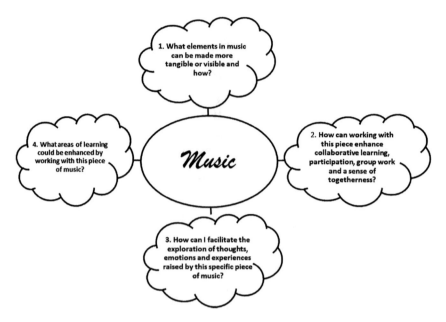

FIGURE 11.2   Making music visible and tangible

Figure 11.2 provides some entry points for thinking about using a piece of music in practice. The music is in the centre, and the four approaches offer the following ways through which to dive in:

- The elements of music.
- The group process.
- Exploring emotions, thoughts and experiences.
- Identifying the transferable skills to other areas of development.

1   What elements in music can be made more tangible or visible and how?
- Does the piece have an interesting rhythmic ostinato or pattern; is it good for experiencing pulse or changing time signatures?
- How could you make the structure of the composition tangible? Can you explore the form, or the orchestration?
- What kind of melodic features are there? Could you pick a melodic idea and add words to help remember it?
- How could you make this a participatory process?
- Does this musical material offer possibilities for improvisation?
- Do the dynamic aspects or different interpretations of the composition offer something to explore?
- Is there something in the harmony/timbre/dynamics/tempo of the music that you could explore?

2   How can working with this piece enhance collaborative learning, participation, group work and a sense of togetherness?

3   How can I facilitate the exploration of thoughts, emotions and experiences awakened by this composition?

- How do the narratives and meanings generated by this composition open possibilities for participants to share and reflect on their thoughts and feelings?

- What could working with this piece offer for respecting and valuing participants' experiences?

4   What general learning skills could be enhanced by working with this piece of music?

- E.g. concentration, listening skills, turn taking and dialogue in communication.

All genres of music are equally valuable in their potential for learning. In order to create rich learning environments, we must welcome encounters with unfamiliar music. This may be challenging because of unfamiliar tonality, rhythms or language, but it allows us to explore outside our comfort zone.

> I was working with family groups with 1-year-olds in a community setting. A father came with his daughter for several weeks. I struggled to find a real connection with him. There was a lack of engagement and enjoyment in the activities. I felt the music group was not giving him a meaningful experience. I asked the parents to bring the music they listened to at home, and selected one of this father's songs to use the following week. The song was an unfamiliar genre for working with young children, but I explored the rhythmic possibilities as a starting point for developing the process.
>
> I was struck by the child's response. She looked from her father, to me, to the CD player, seeming to connect the music from home to this environment. This shared moment of connection and commitment through the child's reaction had an impact on both the father and me, and our sense of joint working. I reflected that I had been able to value the father's choice of music, showing it to be as valuable as the music selected previously for the group.
>
> Looking back, I realise that this gift of a new song widened my landscape of possibilities for music education with young children. The song and the associated activities became a firm favourite for many years.

Jean Sibelius: The Tempest op. 209: Dance of the Nymphs

The structure AABBAACCAA of "Dance of the Nymphs" in Sibelius's "The Tempest" is made tangible by movement. Scarves facilitate free movement in the theme of dancing fairies (see picture 6.17). This composition with its clear structure is a useful one for creating a dance.

Pathway: the Nymphs

You need: scarves

1   Sitting on chairs in a circle, listen to "The Dance of the Nymphs".
    *   Part A – sway on your chair ('home' music – 'home' is your chair).
    *   Parts B and C – movement in the space ('away' music).
2   When you are familiar with the music, develop the movements using scarves.
    *   Part A – sway on your chair at 'home'.
    *   Part B – find a partner and move back-to-back, improvising movements with your scarves.
    *   Part C – one partner moves during the first phrase, and the other for the second.
3   Divide into groups of 4–5 people and without music:
    *   Negotiate whose movements could be used to form a dance for this music.
    *   Rehearse the dance.
4   With music:
    *   Share these dances.
5   Discuss and reflect on this process.

Maurice Ravel: The Mother Goose Suite (Ma Mère L'Oye)

The following workshop ideas are based on the movements: "Sleeping Beauty's Pavane" and "Little Tom Thumb" from Maurice Ravel's Orchestral Suite "Mother Goose". Ravel was inspired by Charles Perrault's fairy tales, we have combined these and the music to suggest ways to improvise, compose and play together with groups.

Diving into a world of music and fantasy is best achieved by non-verbal instructions or a simple "follow me". Too much talk tends to keep us in the everyday, rather than allowing us to experience the imaginative feeling of a story.

Workshop: Sleeping Beauty

Ravel: Sleeping Beauty's pavane

You need: paper, watercolours, brushes and water, feathers, crayons, selection of tuned instruments: e.g. kantele, guitar, xylophones, chime bars, piano (See pictures 6.2 and 6.3 for inspiration).

Tuning

Lie down and close your eyes.

*   Imagine you are someone from the castle of a princess or prince.
*   Listen to the "Pavane".
*   Share your character with the group.

Pathway: exploring the steps of a prince(ss)

Introducing the Pavane steps (ABA form)

- Explore the steps of the Pavane 'in character' without the music and starting with the basic steps:
  - Step to the side with the lead foot (step side). Bring the other foot to meet the lead foot and tap gently. This foot becomes the lead foot for the next step.
  - Step to the side.
  - Continue this pattern until the learners feel comfortable.
  - Add the music when you feel it is appropriate and continue the pattern.
  - Then introduce the pattern of the dance:
  Part A
    - Step, side
    - Step, side
    - Step, step, step, side
    - (Repeat the whole pattern four times)
  - Part B – improvisatory section
    - Think about what your character might be doing in the castle (e.g. combing hair, preparing food, sharpening sword).

Dancing the Pavane

The group dances the Pavane using Part A steps and Part B improvisatory sections.

- Repeat the dance several times, introducing options for Part B (e.g. finding a partner or forming small groups).
- A circle dance can be created using Part A steps, moving around the circle or in and out of it.
- The group selects some of the improvised Part B movements and creates their own Part B piece.

Pathway: dreams

Creating and exploring emotions and our own stories

- Find a comfortable place in the space to listen to the Pavane as if you were asleep.
- What is your character dreaming about?

Colourful dreams

- Gather in small groups around a large piece of paper. Listen to the music with eyes closed, and paint freely as guided by the music.
- Share and reflect together on your group painting.

Creating a rondo form with instruments

- Hearing the dreams ('sleeping rondos'): use these paintings as graphic notation to play a rondo form piece.
  - Choose instruments to suit your painting.
  - Select one part of the painting to be the tutti part (Part A). The group decides how this should be played.
  - One of the group is the conductor. They guide the playing through the tutti part by pointing their way through the painting.
  - The remaining parts of the painting (Part B) are negotiated by the group – deciding how to play them, who plays which parts and with what, what are the tempi, dynamics and timbres etc.
  - The conductor guides the piece by pointing their way through the painting. This role can be shared within the group.
  - The pieces are shared with other small groups.

Pathway: improvising

Improvising using the Part A theme from Pavane.
  Working with phrases and melody.

- Phrases. Listening to Part A music, blow a feather from your hand at the start of each phrase.
- Watch the trajectory of the feather until it falls to the ground (repeat as required).
- Then blow the feather and follow its movement with your body until it falls (repeat as required).
- Melody. Highlight the '**a–c–e–d–g**' melody of the Part A theme by singing it using the words, 'beauty, sleep and dream' (in Finnish, 'nukkuu kaunotar') or words that the group prefer every time it appears in the music.
- Spread large pieces of paper and crayons on the floor.
- In small groups, listen to the piece again and sing the 'beauty, sleep and dream' motif when the '**a–c–e–d–g**' melody appears. Silently draw the rest of the phrases in Part A on the paper. During Part B, get up and walk to another piece of paper; when Part A resumes, repeat the exercise of singing and drawing.
- Now listen to Part A again, singing the, 'beauty, sleep and dream' motif, but instead of drawing, move freely in the space.
- Using the whole piece for movement:
  - Part A – in pairs, one moves during the 'beauty, sleep and dream' motif; the other responds with movement during the rest of Part A.
  - Part B – move alone in the space.

  Improvising with instruments using rondo form with the '**a–c–e–d–g**' theme for pentatonic improvisation

- Find the '**a–c–e–d–g**' motif (a-minor) on a tuned instrument (xylophone, piano, keyboard, guitar, kantele etc.). This forms the tutti ('beauty, sleep and dream').

- Working in pairs, play with a 'question and answer' improvisation on your instruments using '**g–a–c–d–e**'.
- The group creates a piece in rondo form. The '**a–c–e–d–g**' motif is the tutti Part A.
  - How does the story continue? Play the motif together 4 times and then improvise with the '**g–a–c–d–e**' to form the Parts B, C and D of the rondo.
  - The group plays the rondo ABACADA with a conductor signalling the return to Part A after the improvised sections.
  - The improvised parts of the rondo can be solo, small group or whole group improvisations.

Closing

There is a celebration at the castle, and every character brings (imaginary) gifts for members of the group.

- Walk in the space to the Pavane music; when you meet another person you give them their gift.
- To add variety, Part B of the Pavane could include improvised stately dance moves with partners.
- Share the experience of giving and receiving gifts as well as reflections on the whole process.

Workshop: Tom in the forest

Ravel: Little Tom Thumb

You need: a short version of Perrault's *Little Tom Thumb*, brown paper, jars of water, paintbrushes, a selection of instruments.

Tuning

- Lie down and close your eyes.
- Someone volunteers to read a short version of Little Tom Thumb to the group as the music plays.

Pathway: lost in the forest

The music has an ungainly rhythm, which could be imagined as Tom Thumb wandering in circles in the forest.

- With brown paper on the floor and jars of water and paintbrushes to hand, the group paints the forest paths as they listen to the string section (this also could take place outdoors, or in the sand-tray, or using flour).
- Walk some of these routes, joining hands to form a line that moves in the space. The leader at the front of the line leads the group into spirals, circles or wiggly lines. Change the leader from time to time.

- In the story, Tom Thumb is led to a house in the forest.
  - With the Tom Thumb music playing, in pairs, one leads their partner in the space holding just one finger; the other has their eyes closed.
  - Then, without the Tom Thumb music, one leads the other (eyes closed) using an instrument as a sound source. Having a wide selection of instruments is useful so that followers can identify their own leader's sound.

Pathway: challenges and survival

Challenges

Little Tom Thumb finds secret powers in the boots he discovers. These help him overcome his challenges and survive.

- With the music playing, walk in the space thinking about recent challenging events for you. Focus on the secret powers you have that will help you find a way through your challenging situation.
- Share your thoughts with another person.

Survival

- Working in small groups
  - Group members share their secret powers.
  - They devise a scenario in which these powers combine to form a survival strategy.
  - They compose a dramatised sound and movement piece – 'battle for survival' – using their secret powers as inspiration.

Sharing battle stories

- Share the pieces with the whole group.
- After each performance, the audience gives positive feedback to each performer on what they have seen, e.g. "Laura, I so admire your powerful secret power and the way you used it in the battle. I wish I had your secret power!"
- The pedagogue ensures that everyone gets feedback.

Closing

Music suggestion: 'The fairy garden' movement from The Mother Goose Suite

- Divide the group in half.
- One half of the group is clay; the other half is a music sculptor (this can also be done in pairs).
- Without speaking, the sculptors work together to create one big sculpture out of the 'clay' participants, moving and shaping them.
- The whole group finds a suitable name for it.

J.S. Bach: Cello Suite No. 1 in G major

Pathway: active listening

Active listening to music can be fostered and developed. This multimodal activity acts as an example to explore this topic and to inspire ideas for new creations. Using dim lighting helps participants to focus on listening to the music and responding with movement and colour instead of the visual product on paper.

You need: dim lighting, large pieces of paper (e.g. backing paper), crayons, charcoal, glue or sticking tape.

In small groups, sitting around the paper, using the movements of Bach's cello suite:

1   Prelude: take a crayon in your non-dominant hand and let the music move your hand over the paper.
2   Allemande: put this crayon down and select another colour for your dominant hand and if you feel comfortable, close your eyes and let the music move your hand over the paper.
3   Courante: choose another colour in whichever hand you wish and repeat as before.
4   Sarabande: take a colour in both hands and repeat as before.
5   Minuets 1 & 2: take a new piece of paper for the next activity. Take a piece of charcoal, and using whichever hand you wish, move to the sounds of the music on the paper.
6   Gigue: select some colours and repeat the process around the charcoal marks.

Turn the lights on and admire the artwork. Discuss the process and which parts of the music inspired which movements and colour choices.

After these activities:

• Each group passes their pieces of art to the next group.
• This group transforms these pieces by cutting, folding, sticking or tearing them to create one new piece.
• This piece is passed to the next group who uses it to inspire words, which they write down.
• These words are passed to the next group who create a sound-movement composition from them.
• These are shared with the group.

Contributing to the expressive works of others by sharing artworks within the group engenders a sense of shared enterprise that builds community feeling.

(For ideas on listening to Bach with movement, see p. 122)

Jukka Linkola: Snowqueen

Workshop: adventures with the Snowqueen story

This atmospheric piece was written by Linkola for a Finnish film, *The Snowqueen*, based on Hans Christian Andersen's eponymous fairytale. Sections of the composition are used in this Workshop.

You need: brown paper, jars of water, paintbrushes, crayons or paint, plasticine, instruments, old newspapers.

Tuning

The group lies on the floor and listens to "Linkola's Space".

• Listen to the music.
• Then slowly move to stand facing each other.

Pathway: Kai and Gerda playing together

Linkola: Kai and Gerda on the beach
  This music excerpt will be listened to many times during this activity.

• Follow the leader. The group forms a line with the leader at the front.
  • Moving as a group in snake-like fashion, the leader improvises movements to the music and the group follows. The leader finishes their turn by moving to the end of the line; the next person is then the leader.
• Paint with water on brown paper (playing on the beach).
  • The group explores the music with a brush in their hands, painting with water on brown paper.
• In small groups, create a circle dance.

Pathway: freezing

Linkola: The dance of the Snow Queen
Linkola: Space

• The group moves freely to the music. One participant is the Snow Queen; she freezes everyone with the sound of a triangle – everyone freezes on the spot. This role changes as required.
  • When the group is frozen, the Snow Queen creates ice-sculptures, forming and changing the positions of frozen group members.

Pathway: the spring

Linkola: Spring carnival
  This excerpt's structure includes a rhythmic opening, a legato section and a section in waltz-time.

• Rhythmic opening: Walk with staccato movements in the space.
• Legato section (flying): Move with legato and circular movements to this soft and gentle music.
• Waltz section: Improvise a circle dance.
• Explore other ideas for this structure.

Pathway: the Snow Queen casts her spell

Linkola: Limpid

- Imagine invisible threads are pulling you.
- Working in pairs:
  - One pulls the invisible threads and the other moves in response.
  - Experiment with moving where sound is an invisible, pulling thread.

Pathway: the box of treasures

Linkola: The charm of the music box

- Listen to the music, and paint or draw the contents of the box of treasures.
- Use instruments to play these pictures.
- Create sculptures of the treasures.

Pathway: the challenge – Gerda's journey trying to find Kay

Linkola: Northbound, The forest

- Listen to the music while walking in the space and thinking about any personally challenging situations that come to mind.
- When you have identified your challenge, concentrate on it and think about the secret powers you have that can help you.

Pathway: meeting the challenge

Linkola: On the glacier, The sorceress

- Divide the group in half.
  - One half are 'dangers', moving in the space; the other half form pairs and guide each other through the dangers.
  - Negotiate the rules in the group beforehand, e.g. limitations of the space available, 'dangers' might only be able to move their hands, not their feet.

Pathway: the fight

Linkola: The power of the Snow Queen

This excerpt has a strong rhythmic pattern with changing time signatures.

MUSIC 11.1

Using swords made from newspapers, mark the first beat of each bar in combat with others – initially a partner and when the pattern is established, the group.

Linkola: Struggle of light and darkness

In small groups, create a performance that includes the secret powers, a fight, a solution and a happy ending.

Closing: coming together

Linkola: The fool, Memories, Gerda and Kai, The forest, The castle

- Listen to these musical suggestions in sequence while shaping a piece of Plasticine to symbolise what you have gained from the Workshop.
- Discuss and reflect together.

Miguel Castro: Cadence of Waters and Brigamo

Pathway: rhythms of water

- Listen to "Cadence of Waters" while lying on the floor.
- Introduce "Brigamo" and move to the music while still lying on the floor.
- Stand and explore the poly-rhythmic music through movement.
- Split into pairs and improvise movement together.
- Select one rhythmic pattern in the music and interpret it through body percussion. Find ways to memorise this pattern either by writing it down or finding words to match the rhythm.
- Transfer this rhythm pattern to instruments.

Working in a small group:

- Compose a 'water-piece' using your chosen rhythmic patterns from *Brigamo*.
- Draw the structure of the piece.
- Perform the piece and reflect on the process.

Listen again to the two pieces by Castro.

- Compare the listening experiences before and after working with the material.
- Share reflections and discuss.

Maria Kalaniemi: Iho

Pathway: changing time signatures

The piece of Finnish folk music, *Iho* (the skin) by Kalaniemi has an interesting structure and changing time signatures.

- Choose a topic for this dance and find related words to represent the changing time signatures.
  - Part A: 2 + 3 + 4 (e.g. Crocus, Buddleia, Gladioli).
  While listening to Part A, introduce the words with simple gestures that stress the first beat in the bar (e.g. with hands or feet).

- Create dance steps for Part A.
- Practise the dance using the words to help.
- Divide into small groups.
- Listen to *Iho* Part B and try to make sense of the time signature patterns.
  - Part B: 2+3+4+3   2+3+2+3
  - Find words to help recognise the changing time signatures (e.g. Crocus, Buddleia, Gladioli, Buddleia and Crocus, Buddleia, Crocus, Buddleia).
- Create movements for Part B (using the words to structure the piece).
- Share the various Part B dances by dancing the whole piece together. Part A is a 'tutti' part where everyone dances together the shared dance. Each small group introduces their Part B when the Part B appears in the music. Part C could be improvised by the group (it uses the same pattern as Part A).

 Reflection and discussion

IMAGE 11.1 Listening to music through movement can sometimes overwhelm

1 Think about music you love and enjoy. Start to build ideas for a process around that music using Figure 11.2 p. 136.

Reference

Merleau-Ponty, M. (1962). *Phenomenology of perception.* London: Routledge.

Theme 5

IMPROVISING AND LEARNING MUSIC WITH INSTRUMENTS

This theme applies learner-centred pedagogical notions and approaches to instrumental music teaching. This might be a group of beginner recorder students or one-to-one piano teaching. How do we maintain a playful musical dialogue in what might be considered to be a formal teacher-directed learning situation? We will explore the use of improvisation and composition to keep the learner at the centre. This focus may overcome the perceived need for some kind of transition from playful early childhood music learning to a more formal situation, where some might say that 'real music teaching and learning' takes place. The inclusion of creative and improvisational elements can feed both the learner's artistic capacity as well as the technical skills necessary to master the instrument. Juha Ojala and Lauri Väkevä (2013) suggest that nurturing a creative relationship to music alongside more traditional, performance-focused music teaching would be valuable. They also point out that the Finnish education system's creative approaches to teaching music have traditionally been strong in early childhood music education, but weaken when teaching older children and young adults. One reason may be the focus on the rehearsal and practise of ready composed music for performance as the means of learning to play an instrument. They argue for a more open-ended teaching paradigm where music is experienced through exploration and individual meaning-making (Ojala & Väkevä, 2013). Creative collaborative processes have been found to enrich learners' belief in their musical capability and agency (Muhonen, 2014); there are learning benefits for young children composing together (see Burnard, Boyack, & Howell, 2017, pp. 39–59).

 My enjoyment of music began with my first recorder lesson at school when I was about 7 years old. We were taught how to play B, A, G and then sent

> *home with our recorder to write our own piece to bring to the next class. I loved*
> *this activity, and my mum helped me work on a song to go with the piece. We had*
> *a fun time together. I knew I wanted more of this.*

In this example, the learner was given sufficient musical information about how to hold the instrument, how to make a sound with it, and some basic building blocks. The pedagogical action that helped the learner take ownership was being allowed to create, and being treated as a competent musician without constraint: the words, the song were unrequested additions but meaningful for the learner.

Ownership of music and learning has been found to be the foundation stone of musical study. Research conducted in Finnish music institutes (with children aged 7–13 years-old taking instrumental lessons) implies that guidance and the pedagogical approach both play key roles in enhancing positive and meaningful learning in music. Appreciating the initiatives and aims of the children is vital. They need to feel that their own goals and proposals affect the teaching practice, which seemed to be the most important factor in explaining their achievement in music learning (see Tuovila, 2003, p. 5). The sense of being an agent in our own learning is important; all tuition should reflect this. Feelings of making a difference, taking part in the process and navigating together create an environment where individually meaningful learning can take place. Wenger (1998) states, "participating – is both a kind of action and a form of belonging. Such participation shapes not only what we do, but also who we are and how we interpret what we do" (p. 4). Dialogue, ownership and agency are related to learning in music. In the early stages of learning an instrument, what was essential to the learners' commitment and motivation was a warm and friendly pedagogue and a relaxed learning atmosphere. This demonstrates that pedagogical sensitivity (see Chapter 4), apparently unrelated to the transfer of music knowledge and skills, is actually vital at this fragile time (see Davidson, Moore, Sloboda, & Howe, 1998).

This is also important when training students of music teaching. A report on vocal and instrumental teaching in European higher education (Hildén et al., 2010) found that conservatoires were challenged by the need to find effective ways for students to integrate their musical and pedagogical knowledge. A critical question emerging from the report was "What kinds of competences are needed to create a lifelong interest towards music and enable a wide access to music education for the whole community?" (p. 30).

> *I was working with a 9-year-old piano student who reached a point in a*
> *Bach Prelude where he had difficulties with the fingering. I suggested that*
> *we work together with the awkward five-note-fingering pattern as a theme for*
> *improvisation – adding our own ideas to the piece.*

A pedagogue's practice may be influenced by the deep roots of the Western classical music training tradition and their own experiences of learning an instrument. Bruner (1996, p. 147) uses the example of a fish not knowing it lives in water, and Rogoff (2003, p. 24) also argues that one is unaware of a community's practices if one is a member of that community. All our values, prior experiences and assumptions about learning an instrument impact every instrument teaching situation we encounter, including young children's experimentation with chime bars as well as a violin lesson. Therefore, it is crucial to be aware of this underlying value-system about music.

All conceptual music theory knowledge, such as the names of the notes, the stave and the clefs are labels that can be attached to inner knowing already embodied in the learner; as Robert Schenk says, "Play with or without notation? Yes, amongst other things." (Schenck, 2000, p. 237). Many of the Grand Methods are based on these ideas (e.g. Suzuki, Dalcroze). In the Western music tradition, the importance of notation, sight-reading and theoretical conceptual knowledge take precedence over experiential learning and embodying the music.

However, notation is a useful means of conveying meaning in music and finding out the inner thoughts of ourselves and others (those of Mozart as well as my peer). When we start to learn an instrument, conventional notation may not be the best way to record our compositions and ideas.

Guidance for creative improvisation:

Schenck (2000, p. 248) offers helpful insights from his experience of facilitating creative improvisation:

- A safe and accepting group environment.
- Creative boundaries can help creative potential to flourish.
- An atmosphere in which every attempt is welcomed.

The following workshop allows us to reflect on these issues.

Workshop: spring tune

You need: hats, instruments, watercolours, brushes, water, paper.

> *One calm and cloudless evening, toward the end of April, Snufkin found himself far enough to the north to see still unmelted patches of snow on the northern slopes. He had been walking all day through undisturbed landscapes, listening to the cries of the birds also on their way northward, home from the South.*
>
> *Walking had been easy, because his knapsack was nearly empty and he had no worries on his mind. He felt happy about the wood and the weather, and himself. Tomorrow and yesterday were both at a distance, and just at present the sun was shining brightly red between the birches, and the air was cool and*

soft. "It's the right evening for a tune," Snufkin thought. A new tune, one part of expectation two parts of spring sadness, and the rest just the great delight of walking alone and liking it.

He had kept this tune under his hat for several days, but hadn't quite dared to take it out yet. It had to grow into a kind of happy conviction. Then he would simply have to put his lips to the mouth-organ, and all the notes would jump instantly into their places.

(©Tove Jansson, 1962/1963, pp. 3–4 (in the English translation). Moomin Characters ™)

Tuning

- Read the excerpt from 'The Spring Tune'.
- Sit in a circle. The pedagogue passes a hat around the circle.
  - When the hat reaches a participant, they make the sound that the hat speaks to them with. This can be a tiny sound, a vocalisation, or a loud, extended, lengthy improvisation.

Pathway: sound from the hat

- Divide into small groups to compose a short piece of vocal improvisation found in the hat.
- Share the small performances.
  - Each group performs their piece. The other small groups listen to the piece once, thinking about the hat from which the piece has emerged.
  - They perform the piece again, and the other groups form the hat they were thinking of (no speech) or move as if they were wearing that hat.
- Share reflections on hats, compositions and experiences.

Pathway: the spring tune

- Find a place to walk alone in the space.
  - How do you feel?
- Can you add a portion of 'great delight' to your movement? How does that feel?
- Volunteers can produce an improvised accompaniment to those continuing in the 'great delight of walking alone'.

Experimenting with different emotions

- Move with a variety of emotions. 'Expectation' or 'Spring sadness'? How do these affect your movement?
- Part of the group moves and part improvises different emotions with instruments.
- Paint watercolour pictures to reflect some of these emotions.

- In small groups, create a graphical score using these watercolour pictures (cutting, shaping, ripping, folding to create the desired forms). Create a structure for the compositions, 'One part expectation, two parts spring sadness and the rest just the great delight of walking alone'.

Pathway: the tune of the brook

IMAGE 12.1   The tune of the brook

The brook was a good one. It went rushing clear and brown over wads of last year's leaves, through small tunnels of leftover ice, swerving through the green moss and throwing itself headlong down in a small waterfall on to a white-sand bottom. In places it was singing in major as a mosquito, then it tried to sound great and menacing, stopped, gurgled with a mouthful of melted snow and laughed it all.

Snufkin stood listening in the damp moss. "I must have the brook in my tune also," he thought. "In the refrain, I think."
(©*Tove Jansson, 1962/1963, p. 5 (in the English translation).*
Moomin Characters ™ In the excerpt "was singing in major" follows Tove Jansson's original wording. We are using this here with the permission of Moomin Characters™. This was translated in the English version as "droned sharp".)

- Read the excerpt above.
- Pick out the words that describe the sound of the brook and combine them (further words can be added to enhance the spirit of their brook).
- In small groups, now continue with either the composition created in 'The Spring Tune' Pathway or start a new composition based on the descriptive words – using these words as a graphical score. Decide on the order for the parts of the brook tune and how they are to be played.
- Play the tune together.
- Make another version: the brook takes another turn . . .
- In small groups use both tunes to create a composition and notate it.
- Each group shares their piece.
- Read the following excerpt.

A small stone suddenly came loose near the waterfall and raised the pitch of the brook a whole octave.
"Not bad," Snufkin said admiringly. "That's the way to do it. A sudden change, just passing in. I'll have to find that brook a tune of its own."
(*Tove Jansson, 1962/1963, p. 6 (in the English translation). Moomin Characters ™)*

- The small groups add the 'sudden change' to their compositions.
- Share these new tunes and reflect on the process of creating the brook with its twists and turns.

Closing

The tune was quite near at hand, easy to catch by the tail. But there was time enough to wait: it was hedged in and couldn't get away.
(©*Tove Jansson, 1962/1963, pp. 6–7 (in the English translation). Moomin Characters ™)*

Paper hats

Using the remaining watercolour paintings, make paper hats while listening to a composition with a watery theme (suggested music below).

- They can move as they wish.
- The group share the emotions they found in their hats. The hats are passed around the circle.

Listening

Music suggestions

Ludwig van Beethoven: Symphony 6 in F op. 68 (Pastorale), part 2 'Scene am Bach'
Bedřich Smetana: Moldau
Miguel Castro: Cadence of waters

A group listening activity facilitated with a piece of Lycra and a suitably heavy ball that can be passed smoothly and gently over the Lycra while listening to the music.

 Reflection and discussion

1   Can you remember the point at which you felt music was 'for you'?
    •   What were the factors that contributed to this understanding?

Imaginative instruments – beginning to explore improvisation

Some adults and children have lost the confidence to explore musical instruments, in the way babies might explore them. This can affect their facilitation of the creative capacity in others. If an instrument prompts thoughts of "Am I good enough?" or a need to focus on the technical side of playing it, we miss other important aspects of learning music.

The physical environment can be constructed as a place for adventures in sound and to encourage improvisation. This reduces anxieties about playing music and makes musical play accessible to everyone, irrespective of age or skill. In this way, instruments are encountered as powerful tools to explore creative potential and imagination.

•   I can contribute musically even without technique.
•   I can create, play together and have fun with learning music.

We can start to explore improvisation with a basket of kitchen implements (or shoes, buttons, or stones, see pictures 6.8, 6.9 and 6.19); this reduces the baggage that we may inadvertently bring to such situations.

Some ideas to explore:

•   Kitchen instruments (egg cutter strings can be played)
•   Toys: Lego, cars (especially the wheels)
•   Furniture: chairs, tables, radiators
•   Shoes
•   Different sizes and shapes of bottles can be played.
    •   Plastic bottles make a pleasing sound (like boomwhackers) and can be played easily while moving.
•   Branches and natural materials

IMAGE 12.2   Kitchen instruments

- Internet applications offer complex sound-palettes for play
- Traditional instruments can be explored in new ways:
  - Try sand, pebbles or marbles inside a drum
  - Play a guitar or similar with a pencil or knitting needle
  - Play the kantele by dropping a small ball on the strings (a technique invented by a 1-year-old musician, see picture 6.1).

The focus of this theme is the pedagogical thinking behind using instruments with children. The body and voice are our first instruments; all other instrumental playing should be seen as an extension of this. The next section combines the idea of embodied experiences with the imaginative instruments above.

 Reflection and discussion

Choose a musical activity. Plan how you can create learning possibilities for playing with instruments using one idea from the list below:

- Experiencing pulse.
- Rhythms – often a rhyme/words/poem helps to remember rhythmic patterns.

- Find an ostinato, or a continuing rhythmic pattern.
- Create a sound-track for a poem or story.
- Create a sound landscape (e.g. a forest, a market place).
- Create arrangements using instruments to accompany a song.
- Share your ideas and activity with the group.
- Reflect on how your activity created possibilities for learning.

Jumping into the unknown – a world of improvisation

Improvisation can feel like a jump into the unknown; in order for it to flourish, some scaffolds can be helpful, e.g. someone to encourage us as we jump and a visible landing point. As we get used to the experience, we can take on extra challenges.

Facilitating and encouraging improvisation:

- Instructions are vital; without them there can be acoustic and physical chaos.
- Signs for silence and playing.
- Signs for 'your turn', 'my turn' and 'play together'.
- Build up the layers, beginning with body percussion and movement.

IMAGE 12.3 Improvisation can be a leap of excitement

- Routines can be helpful. For example, rituals for selecting instruments, for putting them away or for playing them. These structures provide safe boundaries.
- Creating graphical notation helps to remember and organise the process.

> 💬 *I was working with a group of 5-year-olds in the first week of the Autumn term; they wanted to tell me about their summer holidays. They each recounted an important summer experience and selected an instrument to play this story. We negotiated the structure and turn taking required by drawing a sign for each story. Then we played the summer experiences piece with the instruments.*

Workshop: shoes – sounds, steps and stories

You need: different kinds, colours and sizes of shoe, even dolls' shoes can be included (see picture 6.19 of imaginative shoes) as they don´t need to fit the participants. Charity shops might be a good source of the 30 or more shoes you may need.

IMAGE 12.4 Sounding shoes

Tuning the group to the process

Close your eyes and find a tempo that feels good for you

- Start walking in that tempo (beat).
- Then invent a movement to that beat.
- Transfer this movement into sound.
- The leader guides the group through the stages using the instructions 'walk – move – sound – stop'.

The group as an instrument

- Participants walk at their own tempo.
- They then find a shared walking pulse together.
- The pedagogue adds instruction to 'stop – go' to the activity.

Introducing the shoes

- Choose a shoe and get acquainted with it, asking:
    - What does it look like?
    - What kind of shoe is it?
    - How does it feel in the hand?
    - Where does it come from?
    - Does it have any secrets?
- If this is the first time the group has met, participants can introduce themselves while introducing the shoes. You can ask the participants to share their expectations and feelings about the session.
    - If the group is large or participants are nervous, begin this activity in pairs.

Pathway: moving with shoes

- Think about your shoe; imagine the person who last wore it – how would they have moved in it?
    - Some shoes prefer tiptoeing, others like walking, some insist on dancing . . .
- Move in the space as your shoe leads you.
- First concentrate on your own movement and then become aware of how others are moving, accompanied by improvised music played by the pedagogue or recorded music.
- Divide the group in half.
    - One group accompanies (with instruments, sounds made with mouth, hands, feet etc.) the movements of the others. Swap roles.
    - A leader is selected. When they put their hand on the shoulder of a moving person, they stop and their sound maker also stops.

- Moving with someone:
  - Find another shoe and its owner to dance with; together improvise a dance inspired by your former sound and movement ideas.
- In small groups, make a Shoe-Dance.
  - Pick movements from ideas you have seen and enjoyed. Decide which movements can be combined to form a Part A and a Part B composition.
  - Rehearse. The small group dances the whole dance. Find a suitable name for each movement, e.g. 'shoe in hands' or 'jumping shoe', to help remember the whole dance.
  - Perform for the whole group.

Pathway: shoes – imaginative instruments

Sitting in a circle

- Choose a shoe and get acquainted with it, asking, 'What kind of instrument is this shoe?'
- Share the different sounds it produces and how it can be played.
- Ostinati
  - Devise an ostinato with your shoe instrument.
  - Solo and tutti: one participant shares their ostinato, and the rest of the group copies with their own shoe.
- Make an orchestra
  - One participant begins and then others join in in free order playing their own patterns.
  - One person is the conductor, guiding the performance through their body movements, experimenting with soli, tutti, rests and dynamics.
- Composing
  - In small groups, using the material above, create a composition.
  - Write a story to link the composition together.
  - Share with the larger group.

Closing

Concentration

The group put their shoes in the middle of the room and sit in a tight circle around them; with eyes closed, they try to find their own shoe just by touch.

Shoes lead each other

In pairs, each holding their own shoe so that they touch sole to sole, one leads and the other follows (with eyes closed if they wish). The pairs move in the space to relaxing, slow music.

Reflection and discussion

1   How would you apply these ideas and approaches with your group of learners?

2   What do your experiences in this workshop tell you about learning to play an instrument?

3   Focusing on your experiences of improvising and composing in the group process, which aspects did you find interesting?

4   What are the possibilities for learning in this process?

5   What else was notable?

6   What other elements of music could be explored with shoes?

7   Make a list of stories, poems and songs about shoes. Share them with the group and think how you could use them in your practice.

8   Develop a small activity with pictures. What kind of shoes can be found in them? What are their stories? What sounds surround them?

Examples: composing from pictures/postcards in a group

You need: around 45 postcards or art pictures, paper, watercolour paints, paint-brushes, jars of water.

Example 1

• Pick a postcard.
• Using body percussion or voice, find a sound or ostinato rhythm in your picture.
• Share these sounds with the group.
• Form small groups.
• Organise your sounds to form a composition, using the postcards as graphical notation.
• Each group performs their piece.
• Transfer these compositions to instruments.
• Share these revisited compositions.
• The small groups discuss the other groups' compositions and write an 'idea' to develop each piece.
• All these ideas are incorporated in the compositions and performed again.
• Reflect on the experiences.

Example 2

• Pick a postcard.
• Write three words about the picture.

- Share these words with the group.
- Form (at least three) small groups.
- Each group composes a poem using their words. Additional words may be added, if needed.
- Each group shares their poem with another group.
- They compose a musical piece for the poem they receive.
- They perform their composition to the group, showing the original postcard.
- Reflect on the experiences.

Example 3

- Pick a postcard.
- Write three words about the picture.
- Form (at least three) small groups.
- Each group writes a story using their words, adding more words if needed.
- Each group shares their story with another group.
- They compose a musical piece for the story they receive.
- They perform their composition to the group.
- Each participant paints a watercolour picture inspired by their group's story.
- Reflect on the experiences.

Learning music with instruments

Observation of young children reveals their gross and fine motor abilities. Young children tend to respond with their whole body first, and gross motor movements come more naturally as a result. Children often tap with both hands on surfaces. Motor development becomes refined with age and maturation. Pointing fingers can indicate that it is time to work with fine motor activities: e.g. offering instrument strings to be plucked or played.

Our experience in early childhood music practice has convinced us that instruments are not age-specific. What is key is the way the instrument is introduced, and the different scaffolds and supports needed for children at different stages of development.

I wanted to give a 1-year-olds' baby music group a close interaction with the violin. One child was able to stand and came over to me; I rested an 1/8 size violin on his shoulder, helping him to hold it, and together we held the bow and played an open D string, and the group sang a familiar song. He looked amazed and proud. Another child showing interest was not able to stand and was a bit shy, making eye contact with me. I held the violin in front of him and after his mother had plucked the D string, he joined in. His mother let him continue, and we sang the song again. He looked curious and interested.

In family music groups it is worth remembering that both the children and their parents/carers are members of the group. Therefore you can use almost any instruments, if you are sensitive to the way they are introduced. Parents can play, and children can listen or explore the sound; they can play together or the child can play (perhaps with adult help). Moving away from playing the beat and introducing more complex rhythmic ideas can be nourishing for the parents as they play for their children. Young (2003, p. 68) talks about the multi-layered complexities within family music group dynamics, and Pitt (2014) speaks about parents as co-participants in music groups. Including the needs of the parents/carers, and their agency, can give them a fulfillment in learning music. They become active participants rather than detached assistants (feeling that they can chat or check their phones until they are needed to support their child).

Instruments – pedagogical dimensions for early childhood music practice

- It is best to use instruments of the highest quality you can afford, with a pleasing timbre. Choose instruments given to babies carefully – their movements may not be controlled, and the soundmaker they are using may pass very close to their ears.
- **Maracas/egg shakers, drums and bells** are easy to hold and play.
- **Large gathering drums** can encourage social interaction when children are ready to move away from the safety of their carer's lap.
- **Djembes** can be used by carers to assist a young child to play this larger drum, or the children can sit on the 'waist' of the instrument to feel the sound.
- **Claves** can be used with very young children; an adult plays them, and the baby gets a sense of the instrument by touching it. Alternatively, the child holds one clave, which the adult plays with the other. Babies love to explore their environment with a clave in their hand, playing interesting sounds on chairs, floor etc. Generally, a child that can master hitting objects together can play claves. Lightly holding the instrument produces the best sound.
- **Boomwhackers** are easy to use, provide pitch and can be used to accompany songs with chords.
- **Individual chime bars** can be a more flexible option for use with young children than a xylophone/metallophone. Adults can offer support by moving a single chime bar to meet the child's attempt at using a beater. Two chime bars representing a fifth (do–so) can be used to accompany many songs and activities with an ostinato.
- **Xylophones and metallophones** are beautiful sound makers for babies to tap and scratch with their fingers. Beaters can be used when motor skills are sufficiently developed to bring out the resonating sounds. A variety of beaters adds interest. It is possible to remove unwanted bars from the instrument (if you wish to create a pentatonic scale, for example).
- **Including your musical expertise as a resource.** Playing your instrument to a group allows members to listen and be inspired by it. Being able to feel,

pluck and blow for themselves may add to the experience. The body of many instruments produces vibrations that are wonderful for small babies to sense, and many can be useful for accompanying group singing or playing. Unfamiliar instruments, e.g. an African finger-piano, afford interesting listening experiences and may be played by the smallest fingers.

- **Other melody instruments**
  - Kanteles – the Finnish national instrument – are widely used in early childhood music education in Finland as it offers an easy way to produce tonic, dominant and sub-dominant chords as well as the possibility of plucking five-note melodies. Similarly, guitars and ukuleles are enjoyable plucking instruments.
- Ocarinas (be aware of hygiene issues!) are good to practise blowing and fine motor skills. Simple melodies or an ostinato accompaniment can be played.
- **Percussion instruments**

Flavour and timbre can be added by un-tuned percussion including:

- Guiro
- Agogo
- Cabasa
- Rainstick
- Indian bells
- Triangle (assistance may be needed to make a pleasing sound)
- Windchimes
- Ocean drum
- Home-made instruments

Young children make sense of the world through their curiosity, exploration and experimentation. Music pedagogues can encourage this curiosity through the way we offer instruments in a group setting. There is a tension between learning the 'right way to play' and having freedom to make your own music. This may begin unconsciously with the youngest children in group music situations (see also Schenck, 2000, pp. 43–47). It is a delicate balance; there is a time for practising a composed piece or modelling the technical aspects required, and there is also a time for creating your own repertoire for performance or improvisation that reflects the current mood and learners' capabilities (e.g. one can feel interrupting free play and imposing a steady beat is wrong, or conversely, letting children improvise is not music teaching). Sensitivity is required to avoid one aspect of teaching dominating and inhibiting the others.

These approaches and issues apply to many learning situations: beginner instrumental students, children with additional needs, adults and groups of the elderly. Taking a learner-centred approach to instrumental tuition requires reflection on the professional competencies needed (see Hildén et al., 2010, p. 55; Elliott & Silverman, 2015) and on the pedagogical choices and actions in the moment that facilitate fruitful learning.

IMAGE 12.5

 Reflection and discussion

1 Review the resources and instruments found in this theme, and think about how you might use these in your practice.
2 Share and reflect on your pedagogical ideas with others.

Learning to play an instrument in a group

In the discourse of instrumental tuition, there are opposing views on one-to-one teaching and group tuition. They could be viewed as complementary as they can both open possibilities for learning, although each has a different focus. One-to-one teaching is the usual position for learning an instrument; in recent years group instrumental teaching has become more common.

Thinking about the group as a learning environment, the following section focuses on those elements to be aware of in beginners' instrumental learning. The musical process and the artistic trajectory remain vital foundations, although it is difficult to maintain artistic musical integrity when beginning to learn an instrument. The preliminary steps in learning often do not satisfy the budding musician. It is helpful to hold in mind the need to incorporate wider and richer musical components to nourish each learner's inner artistic capacity.

Things to consider

- **Tuning the group** is as important in this context as any other. It creates a safe atmosphere, acceptance, a sense of togetherness in learning an instrument and builds a community of practice (see Wenger, 1998).
- **Pathway**
  - Build on the group's shared experiences, prior knowledge and skills by:
    - Using familiar songs
    - Learning songs together to form common ground to build on
  - Nurture peer-to-peer learning through a shared process, reflecting together to strengthen the community of practice. A peer can scaffold another's learning of a new piece if they are finding it easier.
    - Use different roles and modalities within the learning process, e.g. one plays while the others make a circle dance – in a shared moment not for performance.
  - Improvisation and composing. The pedagogue can nurture creativity with a framework to structure the improvisation (e.g. Sleeping Beauty's "Pavane" – Theme 4 p. 138). Learners can compose simple tunes after the first session (see vignette example of recorder lesson). There are some helpful systems of notation available, such as figurenotes (see www.resonaari.fi/international), to help learners compose without needing to understand stave notation. Learners can, of course, create their own graphical score; this gives them agency by regarding them as musicians and composers. Improvisation can encourage practise between sessions. Johnson-Green (2016) shared an example of young children in a group keyboard learning situation composing their own pieces over many weeks using Lego to remind them of their composition and to develop it.
  - Be aware of the group's energy and concentration levels. It is not beneficial for children to focus solely on one particular challenge for the whole lesson. Varying the activities within the working process, including some that demand less focused attention (e.g. gross motor exercises to feel 6/8 rhythm), helps to maintain intensity and engagement.
  - Engender motivation, enjoyment, fun and achievement. Music pedagogues play a role in all stages of the learner's journey in music, helping them through a reluctance to practise and school pressures, so that they can

experience the rewards. With sensitive scaffolding and dialogue, everyone can have the chance to learn to play an instrument.
- When beginning to learn, there are many skills to develop at the same time, so caution is needed when focusing on one area in particular, e.g. the correct posture to hold a violin, as one can quickly lose sight of the fundamental elements of making music visible and tangible.

- **Closing**
  Closing the session is as vital as tuning at the start. Find your own way of celebrating and marking this with your learners. Here are some ideas:
  - A song
  - A circle dance
  - A listening activity
  - Reflection around the circle

> Teaching a group of beginner piano students helped me understand the importance of not imposing my targets for learning and of respecting the children as unique musicians. Some children stopped coming, and others lacked the motivation to carry out the tasks I gave them. I discovered a different way of working with the group, where 'less was more'. We formed a learning community, where a shared inquiry in music playing avoided unhealthy comparison and competition. I learned that there are transferable skills of social interaction that are essential to motivation and learning to play an instrument. There is a time and place for everything. Pushing can sometimes help, but pushing too hard and at the wrong time on technical or theoretical elements can be destructive.

Example: working with silence

You need: a selection of tuned or percussion instruments.

- Select an instrument.
- Decide how long to sit in silence, and elect a participant to play first.
- 'Attend' to the silence, experiencing its quality and how it feels to be silent with others.
- The nominated 'silence breaker' keeps the time and chooses how to break the silence with their instrument.
- The rest of the group play their instruments into the silence when they feel moved to do so.
- Reflect together about the presence of silence and the absence of sound. How did it feel to be the silence breaker?

IMAGE 12.6   Listening to silence

 Reflection and discussion

1   What are your childhood experiences of music or instrumental learning?
2   Share these with the group. You can also interview a few people as an assignment and reflect on:
   • The shared features in these experiences?
   • The differences?
3   Look back to Workshop Spring Tune p. 150. Think about how to adapt the ideas to suit a beginner learning group.
4   How would you address the following elements in a beginner learning group? Create some activities to practising them:
   • Concentration
   • Respecting other musicians and their contribution
   • Waiting your turn
   • Solo-tutti
   • Rehearsing a piece
   • Playing together
   • Follow the leader
   • Notation
   • Improvisation

References

Bruner, J. S. (1996). *The culture of education.* Cambridge, MA: Harvard University Press.

Burnard, P., Boyack, J., & Howell, G. (2017). Children composing: Creating communities of musical practice. In P. Burnard & R. Murphy (Eds.), *Teaching music creatively* (2nd ed., pp. 39–59). London: Routledge.

Davidson, J. W., Moore, D. G., Sloboda, J. A., & Howe, M. J. (1998). Characteristics of music teachers and the progress of young instrumentalists. *Journal of Research in Music Education, 46*(1), 141–160.

Elliott, D. J., & Silverman, M. (2015). *Music matters: A philosophy of music education* (2nd ed.). New York: Oxford University Press.

Hildén, K., Ardila-Mantilla, N., Bolliger, T., Francois, J.-C., Lennon, M., Reed, G., Stolte, T., & Stone, T. (2010). *Instrumental and vocal teacher education: European perspectives.* Polifonia Working Group for Instrumental and Vocal Music Teacher Training. Utrecht: AEC Publications-Handbook.

Jansson, T. (1962). *Det osynliga barnet och andra berättelser.* Helsinki: Schildts & Södeström. English translation *Tales from Moominvalley* (1963) Ernest Benn Ltd.

Johnson-Green, E. (2016). *Patterns and play: Teaching kindergarteners music composition through musical-mathematical design.* Spoken paper presentation (26th July, 2016): 32nd ISME World Conference, Glasgow, 24–29 July, 2016.

Muhonen, S. (2014). Songcrafting: A teacher's perspective of collaborative inquiry and creation of classroom practice. *International Journal of Music Education, 32*(2), 185–202.

Ojala, J., & Väkevä, L. (2013). Säveltäminen luovana ja merkityksellenä toimintana. In J. Ojala & L. Väkevä (Eds.), *Säveltäjäksi kasvattaminen. Pedagogisia näkökulmia musiikin luovaan tekijyyteen.* Oppaat ja käsikirjat 2013:3. Helsinki: Opetushallitus.

Pitt, J. (2014). *An exploratory study of the role of music with participants in children's centres.* (Unpublished doctoral thesis), University of Roehampton, London. http://hdl.handle.net/10142/321585

Rogoff, B. (2003). *The cultural nature of human development.* New York: Oxford University Press.

Schenck, R. (2000). *Spelrum – en metodikbok för sång och instrumentalpedagoger.* Göteborg: Bo Ejeby Förlag.

Tuovila, A. (2003). *"Mä soitan ihan omasta ilosta!" Pitkittäinen tutkimus 7–13-vuotiaiden lasten musiikin harjoittamisesta ja musiikkiopisto-opiskelusta. ["I play entirely for my own pleasure!" A longitudinal study on music making and music school studies of 7 to 13-year-old children].* Studia Musica 18. Helsinki: Sibelius-Academy.

Wenger, E. (1998). *Communities of practice.* Cambridge: Cambridge University Press.

Young, S. (2003). *Music with the under-fours.* London and New York: RoutledgeFalmer.

Theme 6
CREATING LEARNING ENVIRONMENTS THROUGH IMAGINATION

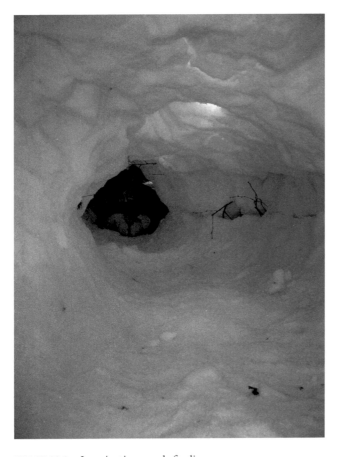

IMAGE 13.1   Imagination needs feeding

This chapter focuses on the world of fairytales, imagination and fantasy as an environment for learning and experiencing music. Through the combination of the spoken word and excerpts of composed or co-created music, learners experience an adventure with the story as a framework for the learning process. Many of the elements of music such as pulse, tempo and dynamics can be explored, and the fantasy world provides a rich environment for improvisation or multimodal transpositions of words into dance. Through the process of adventure in story, we can inhabit the art form (music and story) to gain deep insight and learn musical aspects from 'within' rather than being 'taught' them from the outside.

A story forming the learning environment and the structure for the process

The story affords an holistic learning environment and can act as a source of inspiration for a pedagogue. It offers the chance to be fully immersed in a different dimension that can enable the casting off of a layer of being a teacher. It can open up ways of co-creating in dialogue with learners, through imagination and discovery in the fantasy world. Workshops based on *Moominvalley in November by Tove Jansson* offer adventures for professional development. We are using this story because it is full of music! The words mesmerise the reader to listen, and to open their eyes and ears to the artistic elements around us in life. It is ideal material for composing music, creating (e.g. dancing, painting) and improvising. Listening to music leads to movement; the dance is built literally word by word from the story (see Mymble's dance on p. 182). Musical improvisation and composing can be found in the text; you just need to close your eyes and let your imagination take you to the Moominvalley. Jansson moves naturally in the world of different art forms with her words; she creates a story where music and arts education is inbuilt.

Using a story to create the learning environment carries a message: imagination, stories and creativity are all within our reach and do not rely on expensive materials. The colourful characters of Moominvalley highlight the variety of personalities that we encounter and encourage us to embrace diversity.

An interesting feature in this story is 'music' living its own life: Snufkin is trying to find his missing five bars, but it is not that simple:

> *he had hit upon five bars which would undoubtedly provide a marvelous beginning for a tune. They had come completely naturally as notes do when they have been left in peace. Now time had come to take them out again and let them become a song about rain.*
>
> *Snufkin listened and waited. The five bars didn't come. He went on waiting without getting impatient because he knew what tunes were like.*
>
> **(©Tove Jansson, *1970/1971, p. 27* (in the English translation). Moomin Characters ™)**

This idea is a tempting one for music education. Rather than thinking about music as something you can reduce to its component parts and teach bit-by-bit, it could be thought of as something to be tamed, searched for and waited on because we know what tunes are like. This alternative view of the music learning environment captures something about the magic of music that is difficult to grasp with words. It allows the learner to search for their own music.

> I've lived with this material for the past 6 years; it started with Snufkin searching for the five bars of the spring tune at my first meeting with the students at the start of their academic year, and we improvised with our voices. This story carries a special meaning because it is familiar to me from my childhood; I've read it with my children, and I now use it with my students. The deeper meaning might be that this is what being a music pedagogue is for me – this possibility of walking beside these future pedagogues, learning from them. These workshops have evolved over time and include the influence of every participant. The Moomin characters offer understanding about difference at a metaphorical level. We are all different; when thinking about additional needs they show that we are all unique – they need and support one another.

The musical and creative journey with a story can be built through many pathways. In Figure 13.1 some are illustrated. This framework helps when creating new processes for using stories in music education.

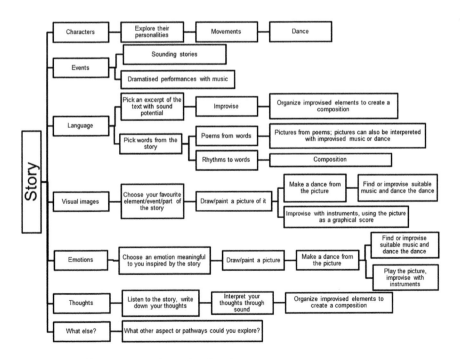

FIGURE 13.1   Story as a starting point for a journey

Tuning the group to listen to the story

- Reading the story is an easy way to tune ourselves to the theme and enter the world of imagination.
- Make sure you are calm by taking some deep breaths before you start. Your voice is the mediator of this magical story-world. It needs to express the story in all its dimensions!
- Listening to a story for a long time, being still and concentrating is not easy – it is often unsuccessful and can cause feelings of failure. This applies as much to adults as to children. It can therefore be beneficial to try alternative ways to facilitate listening. You can vary the way you use it with a group in different sessions. You can ask listeners to sit or lie on the floor; they can have their eyes closed or open; they can sit on the floor in pairs leaning against each other's backs.
- Reflect on these different ways for listening – note which worked best for you. This can be helpful in understanding your own learning, which can, in turn, increase your understanding about what may work for others.

Workshop: morning with a feeling of moving on

> *Early one morning in Moominvalley Snufkin woke up in his tent with the feeling that autumn had come and that it was time to break the camp.*
>
> *Breaking camp in this way comes with a hop, skip and a jump! All of a sudden everything is different, and if you're going to move on you're careful to make use of every single minute, you pull up your tent pegs and douse the fire quickly before anyone can stop you or start asking questions, you start running, pulling on your rucksack as you go, and finally you're on your way and suddenly quite calm, like a solitary tree with every single leaf completely still. Your camping-site is an empty rectangle of bleached grass. Later in the morning your friends wake up and say: he's gone away, autumn's coming.*
>
> (©Tove Jansson, 1970/1971, p. 9 (in the English translation). Moomin Characters ™)

Tuning

- Read the excerpt.
- Select instructions for listening to suit the group and the moment (sitting or lying on the floor, eyes closed or open, sitting on the floor in pairs leaning against each other's back).

Pathway: waking up

Music: J.S. Bach: The Brandenburg Concerto No. 5 BWV 1050 in D major. 1st movement. Allegro

Waking up your body is necessary, because it is your instrument! Concentrate on the 'here and now', experiencing your body, how far it can stretch and reach. This also serves as a preliminary exercise for the next activity that follows in the walking and waking up Pathway.

How can you wake up your body?

Make yourself

- as big as you can, reaching up,
- as small as you can,
- as wide as you can,
- as narrow . . . etc.

Can you move only your

- hands,
- feet,
- head,
- elbows etc.

Pathway: walking and waking up

Music: J.S. Bach: The Brandenburg Concerto No. 6 BWV 1051 in B Flat major. Allegro

In this music, there is 'walking music' and 'waking-up music'.

- Participants use the space to walk in the steady rhythm of the 'walking music', greeting other walkers when passing.
- In the 'waking-up music' they move different parts of their body. The leader can use instructions such as:
  - move your hands,
  - move your legs (in your place),
  - move your head etc.

The physical activity follows the structure of the music, and it enhances listening. This Pathway shows how to 'listen to music with your body' and also use it as a 'moving instrument'.

Example: hop, skip and jump

> *"Breaking camp in this way comes with a hop, skip and a jump"*

Experiment with different types of jumps in the music. The following pieces can be used:

Music suggestions

Pjotr Tšaikovski: The Nutcracker Suite, Op. 71 a. Dance of the sugar plum fairy
Nikolai Rimsky-Korsakov: Capriccio espagnol, Op. 34. Part: Fandango asturiano

Pathway: leaving or staying

> *There are those who stay at home and those who go away and it has always been so. Everyone can choose for himself, but he must choose while there is still time and never change his mind.*
>
> **(©Tove Jansson, *1970/1971, p. 11* (in the English translation). Moomin Characters ™)**

Music: J.S. Bach: The Brandenburg Concerto No. 6 BWV 1051 in B Flat major. Allegro

Continue to work with the now-familiar music with two different moods. The livelier music is for those who choose to go away, and the more stable (previously 'walking music') is for those who choose to stay. Create a movement for staying in one place.

It is valuable to work with the same music in various ways, because it gets more tangible every time you listen and therefore the listening of it becomes progressively deeper.

Closing

You need: a ball of wool.

Sitting in a circle

*   One person throws the ball of wool to another, while holding the end of the wool. The person who catches the ball says something about the contradictions that make us who we are – staying with the familiar or taking a risk ("those who stay at home and those who go away"). Each person shares something as the ball of wool is thrown from one to another.
*   Finally, the 'picture' made by the wool is placed in the centre of the circle.

 Reflection and discussion

1   What thoughts do you have about using a story as a framework for a pedagogical musical process?
2   How did you feel as a pedagogue when you were reading the story?
3   What was the easiest way for you as a participant to concentrate on listening to the story? Why?

After experiencing this Pathway, what thoughts do you have about:

1 Your body as an instrument?
2 Related experiences you have from working with children?
3 Other possibilities for experiencing and learning that can be facilitated by this activity?

Workshop: sounds of rain and running water

You need: a bottle of water, a bowl, garden fleece, paper, crayons.

Snufkin got a feeling that he wanted to write songs. He waited until he was quite sure of the feeling and one evening he got out his mouth-organ from the bottom of his rucksack. In August, somewhere in Moominvalley, he had hit upon five bars which would undoubtedly provide a marvellous beginning for a tune. They had come completely naturally as notes do when they have been left in peace. Now time had come to take them out again and let them become a song about rain.

Snufkin listened and waited. The five bars didn't come. He went on waiting without getting impatient because he knew what tunes were like. But the only things he could hear were the faint sounds of rain and running water. It gradually got quite dark. Snufkin took out his pipe but put it out again. He knew that the five bars must be somewhere in Moominvalley and that he wouldn't find them until he went back again.

There were millions of tunes that are easy to find and there will always be new ones. But Snufkin let them alone, they were summer songs which would do for just anybody. He crept into his tent and into his sleeping-bag and pulled it over his head. The faint whisper of rain and running water was still there and it had the same tender note of solitude and perfection. But what did the rain mean to him as long as he couldn't write a song about it?

(©**Tove Jansson**, *1970/1971, p. 27* (**in the English translation**). **Moomin Characters** ™)

Tuning

With the group lying on the floor, read this story. The following ideas can be explored:

- While reading, move around the room. Your movements and the voice coming from different directions will be interesting to the listener.
- When you read, use sounds of water (e.g. pouring water from a bottle into a bowl or splashing the water in the bowl) to give inspiration to the listener.

- In addition to the water-sounds, you can add a feeling of water – depending on the participants, you may need to explain what to expect – you can drop water on to the hands of participants, or you can gently spray water from above for a pleasing sensation on the face.

Pathway: composition about rain and running water

> *The faint whisper of rain and running water was still there and it had the same tender note of solitude and perfection.*

In small groups:

- Find six sounds for rain and running water. These sounds can be made using mouths and bodies as well as tapping the floor and chairs.
- Create a composition using these sounds, choosing and ordering the types of rain to play (a heavy shower, drizzle etc.).
- Write down simple signs (graphical notation) to indicate the different phases of their composition and to help remember it (for inspiration, see pictures 6.13, 6.14, 6.15 and 6.16).
- Rehearse these pieces.
- Share the compositions. The audience can pretend to be Snufkin in his tent, listening (you can make a tent to create the right atmosphere).

Creativity can be encouraged by restricting the options available. Instead of being overwhelmed by a multitude of options, limiting the choice helps one to focus on the creative process.

Instructions about the structure of the composition are vital:

1 How does it start?
2 Does it change?
3 How does it end?

The graphical notations enable rehearsal and make the piece tangible, so that it can be further developed.

Closing

Listen to a composition inspired by water or rain (e.g. *Sibelius: Sadepisarat*) while giving a raindrop massage (tapping on the head with fingers) to a partner.

 Reflection and discussion

1 What did you experience when you listened in different ways?
2 What do your experiences of listening tell you about concentrating or learning?
3 How did you experience the Workshop as a group member?

4   Did you feel safe?
  • Did you enter a sense of flow in your process?
  • If yes, why? If not, why not?
5   How can the pedagogue facilitate composing when using this process with a group of children?
  • What might need to be done differently?
6   Make a list of songs about rain or water and share them with the group. Pedagogues working in places with high annual rainfall benefit from a wide repertoire of rainsongs!

Workshop: Snufkin chasing the five bars

You need: a selection of instruments (including pitched percussion).

> *It was dark in the tent. Snufkin crept out of his sleeping-bag, the five bars had come no nearer. Not a sign of any music. Outside it was very quiet, the rain had stopped. He decided to fry some pork and went to the woodshed to get fuel.*
> (©Tove Jansson, *1970/1971, p. 59* (in the English translation). Moomin Characters ™)

Tuning: listening to quietness

• Lie on the floor, relaxed and with eyes closed. Listen to the quietness. What can you hear within the room, and outside? Let your mind wander. Bring your attention back to the present moment and the sounds around you.

• Next, move your toes, feet, legs, fingers, arms, and open your eyes. Then slowly get up to a sitting position.

Pathway: circle of quietness

• The group forms a sitting circle.
• Pass a maraca around the circle without making a sound.
• Repeat the activity, this time trying to make a continuous sound.
• Close by repeating the silent version.
• Explore the same activity with different sounding instruments or objects.

Pathway: moving with no sound

• The whole group moves freely in the space and tries not to make any sound.
• Explore the same activity with continuous sound.

Pathway: music and stop

We are surrounded by sounds and noise. Recognising the need for quiet can be difficult for pedagogues as well as the people we work with.

The leader plays music with their instrument including rests in improvised music, or deliberate breaks after phrases in composed pieces.

- Group members listen and move while the leader plays.
- They stop moving during rests and pauses.

Pathway: following sounds

> *The fog had brought complete silence with it, the valley was quite motionless. Snufkin woke up as quickly as an animal, wide awake. The five bars had come a little nearer.*
>
> *Good, he thought. A cup of coffee and I'll get them.*
>
> **(©Tove Jansson, 1970/1971, p. 66 (in the English translation). Moomin Characters ™)**

Work in pairs; each pair has an instrument with a different timbre that is easy to move with.

- One of the pair holds an instrument and moves in the space while playing continually.
- The other closes their eyes and tries to follow the sound of that instrument.
- At the end of the activity, they open their eyes and discuss their feelings with their partner.
- They swap roles.

Pathway: the sound cave

- Everyone has an instrument to hold.
- The group forms two lines facing each other.
- One at a time, each participant walks down the centre of the two lines (sound cave) with their eyes closed, while the others play to form a sound cave around them.
- Once everyone has gone through the sound cave, the group discusses their feelings about the experience.

Pathway: guiding and trust

Music suggestion: Jorge Cardoso: Suite portena. 1st movement. Cancion

Work in pairs with fingertips of index fingers touching;

- One person leads the activity while the other has their eyes closed.
- Move in the space – the lead partner ensures they don't collide with anyone or anything.
- The other tries to both trust them and sense movement through the finger touch.
At the end, discuss your feelings – what frightened or felt safe?

Pathway: searching for notes

This piece is shown in three distinct parts. The 'Toodledidee' and 'Searching for five notes' melodies can be learned as stand-alone pieces, either sung as one song, with the parts following on from each other, or sung at the same time by two groups. The additional harmony parts offer more layers to the piece according to the abilities or wishes of group members. All three parts can be performed together as one piece with the conductor adding and removing parts as they wish, to produce different timbral qualities.

Toodledidee tune

Jessica Pitt

Too dle di dee   Too dle di doo,   Too dle di dee   Too dle di doo.

MUSIC 13.1   published with permission from the composer

Searching for five notes
Toodledidee

Jessica Pitt

Search-ing for   five notes   as   I   play,   search-ing for   five notes   on   my   way.

Search-ing for   five notes   as   I   play,   search-ing for   five notes   on   my   way.

MUSIC 13.2   published with permission from the composer

Where are you?
Ostinato

Jessica Pitt

Where   are   you?   Where   are   you?   Where are   you?   Where are

you?   Where   are   you?

MUSIC 13.3   published with permission from the composer

Closing

Read and listen to the following:

> *Snufkin gave up looking for his five bars, they would have to be allowed to come when they wanted to. There were other songs anyway. Perhaps I'll play a little this evening, he thought.*
>
> (©*Tove Jansson, 1970/1971, p. 92 (in the English translation). Moomin Characters ™)*

 Reflection and discussion

1 Following sounds: What is the role of music in this activity?
How would changing the chosen music affect the experience?
2 Discuss trust in group work and in learning music.

Workshop: thunder and lightning

You need: paper, watercolour paints, brushes and jars of water, selection of sound-makers for thunder and lightning.

> *There really was a big storm coming in from the sea. The lightning was white and violet, he had never seen so many or such beautiful flashes of lightning at one time. A sudden pall had descended on the valley. Fillyjonk lifted up her skirts and rushed back through the garden with leaps and bounds and shut the kitchen door behind her.*
>
> *Snufkin sniffed the air, it felt as cold as steel. It smelt of electricity. The lightning was pouring down in great quivering streaks, parallel pillars of light, and the whole valley was lit up by their blinding flashes! Snufkin jumped up and down with joy and admiration. He waited for the wind and the rain, but they didn't come. Only the thunder rumbled to and fro between the mountain peaks, enormous heavy spheres of sound, and there was a smell of burning everywhere. Then there was a last, triumphant earsplitting crash, and all was completely silent, without a single further flash.*
>
> (©*Tove Jansson, 1970/1971, pp. 84–85 (in the English translation). Moomin Characters ™)*

Tuning

- Decide the most appropriate way for group members to be positioned for listening (e.g. sitting or lying on the floor, with their eyes open or closed, sitting in pairs leaning against each other's back).
- Read the excerpt above.

Pathway: paintings of thunder and lightning

- After listening to the story, paint the thunder and lightning with watercolours.

  When the paintings are finished, place them so that everyone can see them. (They can be hung up like washing.)

Some will not be satisfied with their work. Find something to say about every picture and appreciate it as a unique interpretation; all the pictures are equally valuable.

Playing from the pictures

- Choose an instrument or a sounding object (thunder can be effectively played with a thin board or a plastic bag).
- Find a picture or detail that interests you.
- One person leads the playing by pointing at each painting in turn. When each individual's picture choice is pointed out, they play their instrument.
- Make sure that everyone's picture gets played. If any pictures are not chosen, do another round, playing only those pictures!
- The group discusses their experiences.

Composition from graphical notation

In small groups:

- Each group is given the same number of pictures as there are participants in their group. These pictures act as graphical notation.
- Compose a thunder and lightning piece in your group using the pictures as inspiration.
- Rehearse your piece.
- Share your composition with the larger group.

Decide if the participants either play their own pictures or pictures from those outside their group. It is a different experience to use your own material for a group process than material created by someone else. Both options are valuable.

Closing

Listen to different storm music and reflect on the experience. You can use drawing or painting to help reflect on the music.

Music suggestions

Jean Sibelius: The tempest, Suite No. 1, Op. 109 No. 2. The storm
Pjotr Tšaikovski: The storm
Ludwig van Beethoven: Pastoral Symphony 4th Movement
Antonio Vivaldi: Four seasons winter
Gioachino Rossini: William Tell overture

Reflection and discussion

1 How can a pedagogue create a safe atmosphere for painting and self-expression?
2 What feelings did you have during this process?
3 How could this process be used with learners?
4 How can a pedagogue facilitate composition with a large group of children?

Workshop: Mymble's dance

Mymble walked to the middle of the floor, looking very shy and self-conscious. Her hair reached to her knees, and it was obvious that the hair-washing had been a success. She nodded briefly to Snufkin and he started to play. He played very softly. Mymble raised her arms and circled with short hesitant steps. Shoo, shoo, tiddledidoo, said mouth-organ; imperceptibly the music moved into a tune, became more and more lively and Mymble quickened her steps, the kitchen was full of music and movement and her long red hair looked like flying sunshine. It was all so beautiful and jolly! No one heard the Creature, huge and heavy, creeping round and round the house without knowing what it wanted. The guests beat time with their feet and sang tiddledidi, tiddledidoo. Mymble kicked off her boots, threw her scarf on the floor, the paper streamers fluttered in the warmth from the stove, everybody clapped their paws and Snufkin stopped play-ing with a loud cry! Mymble laughed with self-satisfied pride.

Everybody shouted: "Bravo, bravo!" and Hemulen said with genuine admi-ration: "Thank you ever so much."

"Don't thank me" Mymble answered. "I can't stop myself. You ought to do the same thing!"

(©Tove Jansson, 1970/1971, pp. 126–127 (in the English translation). Moomin Characters ™)

Tuning

• Decide the most appropriate way for the group members to be positioned for listening (e.g. sitting or lying on the floor, with their eyes open or closed, sitting on the floor in pairs leaning against another's back).
• Read the excerpt.

Pathway: the dance

Create a composition and a dance with Mymble and Snufkin based on the story. By using a simple harmonic framework, you can support a group of learners in their composition (e.g. using chords I, IV and V as below).

Creating a song and dance

- *Mymble raised her arms and circled with short hesitant steps.*

  Participants try the Mymble steps, with their arms raised and taking short hesitant steps in a circle.
- *Snufkin was playing very softly. Shoo, shoo, tiddledidoo (Part A).*
- Invite musical suggestions from participants to create a tune for Snufkin (chord I).
- *Shoo, shoo, tiddledidoo.* How does this melody continue?
- Participants contribute musical ideas for continuing with the *tiddledidi, tiddledidoo* (IV, V, I) section (Part B).
- The group devises some steps for *tiddledidi tiddledidoo.*
- They sing and dance the whole song.
- Create a circle dance by selecting some dance movements from the group to form a co-created dance.

Playing with tempo

Imperceptibly the music moved into a tune, became more and more lively. Mymble quickened her steps.
Experiment with singing and dancing at different tempi using the melody you have composed.

Developing the song and dance

The Creature, huge and heavy, creeping round and round the house without knowing what it wanted.
Some participants become creatures and form an outer circle using heavy steps. The inner circle dances part A (*Shoo, shoo, tiddledidoo*).

The guests beat time with their feet and sang.
The outer circle becomes the guests for part B, clapping and stamping feet while singing *tiddledidi, tiddledidoo.* The inner circle dances the whole dance.

Dance the whole dance with accompaniment.

A Mymble dance can be created with readily available composed music.

Music suggestions

JPP – New Finnish Folk Fiddling: Oskan ketkupolkka
English/Irish/Scottish folk dance fiddle music
Diddle Dee I Die Die (see song examples, p. 213) can be adapted and used

Closing – relaxing the dancing feet

This is a relaxation exercise performed in pairs:

- One partner lies on the floor; the other holds their feet – one foot at a time.
- The partner lying on the floor tries to let go of their legs and feet allowing them to become very heavy.

- The active partner moves their partner's legs to help the relaxation process.
- Use a calming piece of music to enhance the experience.
- Swap roles and reflect together on the experience of letting go.

 Reflection and discussion

1 What might it feel like to be the Creature, or Mymble?
2 How can we accommodate the needs of both in a group process?

Workshop: song about the rain

You need: potato flour or corn flour, cotton balls, Lycra or garden fleece, selection of instruments, scarves, white crayons, white paper and diluted coloured paint.

The last part of this journey in the Moominvalley takes us to the first snow of winter and finally to finding the song about the rain that Snufkin had been looking for.

Through the building of a process, the musical material is repeated (both recorded and co-created). Recording the music that the group creates can be useful to refer to during the process.

> *A bank of clouds slowly accumulated over the sea, and the whole sky became heavy with them and it was easy to see that they were full of snow. Within a few days all the valleys would be covered with winter they had been waiting for it for a long time, but it was on its way.*
>
> *Snufkin stood outside his tent and knew that it was time to break the camp, he was ready to be off. The valley would soon be cut off.*
>
> . . .
>
> *At first light Snufkin went to the beach to fetch his five bars of music. He climbed over the banks of seaweed and driftwood and stood on the sand waiting. They came immediately and they were more beautiful and even simpler than he had hoped they would be.*
>
> *Snufkin went back to the bridge as the song about the rain got nearer and nearer, he slung his rucksack over his shoulders and walked straight into the forest.*
>
> (©Tove Jansson, *1970/1971, pp. 153–154* (in the English translation). Moomin Characters ™)

Tuning

- Read the excerpt.

Pathway: the song about the rain

In small groups:

*   Use the material the group has created for rain in Workshop 'Sounds of rain and running water'.

(pp. 175–176)

*   Select a simple tune using a pentatonic scale and compose a melody for a song about the rain.
*   Then write some words for the rain song.
*   Use elements from the rain and running water composition as an accompaniment for this pentatonic song.
*   The small group decides a way to notate their song[1] and teaches it to others.

Pathway: first snow

Music suggestion: Leoš Janáček: On the overgrown path. A blown away leaf
The first snow has fallen in the Moominvalley.
The group sits in a circle.

*   Listen to the sound of potato flour (as you rub it between your fingers to make a sound) – it sounds like walking in the snow.
*   Listen to music that suits the atmosphere of falling snow.
    *   With cotton wool balls, experiment with blowing them off your hands. Next, place them on the Lycra or garden fleece and let them dance, to create a quiet first snow fall.

Pathway: freezing

*   The group improvise movements freely in the space while listening to music.

Music suggestions

Jukka Linkola: Snowqueen. Music from the film, The Snow Queen
*   *On the glacier*
Leoš Janáček: On the overgrown path
*   *Good night*
*   When the cold breeze freezes, stop the movement in the middle . . .
    *   Invent a sign for the cold breeze (for example a specific sound from an instrument or a scarf touching).
*   When the whole group has been frozen, make snow-sculptures by inviting someone to mold and shape the 'frozen' group members into one big sculpture.

Closing – a snowy landscape

- Think about cold and snow while listening to music. Some of the group participants lie under the garden fleece while the others move the fleece up and down to assist with listening.
  - This is a good moment to introduce new music or to revisit previous compositions or recorded music from previous activities.
- The group members create a snowy landscape of Moominvalley by drawing with white crayon on white paper, then add diluted watercolour in a contrasting shade on top.

 Reflection and discussion

1   How do we use a story to create a long process?
   - Think about stories from your childhood: create a workshop based on a story that is meaningful to you.
   - Create the first session for that process (see also Chapter 5).
2   Reflect on the process of *Moominvalley in November* (or part of it) using the guide for observation on p. 66.

Creating a story in a group to form the learning environment

Instead of using fairytales, you can create a story as a group process that forms a learning environment. There are many ways to create a story in a group.

1   Music as a starting point:
   - Listen to a piece of music and write down words inspired by it. You can use these words as a starting point for a story.
2   Picture as a starting point:
   - Look at a picture and draft a story based on the picture.
3   Sentence by sentence:
   - The group sits in a circle and passes a ball from person to person; each one adds one sentence to the story as the ball is passed round the circle. (You can record this if you wish to remember exactly what people have contributed.)
4   A box full of different objects:
   - Each member of the group takes one object in turn and incorporates that object into their part of the co-created story.
5   Hats, buttons, shoes:
   - Create a character around an object (a hat, a button or a shoe) and form stories about these characters.

- Example with buttons:
  1 Choose one button.
  2 Imagine to whom it belonged and why it is here.
  3 Share the details of these characters and events in a group.
  4 Divide the group into smaller groups. This can be done with a rhyme or numbers, so it is a surprise to everyone which characters are joined together for the story.
  5 Create a story using these characters and events, write down the story.
6 Storycrafting:
  - There is an approach called Storycrafting (see Karlsson, 2013) that has been used with children. It can be adapted for use with learners of any age. Within this approach, the learner uses their own words to tell a story or recount an event, and it is written down verbatim. They can amend or correct the story as it is read aloud. The underlying premise is that the learner has ownership of their story, shaping it precisely as they want to. No one else can comment.
7 Starting from movement or sound:
  - You can organise improvisatory movements and sounds to craft a story.

 Reflection and discussion

1 Share in a group any examples you have of working with stories.
2 Which of the examples listed above appeals to you as a starting point for story writing and why?

Workshop: music as a starting point for a co-created story

You need: Plasticine/playdough or clay, paper.

Music: Benjamin Britten: Sea interludes. Sunday morning

The form and shape of the musical piece can be explored and perceived through the deep analytical listening that is offered through this example. The process will involve working alone, in pairs and in small groups.

Tuning

- Get a sense of your energy level as you stand, then walk in the space at a natural walking pace for that moment and in that place.
- Become very aware of your walking, how it feels, and concentrate on your movements. Continue walking and establish the rhythm for yourself.
- Speed up your natural pace and then return to your rhythm. How did it feel? Now, walk a little slower and then return to your normal pace. How did that feel?
- Allow the natural pace to become settled and then find another in the group who is walking at a different pace, walk with them, and then find someone walking at a similar pace, walk with them.

- Finally, the whole group finds a way of walking at the same pace together. What kind of adjustment did that need from individuals?

Pathway: Sunday morning

Listening

- Find a quiet place to sit/lie to listen to Britten's 'Sea Interlude – Sunday Morning'. (By using the word 'quiet', the pedagogue directs the focus of the activity towards not speaking).
- Take some modelling wax (plasticine, playdough or clay) to facilitate the listening process and shape it as you listen to the music. There is no expected outcome (it is not necessary to make a figure).
- Find three words to describe your thoughts or feelings from the listening experience; write them on pieces of paper or post-it notes.
- Place these in a circle along with the modelled wax. Listen to the piece again and look at the words and wax creations as a group.
- Select three words and one wax model, one-by-one while listening to the music. Then find three other people to work with.

Writing a story with the words

- In small groups create a short story with the three elements: the words, the wax objects and the shape or form of Britten's piece.

Composition

- Give your story to another group, who create a composition with a visual form based on that story. The form can include movement, sounds and drama and refers back to the piece – with the form that Britten used.
- Listen again if necessary.
- Create a graphical score to help remember the composition.
- It is valuable to explore various ways of representing the structure of the piece: Modelling wax, objects, images, torn pieces of paper, toys or drawings can all be used to visually demonstrate the structure of the piece.

Performances

- Each group performs their piece to the others.
- The stories can also be shared at this point for discussion.

Reflect on the various ways that each member of the group contributed to the process. Every single aspect was needed, including Britten and his thinking and composition.

Closing

- Lie down and let these reflections and experiences dwell – think about what was meaningful for you at this point. Play Britten's 'Sea Interlude – Moonlight'.

Reflection and discussion

1   What is knowledge in this teaching context?
2   What are the indicators of learning?
3   How do pedagogical actions facilitate learning?

Characters of a story as a starting point for exploration

One option for using the creative material of stories is to explore the different characters in them instead of the plot. Different characters give us freedom to step outside ourselves and explore life through their eyes. Each of us has different characters or 'sides' of ourselves that are brought out by others we encounter, or by situations that we find ourselves in. To explore these dimensions as pedagogues, we can gain understanding about *who* we are in various situations so that our reactions to people and events are not reactive but informed and reflective.

In the following section, there are examples of ways to use characters in creative working processes.

Workshop: the dance of different characters

This adventure begins with colourful characters who will lead us on a journey to accept and embrace individual pathways in learning and experiencing music. When

IMAGE 13.2 May I have this dance?

selecting a story to use, look for those that include characters with different person-alities, ways of moving and experiencing the world.

Winnie the Pooh by A.A. Milne describes the positive character of Winnie the Pooh, the melancholic Eeyore, frightened Piglet and so on. Characters from a paint-ing or picture can also be used. Tove Jansson's Moomin characters are used here as an example.

Dance of the Moomin characters

Through the combination of movement, music, the spoken word and co-created compositions, learners experience a creative process, a journey that forms a learning environment. Many of the elements of music such as pulse, tempo and dynamics can be explored, as well as improvised composition or a multimodal transposition of words into dance.

Tuning

- Select a 'tuning the group' exercise, for example: 'Instrument and Player'.

(p. 76)

Pathway: creating a dance

Music: J.S. Bach: Brandenburg Concerto No. 6 3rd movement

- Present the characters either as pictures (placed on the floor in the circle) or written text descriptions. Allow the participants to choose the character they feel most drawn to.
- Invite the participants to find a movement from the picture or text excerpt to depict how this character would move.
- Explore the movements in the space (the whole group moves at the same time).
- In the world of the characters, *Bach's Brandenburg Concerto No. 6 3rd movement* appears, and the characters respond to the music with their movements.
- The musical form provides a framework for shaping the groups' movements into a creative piece. It allows the group to listen to and perceive the musical form of the work. The opening of the 3rd movement encourages walking in the space; the melody then develops with its quicker, rhythmical element, that can be explored by the characters as they meet each other. The participants are invited to listen for the themes as they move.
- Now that a shared pulse has become established, it is possible to explore the movements in silence. Firstly, ask the group to move while keeping the beat with a drum, and then introduce 'stop' at certain moments. The leader can indicate with body gestures that 'stop' means silent listening to the beat. The next step is to ask the participants, whilst moving, to translate their movements into sounds or body percussion. Continue with the three elements of moving

in silence, the use of 'stop', and the sounds and body percussion. Using just three words: 'Move', 'Sounds' and 'Stop', the group can explore how these different elements feel.

- Divide the group into two groups. Group A shows their movements. Group B creates sounds for the movements.
- Share the individual movements of Group A; each member shares their movements, and the rest of the group imitates. Group B accompanies.
- The groups swap roles.
- For further exploration with the material: the accompanist – piano, guitar, drum or melodic instrument – can choose one movement to improvise with. The rest of the group tries to imitate the movement that was selected by the accompanist.
- Making small groups.
  - The whole group starts moving in silence. Find four or five characters with movements that are different from your own to make a small group for the creation of a dance.

Making a dance of different characters

- Compose a small dance based on the movements of the group members (i.e. each group has 4–5 movements).
- You can use the pictures of the characters as a 'score' to remember the structure of the dance.
- Share the dance and the 'score' with the big group.
- The audience play instruments, or make sounds for your dance. Instructions can be given about the sort of accompaniment that is desired for the different sections of the piece as the score is demonstrated.

I was working in continuing professional development with a group of arts-pedagogues; we were based in a museum for the workshop. I invited all participants to walk for 10 minutes alone in silence in the museum to find a creature that spoke to them. I asked them to move as if they were their chosen creature as part of the dance activity. It was a lovely way of integrating the environment into the creative process.

Workshop: creating your own characters

Buttons can be lovely, open-ended inspirations for a creative process (see picture 6.8).

You need: a selection of different buttons (at least double the number of participants), instruments for improvising, large paper and watercolour materials.

Tuning

- Choose a button and think about the character that wore it.
- Write words/story/poem about this person.
- Share these with the group.

Pathway: music for characters

Exploring the movements of one character

- Each participant in turn describes their button-character and requests certain sorts of sounds from the group of musicians.
- Half the group responds by improvising on their chosen instrument. The improvised sound world can be developed by the 'button-owner'/conductor of their piece.
- Everyone in turn creates a sound world for their character.
- The rest of the group improvises movement for these sounds.

Characters meet

In small groups:

- Each group member shares their 'button-character' in their group.
- The groups make short movement (non-verbal) dialogues for their characters.
- These dialogues can be dramatised further and performed with improvised music. Combining two groups together, for example.

> *I was working with a group of 3-year-olds; we were making sounds for different characters; I found that using 'helping' questions gave ownership to the children, e.g. "Is it a big princess sound, or a small princess sound that you'd like?" "What kind of sound is it? Is it airy; is it sharp and pointy?" They could create and select the sounds they wanted. I was wondering if the use of colourful, rich narrative, as in these questions, which avoided musical terminology, would help facilitate improvisation with all learners irrespective of their age.*

Closing: strengths

- Think about your character: what are their challenges? And what are their strengths?
- Share the strengths in a small group and paint 'a strengthening picture' together.
- To close the process, place the buttons in a good place in the picture.
- You can also 'play the picture' in a group with the instruments.
- Discuss and reflect on the process.

Reflection and discussion

1   What do you find you have in common with these characters and why?
2   What could the different characters give to others?
3   How can this exploratory approach to learning be beneficial for:
    •   Learning in and about music?
    •   Exploring and accepting diversity?
    •   Working in a group?
    •   Enhancing self-understanding, self-esteem etc.?
4   Discuss in the light of the workshop how we are similar, how we are different.
5   Reflect together about how this informs our practice as music peda-gogues and the groups of learners with whom we work with their differ-ent pulses, energy levels, interests and preferences.
6   How can we work in a way where everyone feels accepted and enabled to use their own strengths?

You can explore this process with using e.g. different hats or characters that you find in pictures or other artefacts in museums, galleries or other curated spaces to act as inspiration for the creation of characters.

IMAGE 13.3   The starting point for many stories

Note

1 figurenotes – this system may be helpful as it enables beginners to notate their compositions so that they can be played at home and remembered (for more information: www.
resonaari.fi/international; see also Hakomäki, 2013)

References

Hakomäki, H. (2013). *Storycomposing as a path to a child's inner world: A collaborative music
therapy experiment with a child co-researcher.* (Doctoral dissertation). Jyväskylä Studies in
Humanities 204. University of Jyväskylä, Finland.
Jansson, T. (1970). *Sent I November.* Helsinki: Schildts & Södeström. English translation
Moominvalley in November. (1971). Ernest Benn Ltd.
Karlsson, L. (2013). Storycrafting method – to share, participate, tell and listen in practice and
research. *The European Journal of Social & Behavioural Sciences, 6*(3), 1109–1117.

Theme 7
THE MUSIC PEDAGOGUE AS A CREATIVE INSTRUMENT

This theme emphasises the importance of taking care of your professional instrument, in order to enhance your creative thinking and nurture the building of multimodal learning environments in music education. Every music pedagogue has to find their own pathways to nourish the core of their pedagogical professional practice.

IMAGE 14.1 Every music pedagogue has a unique perspective

Continuous professional development as a music pedagogue – reflective practice – in, on and after

There are countless ways to be a music pedagogue. Every music session can become a shared adventure in the world of arts-based practice. We are never completed as a pedagogue; we are always rehearsing and learning, in a state of becoming. It is an individual process and therefore it is important to be true to yourself, as you offer something unique. Reflection is vital in our ongoing learning process.

There are many ways to understand the concept of professional identity (see Beijaard, Meijer, & Verloop, 2004), and finding a shared definition for this is difficult (see also e.g. Regelski, 2007; Woodford, 2002). Despite these different understandings, there are some key features that illustrate a pedagogue's professional identity. The identity-formation process not only addresses the question, "Who am I?", but is also driven by the question, "Who do I want to become?" (Beijaard et al., 2004; also Heikkinen, 2001; Ropo, 2009). A pedagogue's professional identity comprises different dimensions of 'being a pedagogue' (see e.g., Beijaard et al., 2004). It is a dynamic process that aims to find a balance between these dimensions; "professional identity is not something teachers have, but something they use in order to make sense of themselves as teachers" (Beijaard et al., 2004).

Michael Connelly and Jean Clandinin (1999) studied teacher knowledge and discovered that participating teachers, when asked about their knowledge base, were most concerned with who they were as teachers. It seems as if 'knowing', as a teacher, does not really exist without being, and acting, as a teacher. Professional identity and professional knowledge form the landscape for pedagogical thought and action (Connelly & Clandinin 1999, 1995). Becoming a music pedagogue can be seen as a dynamic process of negotiating experiences in dialogue with one's social and cultural environment and significant others (see e.g. Côté & Levine, 2002; Heikkinen, 2001; Ropo, 2009; Wenger, 1998).

Research indicates that a wide and flexible professional identity allows the formation of a professional competence that is holistic in its ability to include the needs of a broad working life across a multitude of contexts (see Huhtinen-Hildén, 2012). The following quotes demonstrate the centrality of reflection as a developmental tool, not only for pedagogical choices and actions, but also for the formation of professional identity. It is a maturation process with no end, as you discover who you are in the continual process of 'becoming' a music pedagogue.

> "For me it is the most important aspect in teaching, how you are in contact with other people."
>
> *(quote from a student of teaching, Huhtinen-Hildén, 2012, p. 120)*

> "That music would be something meaningful and important for the individual, touching every cell of the body . . . That music would be part of everyday life."
>
> *(quote from a student of teaching, Huhtinen-Hildén, 2012, p. 122)*

"I haven't thought for a long time now that you are born to be a teacher, it's more like an ongoing growing and developing process."

(quote from a student of teaching, Huhtinen-Hildén, 2012, p. 123)

 Reflection and discussion

Your pedagogical handprint

On your own, in a group or with a colleague:

- **Part one:** Draw an outline of your right hand.
  - Think about five central things, approaches or ideas that guide your pedagogical thinking, that are the cornerstones of your personal professional pedagogy. Write these on the fingers of your picture.
  - What are the other spices, flavours, colours or meaningful elements to include in your pedagogical picture? Write these in the palm of the hand.
- Take a moment to look at the picture. What does it tell you? Share these reflections.
- **Part two:** Draw an outline of your left hand.
  - This picture is about you as a pedagogue in five years' time. What does this picture look like? What would you like to add to it, make stronger or take away? Draw as above.
- Take a moment to look at the picture. What does it tell you? Share these reflections.

Views from pedagogical pathways

Seven experienced music pedagogues shared their thinking as an inspiration for readers of this book. They described what nurtures their creativity and where they get their inspiration from.

Creating shared stories in music and arts

Eve Alho, early childhood music teacher in Juvenalia Music Institute, Special Kindergarten teacher, developer of Finnish early childhood music education

For me what is important is that making music and creating a shared story in arts together forms a peaceful situation where every participant feels good. I aim to foster this before people enter the room; the presence in that moment tunes towards the shared adventure. Most important to me is to meet everyone as a unique member of our group. I enjoy observing children's learning, but learning is something that follows making music together, creating stories, dancing, playing, painting, singing.

This week, one of the highlights was a musical dialogue with a 6-month-old baby. We improvised with djembe-drums; she played, I answered, I drummed and she reacted to that with her music. This was clearly as joyful to the baby as it was to me and the observing parents. It is such a delight to be connected through music.

I live inside stories; my subconscious works for the pedagogical material for my own teaching in the theme of the story. I feel that I somehow just gather my plans from the air and get inspired! I have also been fortunate that I have been able to create the environment where I work. The room where I teach is located in the largest centre of art galleries in Finland, which enables interaction between different artists and people working in museums. I love introducing our history to children. If we sing a song telling how butter is made, I can bring the tools that were used and show them how it is done. My music groups are also regular visitors in the museums in our building. The integration and dialogue between arts is essential to my practice.

Music is in the heart of the adventures; the shared experiences enable strong connections between people and form a community where everyone – even the youngest baby – is encountered as a unique musician and artist. I feel it's important that children can touch and explore all kinds of instruments. They become familiar when they can touch them and have time to make the acquaintance at their own speed. I also enjoy meeting some families for the second time with their children. It is heartwarming to see the reaction on the mother's face if I manage to find the familiar songs that I used in my sessions, when the mother attended as a child. This work gives you so much positive energy – I am grateful every day!

I recharge my pedagogical ideas and creativity by walking in the forest and collecting items I can use and play with. This year Finland is celebrating its 100 years – I found a hundred-year-old log from the bottom of the sea in my summer cottage. That has been an inspiration for various improvisatory creations and music making. Inspired by the discovery, I have also made adventures with various wooden instruments with the families (see picture 6.20).

Also, my family helps me to find things I can work with; my husband loves fishing and re-introduced the idea – already familiar from Finnish mythology – that you can create sounds from the teeth of a pike with a brush! I have already cooked several pike for dinner and have some lovely instruments of their heads for the whole music group.

Funniness and the power of the 'hive mind'

Charlotte Arculus, Artistic Director of Magic Adventure.
Artist-Educator-Researcher

At the centre of my pedagogical thinking is the child as a competent learner; practice is based on true partnership with the child; I recognise that they have expertise. It's about providing a stimulus and then seeing what they bring and building on that. I work mostly with 0- to 2-year-olds, and what I find important is to be able to communicate before words, using single words and voice play – honouring those as legitimate channels of expressive communication for children. Music making is about communication of ideas, interaction and expressing oneself – all of these things learners will do, given the right open-ended landscape to explore. The more preconceived ideas we have as the teacher, the more limiting we are.

Funniness is a cornerstone; it gives a flavour of possibility, light-heartedness, there being no wrongs. Funniness is deeper than language; it is like a driver for communication. It is an improvisation, involving letting go of those preconceived ideas, responding authentically in the present moment, honouring that as important. It is a practice; the more you practise the better you are. In time, you become very familiar with getting things wrong, not knowing what you're doing and feeling daft; it resonates with young children in education settings. Learning through failure is really healthy.

The process can involve trying things out and reflecting on incidents immediately after practice, "Was I controlling that?", "What was that child communicating?", "Did I stop that there?" It's really helpful to video your work; you see things in film that you might miss at the time. With a piece of film of a moment, others can look at it and get other interpretations. Children's thinking isn't shown in words – it's in their body language, their gestures and facial expressions, their communicative stuff.

I really like working with beauty, visual things alongside music; it's not all about sound; its sound and the context. Inspired by the visual, I am enjoying playing with light, light and music inspired by Brian Eno, a big hero of mine.

But above all it's the relationship between people. Particularly groups of people – the hive mind – the group affect – group-intersubjectivity and creatively getting the conditions right for that to happen.

I have great interest in creating spaces. Going away to play with just a few people. We take the elements that we're interested in, and we play with them, and see what emerges from it, and to provide a forum for discussion.

How do I get my pedagogical inspiration? I dream about something, I wake up and think that's how we'll do it. Ideas also emerge through the practice. You need space for ideas. You can't be growing anything while you're still doing. Give yourself space to think.

Music sessions – a playful time of soaking in music and exploring it with our bodies

Margareta Burrell, Head of Early Years Music Berkshire Maestros

Communication, music, relationships, movement, empathy.

I have always been drawn to things that are away from musical notation, because music is not that, is it? So, anything that is away from that gives me a buzz – folk music or just dancing in general, which I experienced as a child.

Hearing music and understanding it in my heart gives depth to the experience, and the understanding comes through doing.

What guides my pedagogical thinking is my belief that music is to be explored, experimented with and played with; that is my starting principle. My pedagogical approach is based on Dalcroze principles, namely that you need to experience music from within initially, because of that you are likely to spread the impact of music throughout your body rather than just in your head. We have our own instrument, our bodies, to use to experience music.

The urge to communicate and relate to others comes naturally with music and movement. I realised that's what we're trying to achieve with Music Therapy: communicating your feelings and reactions to someone else through the music.

Becoming a Music Therapist transformed my teaching – giving time and waiting for the other to respond musically, when you are the assistant-cum-facilitator-cum-teacher, responding to that, rather than the other way around. It is challenging personally and professionally, to be careful not to manipulate or destroy what is there – by trying to bring it back to your intentions. But to stay in there and respect that person and where they're at. It is not only about making it fun.

There is huge emphasis on fun in early childhood music education. Which can mean that we don't always respect where the children may be at. All emotions should be respected, from even the smallest baby. That's where music can meet us – in all our different emotional states. This demands a huge sensitivity and musical flexibility of us.

If you want to include everyone, then you need to make space for all the characters in the room with an attitude of respect, that is then picked up by the others. Responding physically, non-verbally, giving yourself to that person, with good eye contact implies to the others that we all need to give that time as well. That is the art, isn't it, of holding the group? To be in charge even if you don't have the means to demonstrate that. It is a very tricky business. Experience helps, and the space is hugely important – to help people feel held. The pop up (see Pantomimus – Burrell, 2015) is so useful in this. To have something behind you can be comforting; it gives reassurance and deflects from distractions so that your mind can concentrate. Physically you are contained; it creates a sense of togetherness and inclusiveness. It helps to create a translucent atmosphere where things are allowed to surface.

I nurture my creativity by regularly going to concerts, exhibitions, conferences, courses. I read books; I need other people to articulate what I experience so I do read. I listen to a wide range of music. I am inspired by my daughters and son and husband. I sing in a choir, and play music with my family in different combinations.

Passionate focused attention

Olly Armstrong, Artist-Facilitator (Connector)

A lot of my music work for all ages focuses on two things:

One is passionate focused attention, so what I try to do with a group is focus in on individuals and respond to their responses – to be like an echo chamber for them.

And the second thing is to make all the work hyper-flexible so everything is in response to a response and open-ended. So, I guess it's an interactive style, sort of call and response-esque, and I mean this wider than music – in a bigger way. My work is not about coming with a set thing that I do, but it's more about following a conversation, responding to ideas and words from the children I work with so it's always quite chaotic. Sprawling, sporadic chaos.

But it's chaos within a boundary that I am comfortable with, or at least I am comfortable with my own discomfort. It's a chaos that is bound by my own skillset in understanding the room. From my teens until my thirties, I was a songwriter. I think playing in bands prepares you well for this work because it's kind of performing. Drawing a room, facilitating a room or a space, there are many elements of that skill in the work.

I steal everyone else's ideas. I think what piece of that can I use? I was in a talk the other day, and there were three tiny bits that the woman said that I thought I can use that in a workshop; they're like little triggers.

My primary concern is not to make young children more musical; that is a by-product; I help them to flourish in who they are, and with the most vulnerable in that space to help them feel more at home with who they are in the group. Developing empathy skills and safety for them to feel safe in the environment.

I have realised recently that I've been pouring out and not having any poured in. It's the communal thing that I think society doesn't do very well, and I think to be refreshed as an artist, having a strong community matters.

My inspiration and ideas come from random tangents, when I'm thinking about something else. Take days out to wander, to let your brain tick over. I think I do that; I value being able to just let my brain work in flow in different directions. I make little notes all the time, snippets of ideas, I write random things in.

I have repeatedly been burnt out. I need to take time out. There are so many threads to follow, I need to be aware that it's alright to let the thread go; if you chase every thread you never switch off.

In terms of what do I call myself – I change my title all the time; it depends on what I've been reading or who I've been talking to, but I aim for a non-hierarchical structure, so recently I call myself an Artist-facilitator. But my identity, I don't know, I am just a person . . . I don't know . . . I think all the things I am doing ,the coordination of the arts forum, my one-to-one work and my music work, they're all mediums to connect. Yes, I do know I am a Connector.

Musical improvisation between the teacher and the children

Dr Susan Young, retired University Lecturer

A cornerstone of Dalcroze Eurhythmics that has stayed with me from my training – both while I was a student at the Royal College of Music, London, and then after the RCM, for a year at the Institut Jaques-Dalcroze in Geneva – is for the lesson to be a musical improvisation between the teacher and the children. The teacher takes the musical impulses of the children and creates musical 'events' that then evolve in the lesson. This principle has underpinned my approach, not only in movement work for which Dalcroze is generally known outside of Switzerland, but for all kinds of varied activities. After Geneva, I trained as a secondary music teacher at a time when the John Paynter schools council approach was very influential and very new. The principle of children's music, as music made by children, that John Paynter introduced has also been very influential on my work.

In my professional career, I have moved through several different 'phases'. I think any good pedagogue is constantly evolving and can never say that they have one approach or pedagogical 'picture' – it is always shifting, partly as a consequence of where I have worked, the children I have worked with, but also with trends and developments in the wider fields of music education. When, for example, I worked in a specialist music school, I taught quite formally because the position required me to – my remit was to train musicianship skills. Then when I was a classroom teacher in a primary school, I had the freedom to be much more experimental in my work right across the primary age phase.

But what inspires me, perhaps the most, is any piece of very, very beautiful music – it might be a very simple traditional children's folk song or a complex piece of classical art music. I have one memory that has always stayed with me from my very earliest teaching days when I sung a quite long, quiet, slow, lyrical song about a dove to a class of 5-year-olds, unsure whether they would 'take' to it or not. One boy, when I had finished said, spontaneously and out loud – "That is a lovely song". So, we must always over-estimate children's musicality, responses, ability to engage and the need for beauty – always have the highest expectations. Gert Biesta has written a book, the 'beautiful risk of education', and I really like that thought.

To nurture my creativity, I need time and I need headspace to think. But I can think while I'm gardening or doing simple tasks like housework. But creativity also needs resources; one is never creative out of thin air, so I read a lot.

Originally, I got my pedagogical ideas from other teachers whom I found inspirational. There was one teacher at the Institut Jaques-Dalcroze who taught children's classes late afternoon, and I used to go and watch her as much as possible and write down everything that she did. At the Institut we were taught pedagogy – each week we had a pedagogy class when we observed the lecturer teach children and then we, the students, had to teach a class in front of the other students.

Afterwards our teaching would be discussed. It was the best training ever – very daunting, because I had to teach in French in front of all the other students and improvise at the piano – but the best training ever.

Starting with the little things

Jane Parker, early years music practitioner

I think if anyone came to see me work they'd see play-based, child-centred-approached music learning. I try to tune-in to the children, AND to the adults (staff or parents). I am constantly thinking – am I interacting or am I interfering (as Julie Fisher talks about)? I am trying to listen and value the children's and the adults' ways of being musical – I try to notice their music, to be sensitive to use music as part of any interaction really. I improvise a lot in my sessions, and it goes off at tangents.

I do have a lot of silences in the middle of my songs, to really stretch it out and hold that tension and wait, wait, wait for that response from the child or adult, just elongating it, playing with anticipation. I will reply to a question with another question in a musical sense. I reflect on practice a lot too; I believe that everyone in the room is a researcher. Whether they're the 17-year-old early years carer, the parent or the child. We are all researchers in practice.

Everything starts with the little things and letting it develop from there. I suggest collecting observations of children's musical play, look at the films, talk about it with colleagues and reflect on the musical learning in the little things.

I'm inspired by collaborating and co-working; it really fires me up. It's the richness and wealth of ideas coming together. How will I ever be inspired if I just plod along delivering my material on my own? I wouldn't develop or learn.

I am a perfectionist – I sit late at night when the house is quiet, and I will plan it all out; I use a template; I reflect back on previous sessions and plan with the group in mind. Another thing to say is I rarely follow my plan! I go off on tangents because a child brings in an object that takes us off in a more relevant direction.

I do a lot of observations before I deliver and think about activities that would suit the needs of the group – for example, a group of boys obsessed with sticks, I will think of ideas for sticks.

Fascinated by sounds

Soili Perkiö, Lecturer in music education, University of the Arts, Sibelius-Academy, developer of Finnish early music education and composer of children's songs

In my daily work at the Uni, I have the privilege to teach music and movement class to the first-year students. I am always so excited about this; each year brings different groups. Close to my heart is to open doors for everyone's own way of *teaching music and being sensitive. What I think is most important in the journey of becoming a music pedagogue are the encounters by which we learn to respect the differences between people. We are all unique – also as pedagogues – I can provide my students with a map and compass and perhaps wellington boots, but the routes they have to navigate for themselves.*

We can be mirrors to each other, to reflect, explore, develop and analyse. That is a long, interesting journey. Every teaching situation is an exciting adventure: I am eager to meet the participants, slightly nervous as well. What will happen? Nothing is self-evident. You need to throw yourself into the situation with all your feelings and the willingness for inquiry. I'd like to remind the younger colleagues especially, that not all teaching sessions can be great, and being a pedagogue is demanding, because you'd like to achieve the best possible at all times, and this is unrealistic. It is important therefore to be merciful towards yourself and to focus on the positive aspects in your teaching.

I choose carefully the music I use in teaching. The pieces need to be musically and emotionally meaningful to me, and sometimes I make the decisions to use a specific music in the moment. I am a sound-person: the sound quality of the instrument is of utmost importance and tunes me into the teaching situation as well. I hope to convey the sensitivity towards sounds to my students. It brings the opportunity to take care of yourself: I hide instruments whose sounds I don't like! The arrangements and instrument choices you use in your practice should create quality sounds and music when put together. A pedagogue is a conductor and a composer who is responsible for the music played together being a touching experience. Afterwards there is the miracle and astonishment of the shared process and musical achievement.

I see composing children's songs as a hobby. I create them from my heart and love that process. I send my songs for their own journey for others to sing. The songs are born by desire: sometimes I feel like composing songs, sometimes I feel like eating ice-cream! When I have the tickling feeling that a new song is on its way, I can be really desperate if I don't have a suitable poem to hand. When I use my own songs in my session, I am emotionally connected to them. When children sing the song, it fills me with gratitude.

Professionally I get inspiration from doing very different things: teaching, preparing, writing pedagogical materials, composing songs, teaching CPD courses in many countries. I enjoy meeting lovely colleagues, playing with children and performing in schools and kindergartens, improvising and playing different instruments. Also, being present in the moment and the people I am with gives me energy and joy. In life, I have noticed how a smile creates smiles. Living your life in a good mood, not to be tied to being tired or going over negative incidents in your mind. I am fascinated by the sea: when you are sailing, you need to be present in the moment, know the compass point, know the winds and the sun – otherwise you get lost.

Reflection and discussion

1   Having read through these narratives, how do they resonate with your own thinking and experience?
2   What are your pedagogical views and sources of inspiration? Write your own narrative into the empty space below.

References

Beijaard, D., Meijer, P. C., & Verloop, N. (2004). Reconsidering research on teachers' professional identity. Teaching and Teacher Education, 20, 107–128.

Burrell, M. (2015). Pantomimus: Amazing music space. Paper presented at CFMAE-MERYC2015 Conference, Tallinn, Estonia, 5th–9th May, 2015.

Connelly, F. M., & Clandinin, D. J. (1995). Teachers´ professional knowledge landscapes: Secret, sacred, and cover stories. In D. J. Clandinin & F. M. Connelly. *Teachers´ professional knowledge landscapes* (pp. 3–15). New York: Teachers College Press.

Connelly, F. M., & Clandinin, D. J. (1999). Stories to live by: Teacher identities on a changing professional knowledge landscapes. In F. M. Connelly & D. J. Clandinin (Eds.), *Shaping a professional identity: Stories of educational practice* (pp. 114–132). New York: Teachers College Press.

Côté, J. E., & Levine, C. G. (2002). *Identity formation, agency, and culture: A social psychological synthesis.* London: Lawrence Erlbaum Associates.

Heikkinen, H. L. T. (2001). *Toimintatutkimus, tarinat ja opettajaksi tulemisen taito. Narratiivisen identiteettityön kehittäminen opettajankoulutuksessa toimintatutkimuksen avulla.* Jyväskylä: Jyväskylän yliopisto.

Huhtinen-Hildén, L. (2012). *Kohti sensitiivistä musiikin opettamista. Ammattitaidon ja opettajuuden rakentumisen polkuja. (Towards sensitive music teaching: Pathways to becoming a professional music educator).* Jyväskylä Studies in Humanities 180. Jyväskylä: University of Jyväskylä.

Regelski, T. A. (2007). "Music teacher": Meaning, and practice, identity and position: Teaching. *Action, Criticism & Theory for Music Education, 6*(2). http://act.maydaygroup.org/articles/Regelski6_2.pdf

Ropo, E. (2009). Identiteetin kehittäminen opetussuunnitelman lähtökohtana. In P.-M. Rabenstein & E. Ropo (Eds.), *Identity and values in education: European dimension in education and teaching* (Vol. 2, pp. 5–19). Baltmannsweiter: Scheiner Verlag Hohengehren GmbH.

Wenger, E. (1998). *Communities of practice.* New York: Cambridge University Press.

Woodford, P. G. (2002). The social construction of music teacher identity in undergraduate music education majors. In R. Colwell & C. Richardson (Eds.), *The new handbook of research on music teaching and learning* (pp. 675–694). New York: Oxford University Press.

SONG EXAMPLES

This is a collection of all the songs that have been used or referred to in this book. Some have been used as parts of processes in Part II; others have been suggested in the text as examples for a specific activity – ideas and suggestions for using these can be found here.

Kilele

African Traditional (Ghana)

Ki - le - le, Ki - le - le   a - wo   a-wo, Ki - le - le,   Ki - le - le   a - wo   a-wo, Ki -

le - le,   Ki - le - le   Jes - si-ca, Ki - le - le,   Ki - le - le   Lau - ra,

MUSIC BM1.1   See page 77 this book. Published with permission from the composer.

Kilele means 'let's do it together' (according to the music group Osibisa, who shared their version online).

Whisper Song

Soili Perkiö
(trans. JP & L H–H)

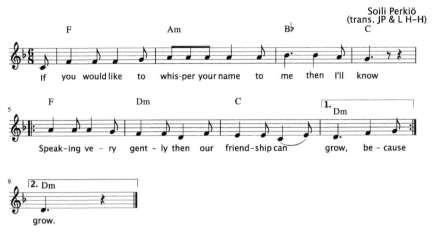

If you would like to whis-per your name to me then I'll know

Speak-ing ve - ry gent - ly then our friend-ship can grow, be - cause

grow.

MUSIC BM1.2   See page 78 this book. Published with permission from the composer.

Searching

Markku Kaikkonen
(trans. JP & LH-H)

Search - ing here and search - ing there. My song has gone to hi - de.
Kier rän, käyn ja kat - se - len ja lau - lu - a - ni et - sin.

Look - ing all a - round who knows what I might find
Mis - tä sen nyt löytä nen, ja mis - tä sen nyt keksin.

MUSIC BM1.3   See page 81 this book. Published with permission from the composer.

The lyrics of the song imply movement, the leader can play the melody while the group improvises movements, or rhythm patterns to suit the words of each verse.

Are you afraid of what you hear?

Hannele Huovi (trans. JP & L H-H)   Soili Perkiö

Are you a - fraid of   what you hear? ssh ssh
Pel - käät-kö pei - kon   ku - mi - naa?

No   no,   no no,   I'm not a - fraid of   sounds I hear
Eh   -   hei, eh - hei,   en   pel kää pei kon   ku - mi-naa!

MUSIC BM1.4   See page 92 this book. Published with permission from the composer and lyricist.

Sounds of the night

Markku Kaikkonen (trans. JP & L H-H)

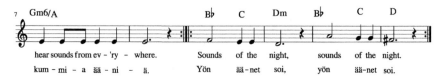

Night   is   here,   sha-dows are   near,   When you can't see   a - ny-thing and
Yö/on - pime - ä,   var - jot pitki - ä,   Pi - mey-des - tä   kuu - luu ai - van

hear sounds from ev - 'ry - where.   Sounds of the night,   sounds of the night.
kum - mi - a ää - ni - ä.   Yön   ää - net soi,   yön   ää-net soi.

MUSIC BM1.5   See page 96 this book. Published with permission from the composer.

Secretive Fish

Hannele Huovi (trans. JP & L H-H) Soili Perkiö

MUSIC BM1.6 See pages 115–116 this book. Published with permission from the composer and lyricist.

Secrets of the Sea

(This song harmonises with 'Secretive Fish')

Laura Huhtinen-Hildén

MUSIC BM1.7 See page 115 this book. Published with permission from the composer.

This song can form an ostinato to be sung with 'Secretive Fish'. Its simplicity offers the opportunity for easy improvisatory explorations when sung alone.

Snowflake Song

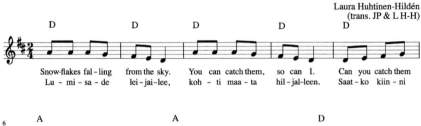

Laura Huhtinen-Hildén
(trans. JP & L H-H)

MUSIC BM1.8   published with permission from the composer

This is an example of a song for a specific purpose; it was invented one morning when in desperate need of a snowflake song, with actions for catching a snowflake, and the need to include accompaniment with tonic-chords for the 5-stringed kantele.

Invent your own words to suit working with other materials (feathers, for example).

Hands up

Jessica Pitt

MUSIC BM1.9   published with permission from the composer

This song emphasises the concepts of up and down and gross body motor movements. Vary the song by using other parts of the body for different verses, e.g. knees up, wiggle toes.

Lala Mwana

sleep child

Traditional Kenyan

La - la   mwa na   la - la   mwa na   la - la   mwa-na   la - la   la

MUSIC BM1.10   published with permission from the composer

This Kenyan lullaby is beautiful when sung gently as a canon in three parts.

Stop

E. Alho, H.Hautsalo, S. Perkiö

Walk - ing,   walk - ing,   walk - ing,   walk - ing,   walk - ing,   walk - ing,   Stop!
Käve - len,   käve - len,   käve - len,   käve - len,   käve - len,   käve - len,   Stop!

MUSIC BM1.11   published with permission from the composer

Variations of this song can include all forms of movement – combined with stop: bouncing, jumping, running, skipping, drumming, tapping etc.

Sei dama dei

Folksong from Telemark

Sei   da-ma dei da-ma   dei dam då,   sei   da-ma dei dam   då - a   Sei   da-ma dei   da-ma

dei dam då,   dei dam då.   Sei   da-ma dei   da-ma   dei   da-ma dei   da-ma   sei   da-ma dei dam   då - a

MUSIC BM1.12

This traditional song from Norway opens a lovely possibility for using body percussion. The easy lyrics (which don't mean anything) help you to concentrate on the movements. Ingrid Oberborbeck (*Stemmen danser – kroppen synger.* Folkeskolens Musiklaererforening, 2001, p. 88) has suggested the following activities:

sei – clap your hands
då – stamp one foot
då-a– step to the right and to the left in your place.

Luuriallallei

MUSIC BM1.13

This song is traditionally sung as call and response. Movements can also be led by the solo singer while walking hand in hand in the space forming spirals, circles and other shapes.

The words of the song can be easily adapted to suit the situation:

It is nice to be here with you – luuriallallei . . .
Let us sing and dance together-luuriallallei . . .
Can you clap your hands together – luuriallallei . . .
Let us copy Jessica´s movement – luuriallallei . . .

The traditional Finnish words tell a story about building the Finnish national instrument, the kantele. The lyrics consist of questions and suggested answers. E.g. What could I put as strings for the kantele? They could be made from a young girl´s hair.

Nanuma

MUSIC BM1.14

This African song can be sung in three-part canon. In some versions of the song, the C sharp in bar 5 is sung as a C natural.

Jaa dan duu

Canon   Soili Perkiö

MUSIC BM1.15   published with permission from the composer

This song can be sung in three-part canon. The haunting melody has words with no meaning that are easy to pick up; the beautiful harmonies of the song are the main focus of attention.

Diddle dee I die die

Margaret Corke   Irish traditional

MUSIC BM1.16   published with permission from the composer

This happy melody inspires movement and dancing and encourages everyone to join in. If you use this with very young children, be on the look-out for their spontaneous movements. Feature these in the verses, naming the child as part of the song. This can help raise awareness of children's participation, even the child who sits very still can be included in a verse ('Can you sit very still, can you sit very still like Hannah over there?').

Toodledidee tune

Jessica Pitt

Too dle di dee   Too dle di doo,   Too dle di dee   Too dle di doo.

MUSIC BM1.17   See pages 97 and 179 this book. Published with permission from the composer.

Searching for five notes
Toodledidee

Jessica Pitt

Search-ing for   five notes   as   I   play,   search-ing for   five notes   on   my   way.

Search-ing for   five notes   as   I   play,   search-ing for   five notes   on   my   way.

MUSIC BM1.18   See page 179 this book. Published with permission from the composer.

Where are you?
Ostinato

Jessica Pitt

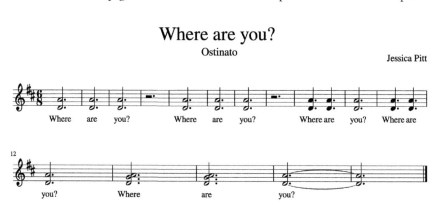

Where   are   you?   Where   are   you?   Where are   you?   Where are

you?   Where   are   you?

MUSIC BM1.19   See page 179 this book. Published with permission from the composer.

EXAMPLES, PATHWAYS AND WORKSHOPS

Theme 3

Theme 4

Theme 5

Theme 6

INDEX

Pages in italics indicate figures on the corresponding pages.